G000162605

London
Shortlist

timeout.com / london

ABOUT THE GUIDE

The *Time Out London Shortlist* is one of a series of pocket guides to cities around the globe. Drawing on the expertise of local authors, it distils their knowledge into a handy, easy-to-use format that ensures you get the most from your trip, whether you're a first-time or a return visitor.

Time Out London Shortlist is divided into four sections:

Welcome to London introduces the city and provides inspiration for your visit.

London Day by Day helps you plan your trip with an events calendar and customised itineraries.

London by Area is the main visitor section of the guide. It includes detailed listings and reviews for the very best sights, museums, restaurants ⑩, pubs & bars ⑩, shops ⑩ and entertainment venues ⑩, all organised by area with a corresponding street map. To help navigation, each area of London has been assigned its own colour.

London Essentials provides practical visitor information, including accommodation options and details of public transport.

Shortlists & highlights

We have selected a Shortlist of stand-out venues in each area, which are marked with a heart ♥ in the text. The very best of these appear in the Highlights feature (*see p10*) and receive extended coverage in the guide.

Maps

There's an overview map (*see p8*) and individual street maps for each area of the city. Venues featured in the guide have been given a grid reference so that you can find them easily on the maps and on the ground.

Prices

All our **restaurant listings** are marked with a pound symbol category from budget to blow-out (£-££££), indicating the price you should expect to pay for an average three-course meal for two (or the equivalent in a café or sharing plates venue) with drinks and service: £ = under £60; ££ = £60-£100; £££ = £100-£140; ££££ = over £140.

A similar system is used in our **Accommodation** chapter based on the hotel's standard prices for one night in a double room: Budget = under £130; Moderate = £130-£250; Expensive = £250-£350; Luxury = over £350.

60

108

75

Contents

Introduction

'It is difficult to speak adequately or justly of London,' wrote Henry James in the 1880s, when the British capital was the most populous and powerful city in the world. 'It is not a pleasant place; it is not agreeable, or cheerful, or easy, or exempt from reproach. It is only magnificent.'

Much has changed since then, but this city's scale and multiplicity still defy description. Despite the collapse of the empire that it once governed, London remains one of only a handful of truly global cities, with more than 300 languages spoken by its nine million inhabitants. Every year, 20 million visitors come to see streets and landmarks dating from Roman times to the present day that have survived fires, bombs, town planners and property developers. And, increasingly, they're being tempted beyond London's bustling core to explore the city's ever-more vibrant suburbs.

Londoners love to complain about the Tube, the traffic and (yes) the tourists, but we know there's nowhere else quite like our city. With its buzzing street life, its hives of government and finance, its world-famous museums and increasingly world-class restaurants, its innovative nightlife and inimitable pubs, the Big Smoke is so vast, diverse and fast-changing that even long-term residents will never manage to see or do all that it offers. So, whether you're here for a day or a lifetime, let this book guide you to the best of our limitless city.

★★★★★
SUNDAY TIMES

'CONJURES THE IMPOSSIBLE!
MAGICAL DOESN'T EVEN BEGIN
TO DESCRIBE IT.'
ENTERTAINMENT WEEKLY

J.K. ROWLING'S

Harry Potter

AND THE
CURSED CHILD

THE STORY CONTINUES ON STAGE

PALACE THEATRE, LONDON
HarryPotterThePlay.com

View from the London Eye

Welcome to London

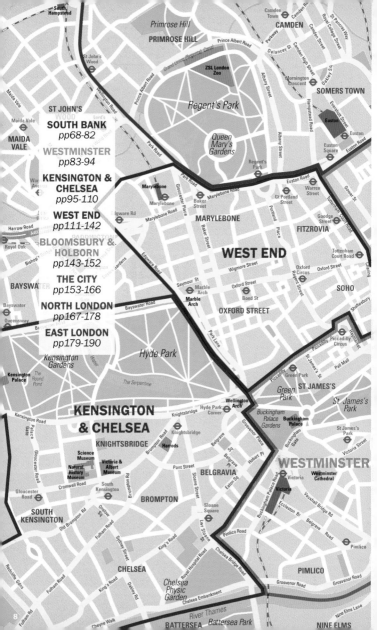

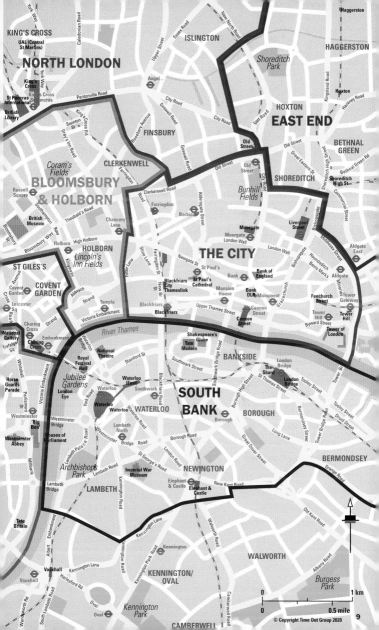

© Copyright Time Out Group 2020

9

Highlights

From historic sights to elegant parks, world-class galleries to cutting-edge theatre, we count down the highlights of this endlessly diverting and diverse city. Other destinations may flit in and out of vogue, but London will always fascinate and inspire: here's why.

1

Victoria & Albert Museum *p101*

Stroll into the V&A's main entrance – that grand hall with its dramatic glass chandelier – and the scale of this museum of art and design, with its combination of stately historical context and cutting-edge modern design, is already apparent. It's gallery after grand and gorgeous gallery, with the Weston Cast Court our absolute favourite. The nearby Science Museum (*see p100*) and Natural History Museum (*see p97*) are fabulous too – but the V&A is unforgettable.

02

Street food *p30*

You can barely swing a tote bag without hitting an artisanal street food stall or provenance-first farmers' market in London these days. They're everywhere, which is great news for foodies on a budget. Take your pick from fish tacos to tea-brined chicken strips to Kim Kardashian-inspired koftas.

03

Houses of Parliament *p87*

The Palace of Westminster is characterised by neo-Gothic buttresses, towers and arches. It contains 1,000 rooms, 11 courtyards, eight bars and six restaurants, for use by staff, MPs, lords and their guests. Members of the public are welcome too. Book a tour to get a sense of how Parliament functions. You can even have afternoon tea at the end of your tour in a room beside the Thames.

04

The Shard *p75*

In the last decade, skyscrapers have been sprouting beanstalk-like all over the capital. Some have striking architecture (the Gherkin), some have great public spaces (Sky Garden), and most offer expansive views, but the Shard is the undisputed kingpin: it's so tall you almost feel you're on a different plane to the ant city below.

05

British Museum *p147*

This is one of the world's greatest museums, a compendium of key artefacts from most of the significant cultures of the world, from Egyptian mummies and the Rosetta Stone to monumental Mesopotamian sculpture and even an Easter Island head. Entry is free, so you can head back as often as you wish.

06

Shakespeare's Globe *p73*

London's West End is a powerhouse of international theatre, but the best bargain is undoubtedly seeing one of Shakespeare's plays authentically staged at the Globe. It costs only £5 if you're prepared to stand as a 'groundling'. If you can't get a ticket, then visit the exhibition and tour the reconstructed theatre instead.

07

St Paul's Cathedral *p160*

As architectural masterpieces go, St Paul's is at the frou-frou end of things, with its frothy Baroque exterior. But the grandeur of the interior is quite breathtaking – and no less so for Sir Christopher Wren's audacity in giving the authorities precisely the cathedral they didn't want.

08

Afternoon tea *p29*

Rolling up to a grand hotel for a meal that consists largely of cake is one of our most indulgent British traditions. Whether you're looking for something outlandish, or the kind of spread that wouldn't be out of place in Buckingham Palace, London has a tea table with your name on it.

09

National Theatre *p81*

The National Theatre remains the country's leading drama showcase, mixing Shakespeare and the classics with exciting new writing and big-budget productions. Don't miss the chance to see UK theatre at its very best in a building that's a masterpiece of 20th-century architecture.

10

Tower of London *p162*

Who doesn't love a castle? The building of this one was started by William the Conqueror in 1078; since then the Tower of London has witnessed many of the key events in London's history. It's a fabulous showcase for the Crown Jewels, as well as home to the traditionally dressed 'Beefeaters' (Yeoman Warders).

11

Westminster Abbey *p90*

The Abbey is Gothic grandeur at its most splendid. It has hosted 16 royal weddings and every coronation since 1066, and it is the final resting place for many of the great and the good of British history. Don't miss the Queen's Diamond Jubilee Galleries and the exquisite Abbey gardens.

12

Maritime Greenwich *p22*

The grand colonnades of Wren's Old Royal Naval College draw you into historic Greenwich Park, a fine introduction to London's most expansive UNESCO World Heritage Site. It combines the National Maritime Museum, the Queen's House art gallery, the gorgeous *Cutty Sark* sailing ship and, yes, the Prime Meridian.

14

13

Tate Britain *p89*

Since its dramatic extension in 2016, Tate Modern (*see p76*) has been hogging the limelight. But we find ourselves drawn back to the original Tate: lovely premises, blockbuster shows every bit as good as those at its bombastic younger rival and the entire chronological span of British art since 1545 to walk through. It's not so busy, either.

14

Liberty *p123*

The capital is blessed with many brilliant department stores, from gloriously gaudy Harrods (*see p104*) to trailblazing Selfridges (*see p119*), but none is lovelier or more London than Liberty. Its jumbled rooms are charmingly old-fashioned but full of cutting-edge international fashion and beauty brands.

15

St James's Park *p93*

One of the city's joys is its chain of incredibly central parks: you can walk from Kensington Gardens and Hyde Park through Green Park to St James's barely touching the tarmac. The last is our favourite. Why? It's the prettiest, with lovely lakes for waterfowl, and has a delicious view of Buckingham Palace.

16

A night out in Peckham *p47*

To experience the city's most inclusive, innovative and thriving night scene, head south on the Overground to Peckham, where some of the capital's most exciting bars, clubs and arts venues are clustered: sip Campari on the roof of a car park; eat barbecue treats in a ticket office; play retro arcade games in a bar and then dance the night away in a record shop.

St Paul's Cathedral

Sightseeing

The key to London's geography is that it is effectively
two cities, not one. The City is the area originally walled
by the Romans, which through its mercantile wealth
and the weakness of English kings secured considerable
independence from Westminster, where the monarchs
and, latterly, Parliamentarians reside. Around these
poles, the patchwork of districts grew up that are now
central London. The problem with a visit to London is – as
it always has been – how to fit it all in. The truth is, you
can't... not in a single trip, not in a single lifetime. So relax
and do whatever you most fancy. If you've only a couple
of days at your disposal, consider following one of our
itineraries (*see p52*).

❤ **Shortlist**

Best historic architecture
Houses of Parliament *p87*,
Old Royal Naval College *p22*,
St Paul's Cathedral *p160*,
Westminster Abbey *p90*

Best for history
British Museum *p147*,
Imperial War Museum *p70*,
Museum of London *p159*,
Tower of London *p162*

Best outdoor attractions
Chelsea Physic Garden *p104*,
Queen Elizabeth Olympic
Park *p189*,
Royal Botanic Gardens, Kew *p20*,
St James's Park *p93*

Best for kids
London Transport Museum *p135*,
Natural History Museum *p97*,
Science Museum *p100*,
ZSL London Zoo *p173*

Best fine art
National Gallery *p86*,
Tate Britain *p89*,
Victoria & Albert Museum *p101*

Best quirky museums
Geffrye Museum *p180*,
Sir John Soane's Museum *p151*,
Wellcome Collection *p148*

Best views
London Eye *p72*,
The Shard *p75*,
Sky Garden *p161*

A whistle-stop tour

The **South Bank** (*see p68*) remains London's key
tourist destination. The principal attractions are well
established: Tate Modern, Shakespeare's Globe (*see
p73*) and Borough Market, the London Eye and the
lively Southbank Centre. Further south, into Lambeth,
is the impressive Imperial War Museum. The Shard (*see
p75*) looks down on all of them from London Bridge.

Across the river, **Westminster & St James's** (*see
p83*) are the focal point of UK politics, location of the
Houses of Parliament (*see p87*), Westminster Abbey
(*see p90*) and Buckingham Palace. Trafalgar Square,
has two brilliant art collections along its pedestrianised
northern edge at the National Gallery and the National
Portrait Gallery. The stately Tate Britain (*see p89*) in
Millbank is also packed with British art.

To the west, **Kensington & Chelsea** (*see p95*) have
a cluster of unmissable Victorian museums – the V&A
(*see p101*), the Natural History Museum and the Science

Museum – as well as famous Knightsbridge department stores, and the boutiques and eateries of the King's Road, not to mention the fabulous Design Museum and enchanting Chelsea Physic Garden.

The **West End** (*see p111*) includes most of what is now central London. We start north of Oxford Street, in the slightly raffish shopping district of Marylebone, with elegant Fitzrovia to the east. South is Mayfair, as expensive as its reputation but less daunting, with fine mews and pubs. A stone's throw away is Soho, a notorious centre of fun, while neighbouring Covent Garden is so popular with tourists that locals often forget its many charms, including the excellent London Transport Museum.

Bloomsbury & Holborn (*see p143*) are respectively London's literary and legal haunts. The former has magnificent squares and Georgian terraces, and the unrivalled British Museum (*see p147*). From here, it's a short hop south to the charming St John's Soane's Museum or east to the plentiful dining options in Clerkenwell.

Bordering Holborn to the east, **The City** (*see p153*) comprises the once-walled Square Mile of the original city. Much more than a financial centre, it has numerous historic attractions, of which the Tower of London (*see p162*) and St Paul's Cathedral (*see p160*) are the best known. Visit the Museum of London to get a grip on the city's bewildering past.

Around these central areas is a doughnut of other districts you won't want to miss: redeveloped King's Cross provides a gateway to **North London** (*see p167*), which includes Camden, Islington, Highgate and Hampstead, while trendier-than-thou **East London** (*see p179*) encompasses the eating, shopping and nightlife of Spitalfields, Brick Lane, Hoxton and Shoreditch, with Dalston to the north. Further east still are the Olympics Park and London Docklands, with historic Greenwich (*see p22*) across the Thames to the south.

Garden Party

Make the most of London's green spaces

Quite apart from the famous royal parks (see p93 St James's Park), which cut a welcome green swathe through the city centre, London is dotted with gardens, where domestic and exotic plants are carefully tended by experienced botanists and amateur volunteers. Chief among these is the **Royal Botanic Gardens** at Kew (TW9 3AB, 020 8332 5655, www.kew.org, £14.90; £3.85-£13.20 reductions), whose half square mile of landscaped beauty features an unparalleled collection of plants begun by Queen Caroline, wife of George II, with exotic species brought back by voyaging botanists (including Charles Darwin). Head straight for the 19th-century greenhouses, filled to the roof with tropical plants, and next door to the Waterlily House's quiet and pretty indoor pond (closed in winter). Rhododendron Dell, designed by 'Capability' Brown, is at its best in spring, while the Xstrata Treetop Walkway, some 60-foot above the ground, is terrific fun in autumn.

Smaller but equally magical spaces can be found all over London. Visit the **Chelsea Physic Garden** (see p104), founded in 1673 by the Apothecaries' Society to grow medicinal plants, or the artsy **Garden Museum** (see p70), whose replica 17th-century knot garden features intricate, twirling topiary. A hidden gem in Holland Park (see p108) is the Japanese **Kyoto Garden**, complete with colourful maples, tiered waterfalls and free-roaming peacocks. Often overlooked but highly atmospheric, **Hampstead Hill Garden** has fine views of the city from its overgrown pergola, draped in flowers and vines. If it's stunning views you're after, the 184-foot-high **Sky Garden** (see p161) is unbeatable, but for another unexpected oasis in the heart of the City, try the **Barbican Conservatory** (see p155), which is home to exotic fish and 1,500 species of tropical plants and trees.

Chelsea Physic Garden

Making the most of it

Don't be scared of London's public transport: it's by far the best way of getting around town. Invest in an **Oyster travel smartcard** (see p201) on arrival or use a contactless debit/credit card to roam cashless through the city by bus, Tube (underground trains) and train, especially the excellent London Overground – which is treated as part of the underground network. The opening of the much anticipated Crossrail will transform travel to the south and east when it eventually opens in 2021.

The Tube is the easiest mode of transport for visitors (avoid rush hour: 8-9.30am, 4.30-7pm Mon-Fri), but buses are best to get a handle on the city's topography. Some good sightseeing routes are RV1 (riverside), 7, 8 and 12, and to a enjoy a classic red bus, hop on the **Routemaster Heritage bus** (*see p200*), which runs from Tower Hill via Monument and St Paul's Cathedral to Trafalgar Square on summer weekends. Note that no London buses accept cash anymore – if you don't have an Oyster, use a contactless debit or credit card.

In the centre, many attractions are surprisingly close to each other and can be easily reached on foot. The **Transport for London walking map** (http://content. tfl.gov.uk/walking-tube-map.pdf) reveals, to cite only the best-known example, that Covent Garden station is only a five-minute walk from Leicester Square station. It looks much further on the schematic Underground map. Alternatively, the **Santander Cycles** bike hire scheme (known as 'Boris Bikes') can be a lot of fun and an inexpensive way to get about (*see p204*).

To escape the worst of the crowds, avoid big attractions at weekends and on late-opening nights, and aim to hit blockbuster exhibitions in the middle of a run; January to March are the quietest months for visiting attractions, July to September the busiest. Last entry can be up to an hour before closing time (we specify when it is more than an hour before), so don't turn up at the last minute and expect to get in.

Whitehall

21

♥ Maritime Greenwich

Greenwich is an irresistible mixture of maritime, royal and horological history, a combination that earned it recognition as a UNESCO World Heritage Site in 1997 and a Royal Borough in 2012. Indeed, royalty has haunted Greenwich since 1300, when Edward I stayed here. Henry VIII was born in Greenwich Palace, which was later redeveloped as the Royal Naval Hospital, now the **Old Royal Naval College** (www.ornc.org). Designed by Wren in 1694, and completed with the help of Hawksmoor and Vanbrugh, the college complex is now a very handy first port of call. Its Pepys Building contains the **Greenwich Tourist Information Centre** (020 8305 5235, www.visitgreenwich.org.uk), and is the home of Discover Greenwich, which provides a great overview of the area's numerous attractions. The public are also allowed into the college's rococo chapel and the Painted Hall, which took Sir James Thornhill 19 years to complete. Walk south between Wren's grand colonnades, which were deliberately placed to frame the **Queen's House** (www.rmg.co.uk/queens-house) – begun by Inigo Jones in 1616 and the first building in Britain to be designed on Classical principles. West of the Queen's House is the **National Maritime Museum** (www.rmg.co.uk/national-maritime-museum), the world's largest such museum, which contains a huge store of creatively organised maritime art, cartography, models, interactives and regalia.

Beyond lies **Greenwich Park**, laid out by André Le Nôtre (1613-

1700), the chief gardener of French King Louis XIV. It's a ten-minute walk (or shorter shuttle-bus trip) south up the park's steep slopes to the **Royal Observatory** (www.rmg.co.uk/royal-observatory) – a collaboration between Wren and the scientist Robert Hooke (1635-1703). It also marks the work of astronomer John Flamsteed (1646-1719), who predicted solar eclipses and laid the groundwork for later advances in navigation. There are superb views out over the Royal Naval College to Canary Wharf, and, at night, the bright green Meridian Line Laser illuminates the path of the Prime Meridian across the London sky.

Elsewhere, shoppers swarm to **Greenwich Market**, a handsome 19th-century building sheltering a mixture of shops and stalls.

Nearby, close to Greenwich Pier, is the 19th-century tea clipper, the **Cutty Sark** (King William Walk, www.rmg.co.uk/cuttysark), as well as the domed entrance to a Victorian pedestrian tunnel that emerges on the far side of the Thames in Island Gardens. The tunnel is rather dingy, due to incomplete repair work, but it's still fun to walk beneath the river.

The best way to travel to or from Greenwich, however, is on board the popular and speedy **Thames Clipper** boats (www.thamesclippers.com), which shuttle passengers to and from central London. Seeing the vistas change as you approach this most historic area of London is an unparalleled joy – redolent of the long period when the city was utterly dependent on its river.

Old Royal Naval College

DINE OUT
WITH US

Time Out critics review restaurants anonymously so they're always without bias.

Search for recommended eateries online at **timeout.com**

THE BEST OF THE CITY

Eating & Drinking

London's restaurant scene is an absolute banger. It's hard to think of a city, save perhaps Tokyo or LA, that surpasses it for sheer thrill factor, as well as cosmopolitan breadth. From gutsy British cuisine to Korean-infused haute-junk, cutting-edge African and modern European fare (plus everything else in-between), you'll find a superlative form of almost every food within zones 1 and 2. What's more, the craft, skill and reverence shown by the capital's best kitchens can also be found in London's finest drinking establishments. You'll find a drinking culture with a conscience, too – with bars focused on sustainability and pubs supporting local brands and producers, especially with the continuing vogue for craft beer and small-batch gin. A combination of rich traditions and a long history of bohemian revelry with a taste for innovation makes eating and drinking in London a real pleasure.

❤ **Shortlist**

Best of British
J Sheekey *p138*,
Regency Café *p91*,
St John *p164*

Best veggie and vegan eats
Cub *p182*,
Farmacy *p109*

Best walk-in restaurants
10 Greek Street *p125*,
The Barbary *p136*,
Padella *p77*,
El Pastór *p77*

Best traditional pubs
Cross Keys *p139*,
Jerusalem Tavern *p165*,
Ye Olde Mitre *p166*

Best cocktails
Connaught Bar *p121*,
Lyaness *p79*,
Swift *p129*

Best for a blow-out
Hutong *p77*,
Social Eating House *p126*

Best of British

Spurred on by the success of **St John** (*see p164*), for a decade in the 2000s, every new restaurant seemed to claim its 'modern British' culinary heritage. The idea was simple: take out-of-favour but flavour-packed cuts of animal (bone marrow, pig's trotters, hearts) and offer them in simple preparations that let the unique qualities of the ingredients shine. Added to this were a couple of key themes: localism (sourcing superb ingredients from as close to home as possible) and the new casual gourmet diner, who was willing to pay for fine food but didn't relish the flim-flam of Mayfair haute cuisine. Today, exponents of and successors to the modern British approach can be found at the likes of **Rabbit** (*see p106*), **Social Eating House** (*see p126*) and the **Marksman** (*see p183*).

In the know
Price categories

All our restaurant listings are marked with a pound-symbol category from budget to blow-out (£-££££), indicating the price you should expect to pay for an average three-course meal for two (or the equivalent for tapas, dim sum, street eats, in a café or at a small plates venue), with drinks and 12.5% service:

£ = under £60

££ = £60-£100

£££ = £100-£140

££££ = over £140

The world in one city

Although it changed the London restaurant scene forever, modern British cooking has long since slid off the cutting edge to be superseded by a succession of international flavours. Eastern Mediterranean cuisine has been riding high for several years, exemplified by the likes of **The Barbary** (*see p136*). It followed on the heels of North African (**Moro**; *see p149*), Peruvian (**Ceviche Soho**; *see p125*); noodles (**Kanada-Ya**; *see p138*) and Nordic cuisine (**Snaps & Rye**; *see p110*) – all of which have had their 'moment' in the last decade and remain very popular. This is hardly a new phenomenon. From the coffee houses that flooded London during the Ottoman Empire in the 17th century, to the mass immigration from Bangladesh in the 1970s, Londoners have welcomed wave after wave of global food and drink. What's notable is how food arrives in London from abroad as cheap national cuisine, becomes dramatically popular, consolidates and is then reinvented as a luxury. But one does not replace the other. The high-end Indian cuisine at **Gymkhana** (42 Albemarle Street, W1S 4JH, 020 3011 5900, gymkhanalondon.com) and others raised the bar for Britain's curry houses, meaning there are now terrific, affordable curry options in the centre of town, at the likes of **Tandoor Chop House** (*see p138*) and **Dishoom** (www.dishoom.com), and even some in the vicinity of Brick Lane.

On the menu

Whichever cuisine they showcase, many of our favourite London eateries have embraced the concept of the 'small plates menu' – a pedestrian description for a parade of exquisite dishes served in reduced portions. Don't miss the superb tapas at **Barrafina** (*see p137*) and **Morito** (*see p149*); *cicchetti* at **Polpo Soho** (*see p126*); Mexican tacos at **El Pastór** (*see p77*) and luxury dim sum at

The Barbary *p136*

Yauatcha (15-17 Broadwick Street, W1F 0DL, 020 7494 8888, www.yauatcha.com). Many have also adopted the trend for vegetarian and vegan food by offering increasingly innovative plant-based menus; exemplars include **Cub** (*see p182*) and **Farmacy** (*see p109*).

Enduring pubs

London may have learnt the art of the bar from the Big Apple – and learnt that lesson surprisingly well – but we continue to own the pub. The 'local' (the public house, with its colourful characters and cosy interiors) remains the symbolic heart of boozing culture in the capital. Although many classic pubs have succumbed to property developers, a handful of historic inns have stood the test of time, holding licences since the 1600s. Although these creaking London legends are the best places to soak up a spot of history, many have been dragged into the 21st century by London's craft beer 'revolution'. Alongside the traditional pints of lukewarm ale, you'll now find hoppy, interesting beers (often brewed in London) served from the keg or in a bottle in even the most retro boozer.

Trending tipples

There are plenty of bars that serve classic cocktails done to perfection, but increasingly, people are seeking out new

💙 Afternoon tea

Allegedly introduced in 1840 by the seventh Duchess of Bedford, afternoon tea was designed to combat what the Duchess described as 'that sinking feeling' around 5pm. This most decadent of meals was eagerly adopted by the capital's grand hotels, who remain the foremost exponents of the classic afternoon tea – think crustless cucumber sandwiches, bone china teapots and fat little scones – but now other venues offer quirkier riffs on convention: how about lager-braised bacon jams, cannabis-infused chocolates or Manolo Blahnik gingersnap stilettos?

For traditionalists, the ultimate tea can be found in the art deco foyer and reading room at **Claridge's** (www.claridges. co.uk; 2.45-5.30pm daily, from £70 pp). Musicians serenade you; the scent of roses surrounds you, as you elegantly stuff yourself on sandwiches and just-baked scones. **Fortnum & Mason** (see p94; from 11.30am daily, from £60 pp) offers an equally lavish spread in the pastel-painted Jubilee Salon. Cosseting staff go beyond the call of duty and the super-buttery scones are exceptional. There's a dedicated children's tea available too. Other trad treats include the English Tea Room at **Brown's Hotel** (roccofortehotels.com, noon-6pm daily, from £55 pp) and the Palm Court at the **Langham** (www.langhamhotels.com, from noon daily, from £62).

For renegades, the options feel limitless. Highlights include a 'Tipsy Tea' at **Mr Fogg's Residence** in Mayfair (see p122;

2-6.45pm Sat, 3-5pm Sun, from £44 pp), where you can get sozzled on bottomless gin tea while surrounded by interesting taxidermy. The plant-based afternoon tea at Westbourne Grove's **Farmacy** (see p109; 3.30-5pm Thur-Sun, £50 pp) includes cannabis choccies, savoury fancies and tea-infused cocktails, while dandy-esque Mayfair pleasure dome **Sketch** (9 Conduit Street, W1S 2XG, 020 7659 4500, sketch. london, from 11.30am daily, from £59 pp) offers a classic tea through the looking glass; don't miss the egg-shaped toilets, where birdsong is piped into each pod.

Finally, if you're on a short trip to the capital and want to cram in as many London traditions as possible, hop aboard **B Bakery's Afternoon Tea Bus** (020 3026 1188, london.b-bakery.com, from £45 pp), which departs from Victoria or Northumberland Avenue several times a day for a tour of central London. Sightseeing? Check. Vintage Routemaster bus? Check. Delicious afternoon tea? Check.

▶ *For more great tea-time options, see timeout. com/london/restaurants/ afternoon-tea-in-london.*

levels of boozy wizardry. One of the leading lights is cocktail maestro Ryan Chetiyawardana, who has become a household name (albeit under his pseudonym, Mr Lyan) thanks to his madcap ideas, techniques and ingredients. Check out his concoctions at **Lyaness** (*see p79*) on the South Bank. Other innovative bars include **69 Colebrooke Row** (*see p176*), which has a lab upstairs, and stripped-back, sophisticated **Swift** (*see p129*). And, you don't have to stay in the West End to sample the finest mixology: rising rents in central London have encouraged a neighbourhood cocktail movement to thrive.

Where to eat and drink

The **South Bank** (*see p68*) has foodie magnets Borough Market and Maltby Street, plus plenty of quality chains strung along the riverside. **Soho** (*see p118*) is still the bohemian centre of the capital with plenty of eating options, both cheap and chic, and

Street food

Now that London is a Russian oligarch's playground, eating out is wildly unaffordable – right? Wrong: some of the most inventive, delicious food in the city is to be found for under a fiver and eaten with a wooden fork. Just don't be afraid to get your hands (and face) dirty.

The Big Daddies of London street food are **Kerb** (www. kerbfood.com) and **Street Feast** (www.streetfeast.com). Kerb was founded in 2012 by Petra Barran, who once ran a mobile chocolate business from an ice-cream van. She saw an opportunity to cluster together the best of the capital's food vendors and bring an element of cooperative organisation to this previously ad hoc industry. Kerb now has six locations hosting a rotating line-up of vendors: at Granary Square, West India Quay, Paddington, the Gherkin, St Katherine Docks and Seven Dials in Covent Garden.

Street Feast was founded in the same year by Jonathan Downey. It hosts markets in derelict and disused spaces to create an urban festival vibe. The Shoreditch hub, **Dinerama** (19 Great Eastern Street, EC2A 3EJ, 5pm-midnight Wed-Sat) is set in a 1,000-capacity former bullion truck yard, while **Giant Robot** (*see p190*) offers an unexpected street-food adventure inside a hulking shiny box at Canary Wharf.

With the support of these collectives, stall-owners are able to trial a foodie idea and make some money, without the burden of renting a London restaurant space. Many have since gone on to greater things. Fried chicken supremos **Mother Clucker** (59-61 Rosebery Avenue, EC1R 4SD, motherclucker.co.uk) were able to open a permanent shop on Exmouth Market thanks to the success of their market stall; **Som Saa** (*see p184*) financed the transition from street vendor to restaurant through an insanely popular crowdfunding appeal; and **Kricket** (12 Denman Street, W1D 7HH, 020 7734 5612, kricket.co.uk), another much-admired restaurant, started out in a shipping container in Brixton.

For those in search of a more traditional London street food experience, **Borough Market** (*see p79*) is still the grandaddy of them all, but the cognoscenti increasingly head a little further east to the less touristy **Maltby Street** and **Spa Terminus** (*see p80*). Another top spot is **Broadway Market** in Hackney (*see p185*), which has supplemented its fruit and vegetables with lobster-infused mac & cheese and roasted duck burgers. Equally charming are Soho's old-world **Berwick Street Market** (*see p129*) and historic covered **Greenwich Market** (www.greenwichmarket.london).

Healthy Yummies, Kerb

Essentials

Payments, service charges and licensing laws

Nearly every restaurant will not only accept but prefer card payments. Contactless payment is increasingly the norm in bars and informal budget eateries, even street-food stalls, but it's wise to have cash to hand too. Service charges are frequently included in café and restaurant bills, but not always. Check: if such a charge hasn't been added, paying a tip of ten to 15 per cent is usual. If you can, tip in cash: it's most likely to go directly to your server that way.

The liberalisation of the licensing laws means that any pub or bar can apply to open late, but noise-nuisance restrictions mean most still close their doors around midnight, with only a handful of places staying open past 1am. In all cases, you'll have to be over 18 to be served alcohol (or even admitted to many venues at night), while many bars embrace a Challenge 21 policy – if you're fresh-faced, expect to have to show ID.

an increasing number of cocktail bars alongside the character-filled pubs. East of Soho, **Covent Garden** (*see p135*) remains a busy tourist trap, but some very decent restaurants have emerged. Expense-account eats are concentrated in **Mayfair** (*see p120*), where celebrity chefs thrive in the dining rooms of posh hotels, and drinks are served with a side of sophistication. To the north, **Marylebone** is another foodie enclave with top-notch delis and cafés, as well as terrific restaurants. The **City** (*see p153*) remains relatively poor for evening and weekend eats but **Clerkenwell** (*see p165*), just beyond the City walls, is a culinary hotspot and the birthplace of many London restaurant trends. Nearby, **Shoreditch** (*see p182*), once the epitome of cool, is still a lively part of town packed with drinkers and a huge number of eating options, but those in the know have drifted north into **Dalston** or south to **Peckham** and **Brixton**, where creative restaurants and bars are flourishing. In fact, the biggest change to the capital's eating and drinking scene has been the growth of exciting new options in more outlying areas.

Shopping

With two of the world's most prestigious design colleges (Central Saint Martins and the London School of Fashion) at its centre, London's fashion scene has an energy that radiates throughout the city. As so often in the capital, it's all in the mix – for every catwalk look on New Bond Street, there's an inspiring street style to be seen in Shepherd's Bush Market; for every neatly attired Dalston hipster, there's a devil-may-care transvestite in a home-made frock. From glossy department stores peddling everything from Prada to panettone, to flower markets and cheap-and-chic high-street chains, there are very few things in this city that money can't buy. And, although you can shop the world's finest if you have the cash, there are vintage stores, market stalls and budget brands on offer if you don't.

❤ **Shortlist**

Best for fashion
Browns *p122*,
Dover Street Market *p92*,
Machine-A *p130*,
Shop at Bluebird *p140*

Best markets
Columbia Road Market *p185*,
Borough Market *p79*,
Broadway Market *p185*,
Portobello Road Market *p110*

Best museum shops
Barbican Centre *p155*,
Design Museum *p108*,
Tate Modern *p76*,
V&A *p101*

Best bookshops
Daunt Books *p118*,
Foyles *p129*,
Gosh! *p130*,
London Review Bookshop *p150*

It's the fashion

We'd argue London is currently the fashion capital of the world. So it should be no surprise that some of the world's finest fashion retailers are here, from small independents – like Soho's **Machine-A** (*see p130*) or the cluster of hipster boutiques on Redchurch Street (*see p185*) – all the way up to the big department stores. Part of the secret is that the big guys who might be in danger of slowing down have learnt to collaborate with the little guys who are still quick on their feet.

Selfridges (*see p119*) is a fine example. Opened in 1909, it is one of a handful of central London department

stores to have thrived ever since the Edwardian shopping boom – and the innovative spirit of founder Harry Gordon Selfridge has remained intact. It pioneered London's first gender-neutral department in 2015; installed a negroni fountain on the roof in 2017; staffed the tech department with robots, and installed its own cinema in 2019. Meanwhile **Liberty** (*see p123*), which still trades William Morris fabrics from grand half-timbered premises like it's 1893, is nevertheless a hotbed of exciting new labels and initiatives, including a hair art salon that weaves Liberty printed scarves into chic new braids.

Big brands use the capital as a testing ground, so Londoners are exposed to all the latest initiatives and launches. After years of perfecting everything from the cut of the silk shirts to the scribbly font on the carrier bags, it was here that the H&M family launched the first branch of **& Other Stories** and its first lifestyle concept store, **Arket**.

Liberty

Only in London

London has more to offer than posh frocks and directional sweatshirts. There's a wealth of niche shops, specialising in traditional umbrellas (**James Smith & Sons**, *see p139*), cheese (**Neal's Yard Dairy**, *see p140*) and gourmet teas

In the know
Opening hours

Shops are generally open 10am-6pm Monday to Saturday, with few closing on bank holidays (Christmas is the sole exception to that rule). Most don't open until around noon on Sundays, which gives you plenty of time to refuel for a day of pavement pounding with a good brunch. In general the shops in central London close later on Thursday nights, with the Oxford Street stores staying open until 10pm.

(**Postcard Teas**, *see p124*), and you can find original funky souvenirs by London artists at **We Built This City** (*see p131*) and **Gallery of Everything** (*see p118*).

Market up

London's markets are another seemingly endless source of creative goodies. Although it's no longer ground zero for alternative culture, sprawling **Camden Market** (*see p172*) remains one of the capital's most popular attractions, with stalls selling everything from handmade crafts to vintage clothes and artisan breads. East London is home to two of the city's best markets: **Columbia Road** (*see p185*) and **Broadway**

Camden High Street

Market (*see p185*). If you're really just after a stroll (and the jam-packed crowds are part of the fun), Columbia Road's the one: stop to smell the roses before investigating the dinky independent shops along the road. Broadway Market is the nexus of dress-down catwalk finds and street eats. For gifts, nip round the corner to **Netil Market**, a great little space dedicated to local designer-makers.

The two other key markets are at opposite ends of town. At the far end of the tourist-magnet South Bank, **Borough Market** (*see p79*) rejuvenated its noble history of food wholesaling with street eats and gourmet snacking – a reinvention that worked so well that the cognoscenti now sniffily head a little further east of London Bridge to **Maltby Street** (*see p80*). Then, in west London, Notting Hill's **Portobello Road** (*see p110*) has stall after stall of vintage goodies – with admittedly few bargains, but great atmosphere. Up-and-coming designers come out in force on Fridays.

Words and music

The bookshop didn't die, it turns out. Like everywhere else, their survival in London comes down to creatively selected stock, helpful and informed sellers, fine events and, wherever possible, a café. At different ends of the spectrum, the **London Review Bookshop** (*see p150*) and **Foyles** (*see p129*) tick all these boxes. The former is a tiny place with stock that's all killer and no filler; the latter is a multistorey book palace, pragmatically redeveloped a few years ago. To these can be added historic beauties like **Daunt Books** (*see p118*) in Marylebone and specialists like comics emporium **Gosh!** (*see p130*). A renewed appreciation of vinyl means that bricks-and-mortar record-selling also survives, even thrives at the likes of **Sounds of the Universe** (*see p131*) and **Rough Trade East** (*see p187*).

IT'S SHOWTIME!

Book the hottest shows,
musicals, events and things
to do via **timeout.com**

TimeOut
THE BEST OF THE CITY

The Monstrous Child,
Royal Opera House p142

Entertainment

To say London has brilliant and diverse entertainment
is an understatement. What other European city offers
anything like such exciting live music, theatre, clubbing
and comedy? With a spectacular array of venues
dotted across the capital, from world-class stadiums
and art nouveau concert halls to warehouse clubs and
secret cinemas, there's energy and creativity at every
turn. These days, big doesn't necessarily mean best,
with many of the smaller venues creating the biggest
buzz. And while the West End has traditionally been
the heart of London's cultural scene, there's plenty of
offbeat, home-grown talent to be found in less central
boroughs. Wherever you venture, one thing is certain:
you won't be bored.

Best for gigs
Corsica Studios *p80*,
EartH *p187*,
Union Chapel *p177*,
Village Underground *p188*

Best theatre
Donmar Warehouse *p142*,
National Theatre *p81*,
Shakespeare's Globe *p73*,
Young Vic *p82*

Best dance clubs
Dalston Superstore *p187*,
Fabric *p166*,
Printworks *p46*,
XOYO *p188*

Best classical music
Barbican Centre *p155*,
BBC Proms *p62*,
Royal Festival Hall *p82*,
Royal Opera House *p142*,
Wigmore Hall *p119*

Film

Londoners still have a feel for the romance of film that out-of-town multiplexes will never satisfy. Perhaps that's why there's such a lively and varied range of screenings in the capital. Leicester Square stages most of the big-budget premières – but it also has the biggest prices. By contrast, the cheap-as-chips **Prince Charles** (*see p133*) repertory cinema is right around the corner and shows films that wouldn't come within a million miles of a red carpet. Outside the mainstream, the **BFI Southbank** (*see p80*) gets top billing for its seasonal explorations of various genres of cinema and TV. After the BFI, the **Curzon** group is the favoured choice for most cineastes; the intimate **Sea Containers** (*see p194*) screening room is inexpensive for its South Bank location.

In the know
Tickets and planning

Always book ahead if there's a specific show that you want to see, and use the theatre or show's own website where possible. If you're flexible or are happy to queue, consider buying from the **tkts booth** (the Lodge, Leicester Square, Soho, WC2H 7NA, officiallondontheatre. com/tkts), which sells tickets for big shows at much-reduced rates, either on the day or up to a week in advance. Many West End theatres hold back a selection of day-seats for each performance, available at a knock-down price on a first-come first-served basis when the box office opens (usually 10am – but get there much earlier for anything popular).

For refurbished art deco gems try the gorgeous, historic **Phoenix** (52 High Road, East Finchley, N2 9PJ, phoenixcinema.co.uk) or the **Rio** (107 Kingsland High Street, Dalston, E8 2PB, riocinema.org.uk) in Dalston. Add to that the vogue for summer screenings in unusual outdoor settings, an enthusiasm for experimental ciné clubs and a world-class film festival, and all you need to do is to get some popcorn and sit yourself down.

Classical music and opera

London's classical scene has never looked or sounded more current, with the **Southbank Centre** (*see p82*), the **Barbican Centre** (*see p155*) and **Kings Place** (*see p171*) all working with strong programmes. Even the once-stuffy **Royal Opera House** (*see p142*) has democratised both its building and its programme, following three years of renovations. And despite recent troubled times at the **English National Opera** (*see p141*), the company has commissioned and produced top-class work from British composers, such as Ryan Wigglesworth's *The Winter's Tale* (2017) and Iain Bell's *Jack the Ripper: The Women of Whitechapel* (2019). Much of the city's classical music action happens in superb venues on an intimate scale. **Wigmore Hall** (*see p119*), **Cadogan Hall** (*see p107*) and **LSO St Luke's** (*see p166*) are all atmospheric places, and several churches make use of their acoustical design to host fine concerts.

Dance

London is the home of two long-established classical dance companies. The **Royal Ballet**, resident at the **Royal Opera House**, is a company of global stature, which managed to lure star Russian ballerina Natalia Osipova into its ranks. Contemporary premières have included Christopher Wheeldon's *The Winter's Tale* and Liam Scarlett's *Frankenstein*, while Wayne McGregor continues to choreograph extraordinary contemporary ballet. The Royal's (friendly) rival is the **English National Ballet**, a touring company that performs most often at the **Coliseum** (*see p141*) and, for the regular *Swan Lake* 'in the round', at the **Royal Albert Hall** (*see p102*), but has expanded into venues more suitable to contemporary dance such as the **Barbican Centre** and **Sadler's Wells Theatre** (*see p177*).

Theatre and musicals

For many people, 'theatre' in London means musicals – and musicals in London are booming. Of late, homegrown musicals have been rather overtaken by Broadway imports: Lin-Manuel Miranda's visionary rap musical *Hamilton* opened in 2017 in the lavishly restored Victoria Palace Theatre and has been selling out ever since, while US musicals *Come from Away*, *9 to 5*, *Waitress*, *On Your Feet* and *Dear Evan Hansen* were all big hits in 2019, an almost unprecedented influx.

But to the discerning theatregoer the real story lies away from the West End: new plays are what the Brits do best, most of them crafted in London's numerous

Sadler's Wells Theatre

subsidised theatres, the **National Theatre** (*see p81*) being the most prominent. The sector itself has experienced considerable change of late: once almost entirely run by white men, theatres that have historically aspired towards diversity, but rarely actually achieved it, have been shaken up by high-profile appointments like Kwame Kwei-Armah at the **Young Vic** (*see p82*) or Lynette Linton at the **Bush Theatre** (7 Uxbridge Road, Shepherd's Bush, W12 8LJ, www.bushtheatre.co.uk). The **Old Vic** (*see p82*) has transformed itself under heavyweight director Matthew Warchus, with an eclectic and busy programme that finds room for plenty of big names, but with a much more diverse and experimental line-up than in years past.

On a smaller scale, Off-West End houses such as the **Young Vic** and the **Almeida** (*see p176*) continue to produce some of London's most exciting, best-value theatre – much of which moves on to the West End. The **Donmar Warehouse** (*see p142*) traditionally lures high-profile film stars to perform at its tiny Earlham Street home, while the **Barbican Centre** (*see p155*) programmes visually exciting and physically expressive work from around the world.

Master Harold, National Theatre

'UNDENIABLE!
SOMETHING
EVERYONE EVERYWHERE
SHOULD COME AND SEE'

NEW YORK MAGAZINE

THE TINA TURNER MUSICAL

Clubbing

When it comes to after-dark indulgence, London has all the variety you could possibly wish for. Yes, we have one of the world's largest and most influential nightclubs, **Fabric** (*see p166*), and the awesome large-scale industrial party space **Printworks** (Surrey Quays Road, Rotherhithe, SE16 7PJ, 020 8498 4934, printworkslondon.co.uk), but spend a few moments hunting on Facebook and you'll unearth fabulous happenings in any number of shop

Printworks

basements and other informal spaces. Check out **The Hydra** (the-hydra.net) and **London Warehouse Events** (www.lwe.events) for a fix of big-name electronica.

Once the hub of the capital's nightlife, Shoreditch has become increasingly commercialised (witness the weekend trails of hen and office parties between Old Street and Spitalfelds), despite the groovy work still being done at live space and club **XOYO** (*see p188*). The city's cool kids now take the bus north up the Kingsland Road from Shoreditch into Dalston, where the **Dalston Superstore** (*see p187*) pulls huge crowds onto its intense pitch-black dancefloor.

There's more of interest to the south. Peckham has put itself at the heart ofLondon nightlife in recent year (*see p47* A night out in Peckham). Brixton has a

❤ A night out in Peckham

Described by *Vogue* as 'the Williamsburg of London' and hailed by *Time Out* as London's coolest neighbourhood, Peckham is buzzing almost every night of the week. Hipsters and culture vultures come for everything from theatre to film, and live music to cutting-edge clubbing. Although it's undeniably trendy, Peckham is open, fun and friendly, with something for everybody out looking for a good time.

Once threatened by demolition, the 120-year-old Bussey Building is at the heart of the area's regeneration. The vast Victorian warehouse was due to be knocked down to make space for a tram depot, but locals campaigned to bring creativity to this corner of south-east London instead. Chronic Love Foundation, a collective dedicated to making positive change through creative projects, rose to the challenge by

opening the **CLF Art Café** (133 Rye Lane, SE15 4ST, www.clfartcafe. org). It's now a hugely successful cultural venue with multiple studios, exhibitions spaces, a rooftop film club and a record shop in the basement that doubles as a late-night clubbing destination.

Across the railway tracks, Peckham's other flagship venue is **Peckham Levels** (95A Rye Lane, SE15 4ST, peckhamlevels. org), a former car park that's now a multi-storey creative hub. It houses tropical-themed cocktail bar **Near & Far** (Level 6, www.nearandfarbar.com), various food traders and the **PeckhamPlex** cinema (0870 042 0299, peckhamplex.com). In summer, the top floor is taken over by non-profit organisation Bold Tendencies (boldtendencies.com), which commissions site-specific music, dance and architecture; it also hosts London's best-loved rooftop bar, **Frank's Café**, which combines cocktails, sculptures and fabulous views.

Nearby, night-time hotspots include **Bar Story** (213 Blenheim Grove, SE15 4QL, barstory. co.uk) for its terrific-value happy hour; **Four Quarters South** (187 Rye Lane, SE15 4TP, geocities.fourquartersbar.co.uk) for craft beers, cocktails and retro arcade games; **Peckham Springs** (22A Blenheim Grove, SE15 4QN, peckhamsprings. co.uk) for late-night drinking in its own winter garden; and **Copeland Social** (133 Rye Lane, SE15 4ST, www.copelandsocial. com) for its lively atmosphere and bangin' sound system.

multitude of venues, not least sleek **Phonox** (418 Brixton Road, SW9 7AY, phonox.co.uk). And the gay village in Vauxhall (*see p45*) is just as welcoming to open-minded, straightrolling types.

To the north, up in King's Cross, there are some good nights at the **Big Chill** (257-259 Pentonville Road, N1 9NL, 7427 2540, bigchillbar.com) and, with its late weekend licence and killer sound system, the **Star of Kings** pub-club (126 York Way, N1 0AX, 7458 4218, starofkings.co.uk). Further north, Camden has credible nights at teeny pub-rave spot the **Lock Tavern** (35 Chalk Farm Road, NW1 8AJ, 020 7482 7163, www.lock-tavern.com) and bourbon-soaked gig haunt the **Blues Kitchen** (111-113 Camden High Street, NW1 7JN, 020 7387 5277, theblueskitchen. com/camden). **Koko** (*see p174*) runs some of the best club nights around, including world-famous cheese-fest Guilty Pleasures (guiltypleasures.co.uk).

Gigs

London's music scene is defined by rampant diversity. You might find yourself watching a US country star in a tiny basement, an African group under a railway arch or a torch singer in a church. While corporations have taken over some venues, there's still rough and ready individuality to be found in the likes of **XOYO** (*see p188*). The **O2 Arena** (*p190*) and **SSE Arena, Wembley** (Wembley Stadium, Empire Way, Wembley, HA9 0WS, 0844 980 8001, www.wembleystadium.com) remain London's most popular stadiums for classic rock and retro gigs. Several nightclubs multitask, staging regular gigs: **Corsica Studios** (*see p80*) is notable.

London has a lively home-grown jazz scene, inspired by freewheeling attractions at the **Vortex** (11 Gillett Square, Dalston, N16 8AZ, 020 7254 4097, www. vortexjazz.co.uk) and the unhinged monthly **Boat-Ting Club** nights (www.boat-ting.co.uk). International names

LGBTQ London

The city's best events, shows, clubs and bars

Acceptance of gay lifestyles in London feels broader than ever. In fact, many clubs no longer bother much about sexual orientation, just as long as everyone gets to have a good time. The closure of key venues, however, has caused plenty of soul-searching. Has Grindr killed the gay bar? Is it rising rents? Noise complaints from intolerant neighbours? London's headline homo event remains **Pride** (see p62), while **BFI Flare** (www.bfi.org.uk/flare) is a major LGBT film festival.

Roughly speaking, London's gay scene is split into three key zones: **Soho** is the most mainstream, **Vauxhall** is the most decadent, and **east London** the most outré. Centred on Old Compton Street, the Soho scene continues to attract the crowds. Notable venues here include **G-A-Y Bar** (30 Old Compton Street, W1D 4UR, 7494 2756, www.g-a-y.co.uk) and **Ku Bar & Club** (30 Lisle Street, Chinatown, WC2H 7BA, 7437 4303, www. ku-bar.co.uk). Meanwhile **SHE Soho** (see p133) is the city's only full-time drinking den for lesbians. The party continues down the road at the legendary **Heaven**, (Under the Arches, Villiers Street, Covent Garden, WC2N 6NG, 7930 2020, heavennightclub-london.com).

Down south, Vauxhall is the place to go if you want to stay up all night and the next day as well. Long-standing alt-cabaret venue **RVT** (Royal Vauxhall Tavern, 372 Kennington Lane, Vauxhall, SE11 5HY, 7820 1222, vauxhalltavern. com) is utterly enjoyable. **Horse Meat Disco** (349 Kennington Lane, SE11 5Y, 020 7793 0903, Eagle, www.eaglelondon.com/ horse-meat-disco) is everything

a good Sunday night club should be: friendly, not too pricey, with an obscenely funky DJ crew.

The most alternative, creative and vibrant of the capital's queer scenes is to be found in east London. In **Dalston Superstore** (see p187) and the **Glory** (281 Kingsland Road, Dalston, E2 8AS, 7684 0794, theglory.co.uk), you'll rub shoulders with fashion and music movers and shakers (plus assorted straight folk), to soundtracks built by ferociously underground DJs.

Ku Bar & Club

Corsica Studios *p80*

can be seen and heard at **Ronnie Scott's** (*see p133*) and there's more good quality mainstream fare at **Spice of Life** (6 Moor Street, Soho, W1D 5NA, 020 7437 7013, www.spiceoflifesoho.com). There's a lot of very good jazz at the excellent **Kings Place**; and both the **Barbican** and the **Southbank Centre** host dozens of big names.

Comedy and cabaret

While the big stadiums – especially the **O2 Arena** and **SSE Arena**, **Wembley** – host the massive shows, it's the circuit of pubs and smaller clubs that defines London's comedy scene. In addition to its stellar programme of plays and cabaret, the **Soho Theatre** (*see p133*) has become one of the best places to see new comics breaking into the scene. Another multitasking venue is the **Union Chapel** (*see p177*), whose monthly *Live at the Chapel* night provides line-ups of big guns (Noel Fielding and Stewart Lee, for example) supported by comics who are headliners in their own right. To see the best cabaret, head to the always interesting **Bethnal Green Working Men's Club** (42-44 Pollard Row, Bethnal Green, E2 6NB, 0207 739 7170, www.workersplaytime.net). **Proud Embankment** (8 Victoria Embankment, Waterloo, WC2R 2AB, 020 7482 3867, www.proudembankment.com) launched in 2018 as a glamorous cabaret and party venue.

London
Day by Day

Trafalgar Square p88

Itineraries

Whether you visit for a weekend or longer, for hedonism or high culture, there's a whole world of things to see and do in the British capital – whatever your budget. While you can't expect to see all of London's sights in one trip, our tailored tours will help you to maximise your time in the city. Choose from Essential Weekend, Budget Break and Family Day Out, or cherry-pick elements from each to create your own itinerary.

▶ *Budgets include transport, meals and admission prices, but not accommodation and shopping.*

ESSENTIAL WEEKEND

The best of London in two days
Budget £200-£250 per person
Getting around walking, Tube and Overground trains

DAY 1

Morning

Start the day in Parliament Square, a UNESCO World Heritage Site, to admire the **Houses of Parliament** (*see p87*) and **Westminster Abbey** (*see p90*). You could spend the rest of the morning on an excellent guided tour of either building, but to pack in as much as possible, saunter north along Whitehall and then on to Horse Guards Parade to watch the Household Cavalry perform the daily **Changing the Guard** ceremony at 11am (*see p60*). After the ceremonials, head through the parade ground into **St James's Park** (*see p93*) to see the pelicans and admire Buckingham Palace (*see p86*) at the end of the lake. A stroll along the Union Jack-lined Mall will take you through Admiralty Arch to **Trafalgar Square** (*see p88*). The centre of London is an impressive sight. Far beneath Nelson on his column, the Fourth Plinth showcases large-scale contemporary art that's always worth a look. The masterpieces of the **National Gallery** (*see p86*) are on the pedestrianised northern side of the square; the **National Portrait Gallery** (*see p88*) is just beyond.

Afternoon

Stroll into Covent Garden for lunch, then catch a heritage Routemaster bus (*see p200*) to **St Paul's Cathedral** (*see p160*), Wren's architectural masterpiece in the heart of the City. If you've booked in advance, you can also visit the **Sky Garden** (*see p161*) on Fenchurch Street for stunning views. Cross over the Thames for a late-afternoon snack at **Borough Market** (*see p79*), followed by a stroll west admiring the sights and attractions of the **South Bank** (*see p68*).

Changing the Guard

Evening

Stay on the South Bank as the sun goes down. Enjoy a play at either the **National Theatre** (*see p81*) or **Shakespeare's Globe** (*see p73*), a film at **BFI Southbank** (*see p80*), or a concert at the **Southbank Centre** (*see p82*). There are plenty of restaurants and bars nearby.

British Museum

DAY 2

Morning

We're not quite done with culture: are you ready for one of the world's finest museums? You betcha – arrive as close to 10am as you can to miss most of the crowds. The **British Museum** (*see p147*) is so full of treasures, you may not know where to begin: try turning left out of the middle of the covered courtyard for the extraordinary monumental antiquities, including the Parthenon Marbles.

Afternoon

Depending on your mood, either mooch around **Covent Garden**, with its varied options for both eating and shopping; or hop on the Tube to Piccadilly Circus for more serious retail therapy at **Liberty** (*see p123*), followed by a fortifying afternoon tea at **Fortnum & Mason** (*see p94*).

Evening

If you're interested in how London's night scene has evolved, it's time to head to **Peckham** (*see p47*) via the Jubilee line and Overground to Peckham Rye. Alternatively, you can stay in the centre to make the most of **Soho**'s cornucopia of eating and drinking options (*see p125*), or with tickets bought in advance, enjoy the razzamatazz of a **West End** show (*see p134*).

Frank's Cafe, Peckham

FAMILY DAY OUT

Keeping the kids amused
Budget £300-£400 for a family of four
Getting around Tube, walking, boat

ITINERARIES

Morning

Have an early breakfast, then catch the Tube to Tower Hill for the **Tower of London** (see p162; book online in advance to avoid the worst of the queues). There's lots to see and do here, with the experience enhanced by the presence of affable red-coated beefeaters. Hustle to the Crown Jewels first thing to glide on the travelator past Her Majesty's baubles before the crowds get too unbearable.

Afternoon

Head east on the District Line and Central Line to Stratford for the **Queen Elizabeth Olympic Park** (see p189). For lunch, try either the Timber Lodge Café, right next to the Tumbling Bay Playground, or the Last Drop café at the foot of the **ArcelorMittal Orbit** (see p190). Have fun in the park, then catch the Jubilee Line to North Greenwich, where you can pick up a **Thames Clipper** (see p203) back into central London, with views of Maritime Greenwich (see p22), Canary Wharf, Tower Bridge and the Shard (see p75) en route. Leave the boat at Bankside Pier (if you want a stroll) or at Festival Pier (if little legs are still tired).

Evening

The **South Bank** (see p68) is particularly magical in the evening when the fairy lights come on. There's often free child-focused entertainment in the foyer of the **Royal Festival Hall** (see p68), but if not, the combination of crowds, entertainers and reliable chain restaurants will keep the nippers happy and well fed. Finish at the **London Eye** (see p72) to enjoy the constantly changing vistas as the sun goes down. (Book your time slot in advance for the cheapest tickets.)

Thames Clipper and the Tower of London

BUDGET BREAK

For the pound-conscious visitor
Budget £50-£70 per person
Getting around Tube, walking

Good news, pound-stretchers. London, although expensive in most terms, is incredibly cheap for culture. Almost all of the key museums are free, only charging for temporary exhibitions. The British Museum, both Tates and all three South Kensington museums are just the start, with many smaller collections (including the Soane, Wallace and Grant) also eschewing an admission price. To ensure your transport costs are as low as possible, get an Oyster card (*see p201*), or use the same contactless debit/credit card for all your journeys. Your fares for the day will be capped at the price of a one-day Travelcard (*see p201*).

Morning

Start at South Kensington tube station, which is a short walk from three of London's – indeed, the world's – finest museums. The **Victoria & Albert Museum** (*see p101*) is our favourite, combining a palatial Victorian setting with absorbing and awe-inspiring collections that are a fascinating history of art and design. The Arts and Crafts-style tea room is a good spot for an early lunch, or take a picnic and head north to **Kensington Gardens** (*see p97*), the lovelier half of **Hyde Park**.

Kensington Gardens

Victoria & Albert Museum

Afternoon

Check out what's on at the **Serpentine** and **Serpentine Sackler** (*see p102*), then jump on the Tube at Hyde Park Corner and whizz across town to Liverpool Street to explore **Spitalfields** and **Brick Lane**, and to mingle with the hipsters on **Redchurch Street** and **Shoreditch High Street**. If it's a Sunday, continue north to **Columbia Road** to get end-of-the-day bargains at the flower market (*see p185*).

Evening

Stay in the East End for the evening, perhaps heading to **Dinerama** in Shoreditch for a plethora of affordable street food in a party atmosphere (*see p30*), or check out the artsy going-ons at the **Village Underground** (*see p188*).

Serpentine

Redchurch Street

FOLLOW
OUR LEAD

Wherever you're exploring, we've got the insider scoop on the world's best destinations.

Travel better with timeout.com

THE BEST OF THE CITY

Diary

Forget about British reserve. Age-old rituals and traditional ceremonies are joined on London's calendar by cultural festivals and arts events that attract crowds of revellers and enthusiasts. Weather plays a part in the timing, with a concentration of things to do in the warmer and usually drier months of summer, but the city's schedule is busy for most of the year, so you'll never be far from a celebration of some kind.

Year round

London doesn't really have an off-season, with interesting things going on all through the year. The weather is never predictable, but nor is it particularly harsh – in winter you might even bless our polluted air, which keeps the temperature a degree or two higher than the surrounding countryside.

Ceremony of the Keys

www.hrp.org.uk/tower-of-london/ explore/ceremony-of-the-keys
Join the Yeoman Warders at the Tower of London as they lock the fortress's entrances in this 700-year-old ceremony. Apply 12-18 months ahead.

Changing the Guard

www.royal.uk/changing-guard
This historic 45-minute piece of pageantry sees the Queen's Guard, in their scarlet tunics and bearskin hats, march down the Mall to Buckingham Palace. The ceremony, accompanied by a full military band, takes place on alternate days from 10.45am (or daily from 10.15am from April to July). Arrive early.

Gun Salutes

www.royal.uk/gun-salutes
Many important royal occasions are marked with gun salutes and dramatic cavalry charges.

Changing the Queen's Lifeguard

changing-guard.com/ queens-life-guard
A less crowded alternative to Changing the Guard, the Household Cavalry regiments mount the guard daily at 11am (10am on Sunday) at Horse Guards Parade. After the old and new guard have stared each other out, they dismount in a synchronised fashion.

Spring

Our favourite time of year. This is a surprisingly green city, with blossoming cherry trees and crocuses, primroses and daffodils in the Royal Parks. Spring weather can be mixed, but Easter holidays aside, there tend to be fewer crowds than in the summer. The Old Smoke can feel lively, pretty and far more cheerful than our fellow Brits would ever believe.

Mar WoW: Women of the World

www.thewowfoundation.com
Discussion, debate and performances about women.

Mid Mar St Patrick's Day Parade & Festival

www.london.gov.uk/events
Sunday parade followed by toe-tapping tunes in Trafalgar Square.

Late Mar-May Kew at Springtime

www.kew.org
Five million flowers carpet the grounds in spring (see p20).

Apr Oxford & Cambridge Boat Race

www.theboatrace.org
Elite rowers from Oxford and Cambridge universities battle it out on the Thames.

Mid Apr London Marathon

www.virginmoneylondonmarathon. com
Some 40,000 elite athletes and fundraisers run, jog and walk their way to the Mall.

Mid May Covent Garden May Fayre & Puppet Festival

www.coventgarden.london /whats-on
All-day puppet mayhem devoted to Mr Punch at the scene of his first recorded sighting in England in 1662.

Mid May Chelsea Flower Show
www.rhs.org.uk/shows-events
Admire perfect blooms in entire
laid-out gardens.

May/June State Opening of Parliament
www.parliament.uk
The Queen reopens Parliament
after its recess, arriving and
departing in the golden State
Coach, accompanied by Household
Cavalry troops.

Summer
At the slightest sniff of fine
weather, Londoners are boozing at
pavement tables like some fantasy
of the south of France. The Tube
becomes a sweaty hellhole, but
suck it up: this is the season of al
fresco cinema, music festivals in
the parks and sipping Camparis
with the trendsters.

Field Day

Late May/Early June All Points East
www.allpointseastfestival.com.
An eclectic ten-day festival takes
over Victoria Park. Four days of
community-driven entertainment
(comedy, film screenings, street
food and more) are sandwiched
between two weekends of serious
music, with 2020 headliners
including Tame Impala,
Kraftwerk, Johnny Marr, Anna
Calvi and Iggy Pop.

June Field Day
fielddayfestivals.com
Acts ranging from weird pop and
indie rock to underground dance
producers and folk musicians.

June London Festival of Architecture
www.londonfestivalofarchitecture.org
Talks, discussions, walks,
screenings and other events.

June LIFT (London International Festival of Theatre)
www.liftfestival.com
Biennial festival featuring
hundreds of artists.

June Camden Rocks Festival
camdenrocksfestival.com
One-day festival of rock and
metal bands.

June Bushstock
www.bushstock.co.uk
Run by independent record label
Communion Presents, focusing on
new talent.

June Meltdown
www.southbankcentre.co.uk
Music and cultural festival at the
Southbank Centre, curated by
a different musician every year,
including Grace Jones in 2020.

Mid June Beating Retreat
www.householddivision.org.uk/ beating-retreat

For two successive evenings in June, a pageant of military music and precision marching begins at 8pm when the Queen (or another royal) takes the salute of the 300-strong drummers, pipers and musicians of the Massed Bands of the Household Division.

Mid June Trooping the Colour

Staged to mark the Queen's official birthday on the Saturday closest to 13 June (her real birthday is in April). At 10.45am, the Queen rides in a carriage from Buckingham Palace to Horse Guards Parade to watch the soldiers, before heading back to Buckingham Palace for a midday RAF flypast and the impressive gun salute from Green Park.

❤ Late June/early July Greenwich & Docklands International Festival

festival.org
This annual week of outdoor arts, theatre, dance and family entertainment is spectacular. Events take place at the Old Royal Naval College and other sites, including Canary Wharf and Mile End Park.

❤ Late June/early July Pride London

prideinlondon.org
This historic celebration of the LGBT community (taking place since 1972, initially in support of the Stonewall rioters) now welcomes a million revellers to a week of events, culminating in a celebratory parade held on Saturday.

Late June-mid July Wimbledon Tennis Championships

www.wimbledon.com
One of the world's most prestigious tournaments.

Early July Wireless Festival

www.wirelessfestival.co.uk
Three nights of rock and dance acts.

Mid July Lovebox Weekender

loveboxfestival.com
Top-quality weekend music festival in Victoria Park, everyone from Sly Stone and Blondie to MIA has headlined.

Mid July Somerset House Summer Series

*www.somersethouse.org.uk/
whats-on/summer-series-
somerset-house*
A dozen big-name concerts in the fountain court.

2 weekends in July British Summer Time Festival

www.bst-hydepark.com
This ten-day event in Hyde Park plays host to some of the planet's biggest musical stars.

❤ Mid July-mid Sept BBC Proms

www.bbc.co.uk/proms
The Proms overshadows all other classical music festivals in the city, with around 70 concerts, covering everything from early-music recitals to orchestral world premières, and from boundary-pushing debut performances to reverent career retrospectives. BBC Radio 3 plays recordings of the concerts.

Mid July-mid Sept Summer Streets

*www.regentstreetonline.com/
events/summer-streets*
Regent Street's classy curve is pedestrianised for a street party.

Early Aug Carnaval del Pueblo

carnavaldelpueblo.com
Loud-and-proud day out for Latin American Londoners, attracting up to 60,000 people to Burgess Park in Southwark.

❤ Aug bank holiday Notting Hill Carnival

*www.thelondonnottinghillcarnival.
com*

Notting Hill Carnival

Sept London African Music Festival

www.joyfulnoise.co.uk
A wonderfully eclectic affair, held over a fortnight in September in multiple venues.

Sept London Design Festival

www.londondesignfestival.com
This festival is the ultimate chance to discover design and craft in the capital at its very best. The V&A serves as the festival hub and is filled with eye-popping installations, but there are other events and exhibitions at dozens of locations throughout the capital, with landmark projects commissioned for major public spaces.

❤ Sept Totally Thames Festival

totallythames.org
A giant party along the Thames, this month of events is London's largest free arts festival. It's a family-friendly mix of carnival, pyrotechnics, art installations and live music alongside craft and food stalls. Events include the Great River Race – a 22-mile marathon for all manner of traditional rowed and paddled boats. The festival is brought to an end with a lantern procession and fireworks.

Sept Emerge Festival

emergefestival.co.uk
Launched in 2019 to replace the Museums at Night initiative, this two-night festival aims to open up the capital's world-class museums, galleries and historic houses to a new, younger audience, with a night-time series of specialist talks, unusual events and one-off exhibitions.

Sept Pearly Kings & Queens Harvest Festival

www.visitlondon.com/things-to-do/ event/26845942-pearly-kings-and- queens-harvest-festival

Two million people stream into Notting Hill for Europe's largest street party. Massive mobile sound systems dominate the streets with whatever bass-heavy party music is currently hip, but there's plenty of tradition from the West Indies too: calypso music and a spectacular costumed parade.

Aug bank holiday South West Four

www.southwestfour.com
London's key dance-music festival, covering everything from trance to house on Clapham Common.

Autumn

Autumn has a good share of clear, crisp days, which often seem to fall kindly for Diwali and Bonfire Night fireworks. The kids are back at school after the summer holidays, but it is rarely unpleasantly cold, so autumn is a great time of year for sightseeing.

Early Sept Tour of Britain

www.tourofbritain.co.uk
Join spectators on the streets of the capital for a stage of British cycling's biggest outdoor event.

A proper Cockney knees-up as the Pearly Kings and Queens lead a parade to St Mary-le-Bow church. Expect maypole dancing, Morris dancers and a marching band.

Mid Sept Open House London
openhouselondon.org.uk
For one weekend only, there's access to some 800 amazing buildings that are normally closed to the public.

Mid Sept London Fashion Week
www.londonfashionweek.co.uk
The autumn edition of the biannual fashion jamboree in Somerset House.

Mid Sept-mid Oct London Literature Festival
www.southbankcentre.co.uk/ whats-on/festivals-series/london- literature-festival
Combining superstar writers with architects, comedians, sculptors and cultural theorists at the Southbank Centre.

Oct Dance Umbrella
www.danceumbrella.co.uk
Innovative celebration of dance covering many styles and choreographers.

Oct London Cocktail Week
drinkup.london
Download a festival pass and get £6 drinks from the capital's best bars, mixologists and drinks vendors. The pass is valid at 300 bars and pop-up parties across London and also for the Cocktail Village in the Old Truman Brewery, giving you the chance to try some of the finest tipples the capital has to offer.

Mid Oct London Film Festival
www.bfi.org.uk/lff
The most significant of the capital's film festivals; expect red-carpet celebs at the BFI Southbank and Leicester Square's Vue West End.

❤ Mid Oct London Frieze Art Fair
frieze.com/fairs/frieze-london
The biggest contemporary carnival in London's art calendar occupies a purpose-built venue at the south end of Regent's Park, where some 1,000 artists are displayed over the four-day festival. Highlights include the daily-changing Projects; debates and discussions as part of the Talks strand; and Live, showing performance-based installations.

Oct/Nov Diwali
www.diwaliinlondon.com
Hindu, Jain and Sikh Festival of Light in Trafalgar Square.

5 Nov & around Bonfire Night
Firework displays all over town, marking the arrest of Guy Fawkes, and the thwarting of the attempt to blow up Parliament on 5 November 1604.

❤ Early Nov
Lord Mayor's Show
lordmayorsshow.london
This big show marks the traditional presentation of the new Lord Mayor for approval by the monarch's justices. The Lord Mayor leaves Mansion House in a fabulous

Bonfire night fireworks

gold coach at 11am, along with a colourful procession of floats and marchers. At 5.15pm, there's a fireworks display on the river.

▶ *The Lord Mayor is a City officer, elected each year by the livery companies and with no real power outside the City of London; don't confuse him with the Mayor of London, currently Sadiq Khan.*

Early Nov Remembrance Sunday Ceremony

Always held on the Sunday nearest to 11 November, this solemn commemoration honours those who died fighting in the World Wars and later conflicts. The Queen, the prime minister and other dignitaries lay poppy wreaths at the Cenotaph. A two-minute silence at 11am is followed by a service of remembrance.

Mid Nov London Jazz Festival

efglondonjazzfestival.org.uk
London's biggest jazz festival features ten days of music from trad to free improv.

Winter

There's plenty of fun to be had in the run-up to the big C, with roaring fires in trad pubs, the giant Christmas tree arriving in Trafalgar Square from Norway and the West End illuminations going up. Just don't count on seeing any snow. Christmas Day is pretty much the only time London closes down: there's no public transport and few attractions, shops or restaurants bother to open.

Dec Spitalfields Winter Music Festival

www.spitalfieldsmusic.org
Multi-genre music events, featuring world-class artists, in unusual venues across East London.

Early Dec Great Christmas Pudding Race

xmaspuddingrace.org.uk

Fancy-dress race in Covent Garden that involves balancing a Christmas pudding.

31 Dec New Year's Eve celebrations

www.london.gov.uk/events
A full-on fireworks display launched from the London Eye and rafts on the Thames.

1 Jan New Year's Day Parade

www.lnydp.com
If your hangover isn't too bad you can join the costumed New Year's Day Parade in central London.

Jan-Mar Vault Festival

vaultfestival.com
A sprawling, crypt-like space near Waterloo Station is the hub for this eight-week fringe festival, featuring some of London's most exciting new and grassroots theatre, cabaret and comedy. There's a packed line-up of immersive experiences, pop-ups, parties, and bags of underground atmosphere.

Jan/Feb London International Mime Festival

mimelondon.com
Theatrical magic in many forms, from haunting visual theatre to puppetry for adults

Shrove Tuesday Great Spitalfields Pancake Race

www.alternativearts.co.uk
Fancy dress teams run through the cobbled streets of Spitalfields flipping a pancake in the hope of winning a specially engraved frying pan.

Feb Chinese New Year Festival

www.lccauk.com
Celebrate the Chinese New Year in style in Chinatown and Leicester Square.

Mid/late Feb London Fashion Week

www.londonfashionweek.co.uk
See p64 London Fashion Week.

Time Out MARKET

THE BEST CHEFS OF THE CITY
Under one roof

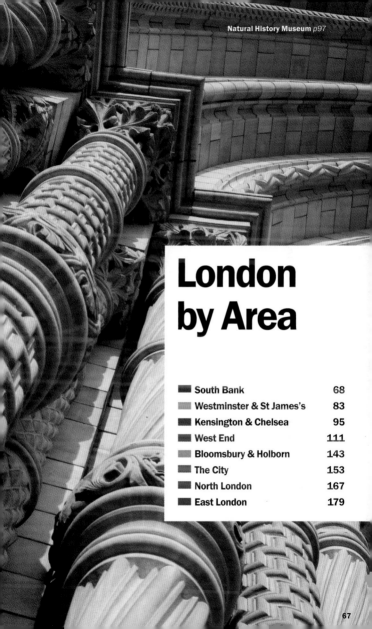

London by Area

South Bank

An estimated 14 million people come this way each year, and it's easy to see why. Between the London Eye and Tower Bridge, the south bank of the Thames offers a two-mile procession of diverting arts and entertainment venues and a host of London's must-see attractions.

Tourists have been visiting the area for centuries, but the entertainments have changed somewhat. **Shakespeare's Globe** remains as popular as ever, but the associated prostitutes, gamblers and bear-baiters have been replaced with art lovers, theatre-goers and culture vultures.

The area's modern-day life began in 1951 with the Festival of Britain, staged to boost morale in the wake of World War II. The **Royal Festival Hall** stands testament to the inclusive spirit of the project; it was later expanded into the **Southbank Centre**, which, alongside the **BFI Southbank** (the UK's premier arthouse cinema) and the concrete ziggurat of the **National Theatre**, has developed into a thriving cultural hub.

The riverside really took off in the new millennium, with the arrival of the **London Eye**, the **Millennium Bridge** and the **Tate Modern**, but has continued to thrive in the years since, with the **Shard** and the Tate Modern's **Blavatnik Building** adding to the parade of show-stopping structures.

Nearby, 13th-century **Borough Market** is a superb foraging place for both street-food enthusiasts and wannabe chefs, though it faces stiff competition from the other eateries and markets nearby.

Meanwhile in Lambeth, the impressive – and steadily revamped – **Imperial War Museum** provides a compelling, frequently hard-hitting history of armed conflict since World War I.

➡ **Getting around**
The area is best accessed by Tube/rail and, once there, most of the sights can be reached on foot. It can take anything from 40 minutes to three hours to walk the riverside path from Westminster Bridge to Tower Bridge.

Sights & museums

Other sights along the two-mile South Bank include the independent galleries at **Oxo Tower Wharf**, the **Clink Prison Museum** (1 Clink Street, SE1 9DG, 020 7403 0900, www.clink.co.uk) and a full-scale replica of Sir Francis Drake's ship, the **Golden Hinde** (St Mary Overie Dock, Cathedral Street, SE1 9DE, 020 7403 0123, www.goldenhinde.com).

Garden Museum

5 Lambeth Palace Road, SE1 7LB (020 7401 8865, www.gardenmuseum.org.uk). Lambeth North tube or Waterloo tube/rail. **Open** *10.30am-5pm Mon-Fri, Sun; 10.30am-4pm Sat; check website for occasional closures.* **Admission** *Museum £10; £5-£8.50 reductions; free under-6s. Tower £3; free under-18s.* **Map** *p71 M11.*
Saved from demolition in the 1970s, the deconsecrated church of St Mary's is a fitting site for the world's first horticulture museum: it was the last resting place of intrepid plant hunter and gardener to Charles I, John Tradescant (c1570-1638) – just one of the 20,000 bodies buried on the site, some dating back to the Norman Conquest. After a £7.5 million redevelopment, the museum's interior features seven galleries containing gardening memorabilia from 1600 to the modern day. The new courtyard extension contains a garden of rare plants, designed by Dan Pearson, and a café. It's a quiet place for reflection too.

Hayward Gallery

Southbank Centre, 337-338 Belvedere Road, SE1 8XX (020 7960 5211, www.southbankcentre.co.uk). Embankment tube or Waterloo tube/rail. **Open** *11am-7pm Mon, Wed, Fri-Sun; 11am-9pm Thur.* **Admission** *varies.* **Map** *p71 N9.*

The 1960s brutalist Hayward Gallery reopened in 2018 after a two-year multi-million pound refurbishment project. Now, 66 glass pyramid rooflights let controlled natural lighting into the upper galleries for the first time, transforming the visitor experience. The improved environment makes the gallery's versatile programme of thought-provoking contemporary art all the more appealing. It has no permanent collection, but has always hosted (often sell-out) exhibitions, among them Anthony Gormley's fog-filled chamber for 'Blind Light,' and Carsten Holler's roller-coaster slides. A highlight for 2020 is the major retrospective of work by the British artist Bridget Riley.

HMS Belfast

The Queen's Walk, SE1 2JH (020 7940 6300, www.iwm.org.uk). London Bridge tube/rail. **Open** *Mar-Oct 10am-6pm daily. Nov-Feb 10am-5pm daily.* **Admission** *£18; £9-£14.40 reductions; free under-5s.* **Map** *p71 S9.*
This 11,500-ton Edinburgh class large light cruiser is the last surviving big-gun World War II warship in Europe. It's also a floating branch of the Imperial War Museum, and is a popular if unlikely playground for children, who tear around its complex of gun turrets, bridge, decks and engine room. The *Belfast* was built in 1936, ran convoys to Russia, supported the Normandy Landings and helped UN forces in Korea before being decommissioned in 1963.

♥ Imperial War Museum

Lambeth Road, SE1 6HZ (020 7416 5000, www.iwm.org.uk). Lambeth North tube or Elephant & Castle tube/rail. **Open** *10am-6pm daily.* **Admission** *free. Special exhibitions vary.* **Map** *p71 O11.*
One of London's great museums – but probably the least famous of

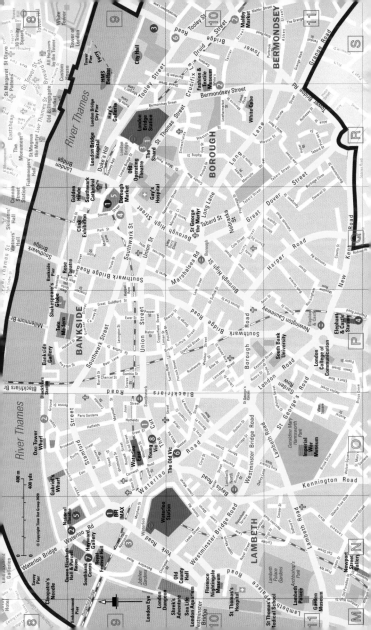

London Eye

them – IWM London focuses on the military action of British and Commonwealth troops during the 20th century. One of the highlights, built to commemorate the centenary, are the state-of-the-art First World War galleries that take a considered, contemporary look at the conflict, examining the Home Front as much as the Western Front. Alongside huge set pieces like a walk-through trench is a heart-stopping collection of small, personal items and medical objects, including a magnet used to pull shrapnel from wounds.

The Central Hall is an attention-grabbing repository of major artefacts: guns, tanks and aircraft hang from the ceiling (not least a Harrier GR9 that saw action in Afghanistan).

The museum's tone darkens as you ascend. On the third floor, the Holocaust Exhibition (not recommended for under-14s) traces the history of European anti-Semitism and its nadir in the concentration camps. Upstairs, Crimes Against Humanity (unsuitable for under-16s) is a minimalist space in which a film exploring contemporary genocide and ethnic violence rolls relentlessly.

London Dungeon
Riverside Building County Hall, Westminster Bridge Road, SE1 7PB (www.thedungeons.com/london). Westminster tube or Waterloo tube/rail. **Open** *10am-5pm Mon-Fri, Sun; 10am-6pm Sat. Times vary during school hols.* **Admission** *£30; £24 reductions; free under-3s. Book online for 30% reductions.* **Map** *p71 N9.*

Visitors to this jokey celebration of torture, death and disease journey back in time to London's plague-ridden streets (rotting corpses, rats, vile boils, projectile vomiting) and meet some of the city's least savoury characters, from Guy Fawkes to Sweeney Todd. A cast of blood-splattered actors are joined by 'virtual' guests, such as Brian Blessed as Henry VIII, as well as 18 different shows and 'surprises' – which could see you on the run from Jack the Ripper or getting lost in London's Victorian sewers. There are two thrill rides too: a turbulent boat trip down the Thames for execution, and a dark drop ride that plunges three storeys in the pitch black.

♥ London Eye
Riverside Building, County Hall, Westminster Bridge Road, SE1 7PB (www.londoneye.com). Westminster tube or Waterloo tube/rail. **Open** *varies.* **Admission** *£30; £24 reductions; free under-3s. Book online for reduced prices.* **Map** *p71 N9.*

The Eye is up there with Tower Bridge and 'Big Ben' among the

♥ Shakespeare's Globe

21 New Globe Walk, Bankside, SE1 9DT (information 020 7902 1400, tickets 020 7401 9919, www.shakespearesglobe.com). Southwark tube or London Bridge tube/rail. **Tours** *9.30am-5pm daily (except during performances).* **Box office** *10am-6pm daily.* **Admission** *£17; £10-£15.50 reductions; £46 family; free under-5s.* **Tickets** *£5.* **Map** *p71 P8.*

The original Globe Theatre, where many of William Shakespeare's plays were first staged and which he co-owned, burned to the ground in 1613 during a performance of *Henry VIII*. Nearly 400 years later, it was rebuilt not far from its original site, using construction methods and materials based on as much historical detail as could be found.

A visit here isn't just a history lesson. The Globe is also a fully operating open-air theatre and the productions are among the best in London. Each season (from 23 April – conventionally regarded as the Bard's birthday – into early October) includes several Shakespeare classics, performed by a company of established and upcoming actors, but works of other writers are also programmed.

The Globe also now offers performances in the Sam Wanamaker Playhouse – a candlelit indoor theatre alongside the Globe, which presents plays in a traditional and intimate Jacobean setting.

Even if you're not attending a play, you can do the Globe Exhibition and Tour: the tours run all year, even out of season (allow 90 minutes for the visit).

capital's most postcard-friendly tourist assets. Assuming you choose a clear day, a 30-minute circuit on the Eye affords predictably great views of the city, with touchscreens in each of the 32 pods providing a guide to what you can see. Take a few snaps from the comfort of your pod and, there, your sightseeing's just about done. The Eye was the vision of husband-and-wife architect team Julia Barfield and David Marks, who entered a 1992 competition to design a structure for the millennium. Their giant wheel idea came second, but the winning entry is conspicuous by its absence. The Eye was planned as a temporary structure but its removal now seems unthinkable.

Newport Street Gallery

Newport Street, SE11 6AJ (020 3141 9320, www.newportstreetgallery. com/about). Vauxhall tube/rail or Lambeth North tube. Open 10am-5pm Wed-Sun. Admission free. Map p71 N11.

Damien Hirst, the Young British Artist par excellence, isn't a man to do things by halves – unless, that is, taking half a street of listed warehouses and converting them into a huge gallery. Across two levels, six exhibition spaces and some 37,000sq ft of floor, his private collection of 3,000 works is displayed in temporary exhibitions: with holdings that include Picasso, Francis Bacon and Jeff Koons alongside YBA chums like Sarah Lucas and Gavin Turk, he's got plenty of art to choose from, but there's also taxidermy, indigenous art from the Pacific Northwest and anatomical models. The space was brilliantly reworked by the architects Caruso St John, who won the 2017 Stirling Prize for their work. The in-house restaurant, **Pharmacy 2**, designed by Hirst, serves a casual modern-British menu overseen by chef Mark Hix.

Sea Life London Aquarium

County Hall, Westminster Bridge Road, SE1 7PB (www.visitsealife. com/london). Westminster tube or Waterloo tube/rail. Open 10am-6pm Mon-Fri; 9.30am-7pm Sat, Sun. School hols varies. Admission £29; £23 reductions; free under-3s. Book online for reductions. Map p71 N10.

This is one of Europe's largest aquariums, and a huge hit with kids – perhaps too huge: it does get awfully crowded in the school holidays and at weekends. The inhabitants are grouped by geographical origin, beginning with the Atlantic, where blacktail bream swim alongside the Thames Embankment. The 'Rainforests of the World' exhibit has introduced poison arrow frogs, crocodiles and piranhas. The Ray Lagoon is still popular, though touching the friendly flatfish is no longer allowed (it's bad for their health). Starfish, crabs and anemones can be handled in special open rock pools instead, and the clown fish still draw crowds. There's a mesmerising Seahorse Temple, a tank full of turtles and enchanting Gentoo penguins. The centrepieces, though, are the massive Pacific and Indian Ocean tanks, with menacing sharks quietly circling fallen Easter Island statues.

Southwark Cathedral

London Bridge, SE1 9DA (7367 6700, www.cathedral.southwark. anglican.org). London Bridge tube/rail. Open 9am-5pm Mon-Fri; 9.30am-3.45pm, 5-6pm Sat; 12.30-3pm, 4-6pm Sun. For service times, see the website. Admission free; suggested donation £4. Map p71 Q9.

The oldest bits of this building date back more than 800 years. The retro-choir was the setting for several Protestant martyr trials during the reign of Mary Tudor. Inside, there are memorials

💜 The Shard

*Joiner Street, SE1 0QU (0844 499 7111, www.theviewfromtheshard. com). London Bridge tube/ rail. **Open** 10am-10pm daily. **Admission** £30.95; £24.95 reductions; free under-4s. Book online for reductions. **Map** p71 R9.*

You can't miss the Shard – which is, after all, the point of the structure. Looking oddly similar to Saruman's tower in *The Lord of the Rings*, it shoots into the sky 'like a shard of glass' – to use the words of its architect, Renzo Piano, who doodled the idea for this vast edifice for its developer, Irving Sellar, on the back of a menu. In 2011, the Shard became the tallest building in the EU, but wasn't to reach its full height until 2012, when it topped out at 1,016 feet (310 metres).

But height isn't everything: it's the shape of this slim, slightly irregular pyramid that makes it noteworthy, an instantly recognisable centrepiece of views

from pretty much everywhere in London – except, ironically, from the Victorian alleys at its foot, where the monstrous building plays peek-a-boo with visitors as they scurry around looking for a good snapshot.

Once you're inside, high-speed lifts whisk passengers up 72 floors to enjoy stunning 360º, 40-mile views, but the real joy of a visit is looking down: even seasoned London-watchers find peering down on the likes of the Tower of London from this extreme height oddly revelatory, like Google Earth in real time.

If you've got a few quid in your pocket, a stay at the Shangri-La (*see p194*) gives you plenty of time to take it all in without the hoi polloi – and with the opportunity to swim in a rather narrow infinity pool on the 52nd floor. But you don't have to be resident to enjoy cocktails at Gŏng (*see p78*) or eat at one of the four restaurants; Hutong is our favourite (*see p77*).

Southwark Cathedral p74

to Shakespeare, John Harvard (benefactor of the American university) and Sam Wanamaker (the motivation and driving force behind the reconstruction of the Globe); Chaucer features in the stained glass. There are displays throughout the cathedral explaining its history. The courtyard is one of the area's prettiest places for a rest; there's also a café.

♥ Tate Modern

Bankside, SE1 9TG (7887 8888, www.tate.org.uk). Blackfriars tube/rail or Southwark tube. **Open** *10am-6pm Mon-Thur, Sun; 10am-10pm Fri, Sat.* **Admission** *free. Temporary exhibitions vary.* **Map** *p71 P8.*

Thanks to its industrial architecture, this powerhouse of modern art is awe-inspiring even before you enter. Built after World War II as Bankside Power Station, it was designed by Sir Giles Gilbert Scott, architect of Battersea Power Station. The power station shut in 1981; nearly 20 years later, it opened as an art museum, and has enjoyed spectacular popularity ever since. The gallery attracts five million visitors a year – twice as many as the original building was intended for, hence the ten-storey extension that rose from the power station's former fuel tanks to completion in 2016. This vast, partly folded tower has increased exhibition space by 60% and features a top-floor viewing level, restaurant, and three new floors of galleries. It has allowed for a 'progressive rehang' of Tate Modern's permanent collection, with more room for lesser-known international art. The cavernous Turbine Hall, used to jaw-dropping effect for the massive Hyundai Commission installation each year, has become what the Tate is calling 'the street' that connects both buildings.

Beyond, the permanent collection draws from the Tate's many post-1900 international works, featuring heavy-hitters such as Matisse, Rothko and Beuys. The polka-dotted **Tate-to-Tate boat** zooms to Tate Britain every 40 minutes, via the London Eye (tickets £8.70, £2.90-£5.80 reductions, free under-5s).

Restaurants

Anchor & Hope ££

36 The Cut, SE1 8LP (7928 9898, www.anchorandhopepub.co.uk). Southwark tube or Waterloo tube/rail. **Open** *Food served 5.45-10pm Mon; noon-5pm, 5.45-10pm Tue-Sat; noon-3.15pm Sun.* **Map** *p71 O9* ❶ *Gastropub*

Open for more than a decade, the Anchor & Hope is still a leading exponent of using offal and unusual cuts of meat in simple but artful combinations, served in a relaxed setting. Bookings aren't taken, so most evenings you'll join the waiting list for a table (45 minutes midweek is typical) and have to hover at the crammed bar. But the food is terrific: beautifully textured venison kofte, say, served on perkily dressed gem lettuce leaves; or rabbit served savagely red, with salty jus, fat chips and béarnaise sauce.

Casse-Croûte £££
109 Bermondsey Street, SE1 3XB (7407 2140, cassecroute.co.uk). London Bridge tube/rail. **Open** *noon-10pm Mon-Sat; noon-4pm Sun.* **Map** *p71 R10* ❷ *French*
Romantically lit, with checked tablecloths and a tiny bar lined with digestifs, Casse-Croûte is a shot of warm, villagey France in Bermondsey. On the site of a former sandwich shop, Hervé Durochat's intimate bistro has space for just over 20 covers and feels genuinely familial. Best of all, the sensibly priced blackboard menu of boldly chosen French classics really delivers. From delicate shavings of calf's head in a tangy sauce *ravigote* to creamy mackerel fillets pepped up with a scoop of mustard ice-cream, dishes are fresh, simple and smartly executed. **Other location** Pique Nique, Tanner Street Park, SE1 3LD (7403 9549, pique-nique.co.uk).

♥ Hutong ££££
The Shard, Level 33, 31 St Thomas Street, SE1 9RY (3011 1257, hutong.co.uk). London Bridge tube/rail. **Open** *noon-2.30pm, 6-10.30pm Mon-Fri; 11.30am-3.30pm, 6-10.30pm Sat, Sun.* **Map** *p71 R9* ❸ *Chinese*
Like the original Hutong in Hong Kong, the Shard version is a glitzy

place with amazing views, ersatz Old Beijing decor, and a Sichuan/northern Chinese menu. The traditionally fiery cuisine, big on chilli and sichuan pepper, has been toned down a little for the *gweilo* (Western) palate, but there's plenty to set the tastebuds alight. Delicate starters of chilled sliced scallops served with pomelo segments or octopus salad with hot and sour sauce are followed by mouthwatering mains such as prawn wantons with *ma-la* ('numbing, spicy hot' sauce), a 'red lantern' of softshell crabs or Mongolian-style barbecue rack of lamb. It's not cheap but then this is the Shard, not Chinatown.

♥ Padella ££
6 Southwark Street, SE1 1TQ (www.padella.co). London Bridge tube/rail. **Open** *noon-3.45pm, 5-10pm Mon-Sat; noon-3.45pm, 5-9pm Sun.* **Map** *p71 Q9* ❹ *Italian*
This sleek pasta bar, from the duo behind Islington's **Trullo** (*see p175*), is ideal for a classy express lunch. There's a changing mix of classics and lesser-spotted varieties, such as *tagliarini* (skinny tagliatelle) or *pici* (a kind of hand-rolled no-egg noodle from Siena), which is smothered in a simple yet moreish *cacio e pepe* sauce of parmesan, butter and cracked black pepper. The eight-hour beef shin ragu served over pappardelle is a perennial favourite, while the smoked eel and cream tagliatelle – with just a hint of Sicilian lemon – is sublime. Dishes are small enough (and, at around £5-£12, cheap enough) to let you to order three between two.

♥ El Pastór ££
7A Stoney Street, SE1 9AA (www.tacoselpastor.co.uk). London Bridge tube/rail. **Open** *noon-3pm, 5-11pm Mon-Fri; noon-4pm, 6-11pm Sat; noon-4pm Sun.* **Map** *p71 Q9* ❺ *Mexican*

El Pastór is a taco joint in a railway arch next to foodie magnet Borough Market (see p79) and it doesn't accept bookings. The wait can, at peak times, be up to two hours. But once you've got a table you might try a tuna tostada, a bowl of fresh guac and a prawn taco on a nicely firm corn tortilla. Or the signature 24-hour marinated 'al pastór' pork – just the thought of which makes us smile. With the pork, make sure you get 'gringa' quesadilla: a dirty and delicious quarter slice of a large tortilla, served 'open-faced', with a messy tumble of meat, melted cheese, coriander and salsa. Every bite brings sweet, salt, fire, squidge and crunch. El Pastór knows how to throw a fiesta, with excellent, Latin-vibey music cranked up loud; staff who are smiley and obliging; and the lighting set to 'looking good, baby'.

El Pastór p77

♥ Restaurant Story £££658

199 Tooley Street, SE1 2JX (7183 2117, restaurantstory.co.uk). *London Bridge tube/rail.* **Open** *6.30-9pm Mon; noon-5pm, 6.30-9pm Tue-Sat.* **Map** *p71 S10* ⑥
British

Story, from starry young chef Tom Sellers, continues this area's rise to foodie heaven, having secured a Michelin star within months of opening. It's set in a sparse room – all the better to emphasise the view of the Shard through floor-to-ceiling windows, and, of course, the food: an enjoyable procession of modernist dishes layered with culinary puns (bread and dripping, for instance, features a lit candle made from dripping) and tastebud challenges (mackerel versus green strawberries).

Pubs & bars

Gŏng

Level 52, The Shard, 31 St Thomas Street, SE1 9QU (7234 8208, www. gong-shangri-la.com). *London Bridge tube/rail.* **Open** *noon-1am Mon-Sat; noon-midnight Sun.* **Map** *p71 R9* ①

Take the express lift up the Shard to the 52nd floor to find London's highest bar. At this altitude, it's actually not so easy to pick out landmarks, but the views of the City are simply spectacular, especially if you book a two-hour slot across sunset. Be warned: you'll pay a premium for drinking in such an elevated location. Look No Hands, for example, made with CopperDog whisky, Triple Sec and Fernet-Branca is a punchy apertif, but you won't get any change from a £20 note.

There's usually a minimum £30 spend per person, but on Sunday, Monday or Tuesday (except bank holidays) you can enjoy the view for up to 90 minutes for just the price of a bottle of beer or a glass of wine.

💜 Lyaness
20 Upper Ground, SE1 9PD (3747 1063, lyaness.com). Blackfriars tube/rail. **Open** *4pm-1am Mon-Wed; noon-2am Thur-Sat; noon-12.30am Sun.* **Map** p68 O8 ❷

More than just a scientist with a snappy dress sense and a curious approach to cocktails, Ryan Chetiyawardana is a master of reinvention. Just as Dandelyan was crowned World's Best Bar in 2018, he announced he was closing it down. Lyaness rose from the ashes, offering the same Thames-side views but with an electric-blue makeover and an overhauled menu of weird and wonderful flavours such as Onyx, Infinite Banana or King Monkey Nut. Go for Fancy Tea or the late-night DJs, but let the drinks do the talking.

Waterloo Tap
Corner of Sutton Walk & Concert Hall Approach, SE1 8RL (3455 7436, www.waterlootap.com). Waterloo tube/rail. **Open** *noon-11pm Mon, Tue; noon-11.30pm Wed, Thur; noon-midnight Fri; 11am-midnight Sat; 11am-10pm Sun.* **Map** p71 N9 ❸

Tucked away in a railway arch a short dash from Waterloo Station, the Tap has bucked the trend towards the new breed of high-alcohol brews and stuck to its roots as a more traditional alehouse. You'll find no filament bulbs or scruffily chalked-up beer lists here. The 20-strong keg collection is British-focused, with the north especially well represented (no surprise, given the original Tap is in Sheffield). If they're on, try something from Manchester's Cloudwater Brew Co, whose one-off, seasonal brews are never around for long.

Shops & services

💜 Borough Market
8 Southwark Street, SE1 1TL (7407 1002, www.boroughmarket.org.uk). London Bridge tube/rail. **Open** *10am-5pm Mon-Thur; 10am-6pm Fri; 8am-5pm Sat.* **Map** p71 Q9 ❶ Market

The food hound's favourite market is also London's oldest, dating back to the 13th century. It's the busiest, too, occupying a sprawling

Borough Market

site near London Bridge. In its long history, Borough Market has survived fire, riot, terrorism and redevelopment - a busy rail line has been thrice installed and extended above the market itself. Now all it has to contend with are the hordes of tourists and Londoners who flock here to grab a gourmet goodie: from fresh loaves and rare-breed meats, via fish, game, fruit and veg, to cakes and all manner of preserves, oils and teas; head out hungry to take advantage of the numerous free samples. Market Hall, facing on to Borough High Street, acts as a kind of greenhouse for growing plants (including hops), as well as hosting workshops, tastings and foodie demonstrations. You can also nip in with your snack if the weather's poor.

▶ *Borough Market's weekend trade has been challenged by former stallholders who have set up camp under the arches around Maltby Street (Ropewalk, SE1 3PA, www.maltby.st). The website www.spa-terminus. co.uk has a useful map showing locations and opening hours.*

Entertainment

BFI IMAX

1 Charlie Chaplin Walk, SE1 8XR (0330 333 7878, www.bfi.org.uk/ bfi-imax). Waterloo tube/rail. **Tickets** *£17.25-£23; £13.50-£17.50 reductions* **Screens** *1.* **Map** *p71 N9* **❶** *Cinema*
London's – indeed, the UK's – biggest cinema screen at 5,800sq ft (539sq m), the BFI IMAX is in the centre of a busy roundabout next to Waterloo station. As well as the massive screen, you get superlative sound quality and seats arranged at such a vertiginous angle there's no chance of a head blocking your view. It's not cheap – just over £20 for a premium seat – but if you

like your blockbusters vast and noisy, there's really nothing else like it in town. Film aficionados will likely prefer **BFI Southbank** (020 7928 3232, whatson.bfi. org.uk, **❷**), under Waterloo bridge, which screens significant British and foreign films.

Bridge Theatre

3 Potters Fields Park, SE1 2SG (tickets 0333 320 0051, bridgetheatre.co.uk). London Bridge tube/rail. **Box office** *9am-9pm daily.* **Tickets** *£15-£90.* **Map** *p71 S9* **❸** *Theatre*
In 2017 Sir Nicholas Hytner (of National Theatre fame; *see p81*) and Nick Starr opened the new 900-seat Bridge Theatre close to Tower Bridge. It was the first commercial theatre of its size to open in London for decades, and it provides the comfortable seats, plentiful loos, delicious food and, above all, proper new writing that the West End so conspicuously lacks. It is yet to stage a really outstanding transfer-worthy production, but its aim to commission and produce new work attracts big-name playwrights and actors, including Alan Bennett, Martin McDonagh, Rory Kinnear and Simon Russell Beale.

♥ Corsica Studios

4-5 Elephant Road, Elephant & Castle, SE17 1LB (020 7703 4760, www.corsicastudios.com). Elephant & Castle tube/rail. **Open** *8pm-3am Mon-Thur, Sun; 8pm-6am Fri, Sat.* **Admission** *free-£15.* **Map** *p71 P11* **❹** *Events space*
An independent, not-for-profit arts complex, Corsica Studios seeks to breed a culture of creativity. The flexible warehouse space is one of London's most adventurous, supplementing the DJs that play here with bands, poets, painters and lunatic projectionists. Sure, it's rough around the edges, with

💙 National Theatre

*South Bank, SE1 9PX (020 7452 3000, www.nationaltheatre.org. uk). Embankment or Southwark tube, or Waterloo tube/rail. **Box office** 9.30am-8pm Mon-Sat. **Tickets** £15-£52. **Map** p71 N9 ❺ Theatre*

A still-startling jewel of brutalist design, the National is surely the world's greatest theatre. It boasts three auditoriums – the epic, ampitheatre-style Olivier; the substantial end-on space the Lyttelton; and the Dorfman, a smaller venue for edgier work. Nobody says it gets everything right, but it is worthy of a pilgrimage for anybody remotely interested in the arts. Former artistic director Nicholas Hytner rescued the NT from the doldrums, launching endless hit transfers to the West End, got Travelex to sponsor tickets to bring down the prices, and adroitly balanced the programme to mix big, crowd-pleasing stuff by Shakespeare with startling new work and some properly obscure rediscoveries. His landmark successes – Alan Bennett's *The History Boys* and *War Horse* – showed that the state-subsidised home of British theatre could turn out quality drama at a profit.

Successor Rufus Norris has had a slightly more difficult time of it. Big West End money-spinner *War Horse* finally closed, and *The Curious Incident of the Dog in the Night-Time* followed suit, with no obvious sign of replacements. The press has been occasionally unkind, criticising Norris for everything from staging work

that's too weird, to putting on too much new writing and not commissioning enough female writers and directors. If a new West End hit remains elusive, that's not for want of popular, agenda-setting productions, with a starry revival of Tony Kushner's epic *Angels in America*, van Hove's take on the classic '80s film *Network*, starring *Breaking Bad*'s Bryan Cranston, and Annie Baker's *The Antipodes* all keeping the returns queue busy. The Travelex seasons continue, widening audiences by offering tickets for £15, as does the free outdoor performances on the River Stage, held outside the NT during the summer.

THREE SISTERS

a new play by Inua Ellams after Chekhov

makeshift bars and toilets, but the events are second to none. The live-music roster has included gigs from Silver Apples, Acoustic Ladyland and Lydia Lunch.

Old Vic

The Cut, SE1 8NB (0344 871 7628, www.oldvictheatre.com). Southwark tube or Waterloo tube/rail. **Box office** *In person 10am-6pm Mon-Fri, also Sat on performance days only. By phone 9am-7.30pm Mon-Fri; 9am-7pm Sat on performance days.* **Tickets** *£10-£90.* **Map** *p71 O10* ❻ *Theatre*

Matthew Warchus is a seriously heavyweight director with a bold, eclectic approach to serious programming. His USP is new musical work, including *Groundhog Day* and *Girl from the North* (based around the songs of Bob Dylan), both of which transferred to Broadway. In 2019 Duncan Macmillan's brilliant *Lungs* got its first major revival, starring Claire Foy and Matt Smith in rather different roles to those that fans of *The Crown* will be used to.

❤ Southbank Centre

Belvedere Road, SE1 8XX (020 3879 9555, www.southbankcentre. co.uk). Embankment tube or Waterloo tube/rail. **Box office** *In person 10am-8pm daily. By phone 9am-8pm daily.* **Tickets** *£7-£75.* **Map** *p71 N9* ❼ *Concert venue*

The centrepiece of the cluster of cultural venues collectively known as the Southbank Centre is the 2,500-seat **Royal Festival Hall**. Along with the neighbouring 900-seat **Queen Elizabeth Hall** and attached 365-seat **Purcell Room** it programmes a wide variety of events – spoken word, jazz, rock and pop gigs – but classical is very well represented. The RFH has four resident orchestras and hosts music from medieval motets to

Messiaen via Beethoven and Elgar. Beneath the main hall, facing the foyer bar, a stage puts on hundreds of free concerts each year.

Young Vic

66 The Cut, SE1 8LZ (020 7922 2922, www.youngvic.org). Waterloo tube/rail. **Box office** *10am-6pm Mon-Sat.* **Tickets** *£10-£57.* **Map** *p71 O9* ❽ *Theatre*

As the name suggests, this Vic has more youthful bravura than its older sister up the road, and draws a younger crowd, who pack out the open-air balcony and its restaurant and bar on the weekends. They come to see classics with a modern edge, new writing with an international flavour and collaborations with leading companies. Recent winners have included Matthew Lopez's haunting, ambitious *The Inheritance*, about the post-AIDS generation, which transferred to the West End in 2018. That year also saw the homecoming of Kwame Kwei-Armah as artistic director. He hit the ground running with a large-scale revival of Danai Gurira's off-West End success *The Convert*, plus *The Tree*, a collaboration with Idris Elba.

Southbank Centre

Westminster & St James's

The whole of the United Kingdom is ruled from this small portion of London on the north bank of the Thames. The monarchy has been in residence in **Westminster** since the 11th century, when Edward the Confessor moved west out of the walled City, and as the role of British kings and queens became increasingly ceremonial, Parliament was already here to take on the real business of government. Many visitors find the imposing buildings of Westminster more formal than inviting, but it's a key destination, with the most significant area designated a UNESCO World Heritage Site back in 1987.

    Parliament Square has some of the capital's most impressive architecture: the Gothic masterpiece of

Best sights
Houses of Parliament *p87*,
Westminster Abbey *p90*

Best decadent dining
Wolseley *p92*

Best old-school café
Regency Café *p91*

Best shops
Dover Street Market *p92*,
Fortnum & Mason *p94*

Best park
St James's Park *p93*

Best art galleries
National Gallery *p86*,
Tate Britain *p89*

Westminster Abbey has been the site of almost every British coronation, while the **Houses of Parliament** and its '**Big Ben**' clock tower have starred in many holiday snaps. Heading north along **Whitehall** – one of London's most majestic streets – is **Trafalgar Square**, where visitors flock in their thousands to pose for photographs in front of **Nelson's Column**.

Westminster is also packed with culture. The **National Portrait Gallery** and **Tate Britain** – often overlooked in favour of its modern cousin on the other side of the river – offer a walk through British history. The perennially popular **National Gallery** continues to draw visitors with one of the greatest collections of paintings in the world.

And for such an important part of London, the area is surprisingly spacious. **The Mall** offers a regally broad approach route to **Buckingham Palace**, which presides over lovely **St James's Park**. Traditional, quiet and exclusive, the residential area of **St James's** is dignified and unhurried, whether you're shopping at **Fortnum's** or entertaining at the **Wolseley**.

➜ **Getting around**
This central area is very well served by tube and bus, but you'll see more if you walk. Most sights are within half a mile of each other.

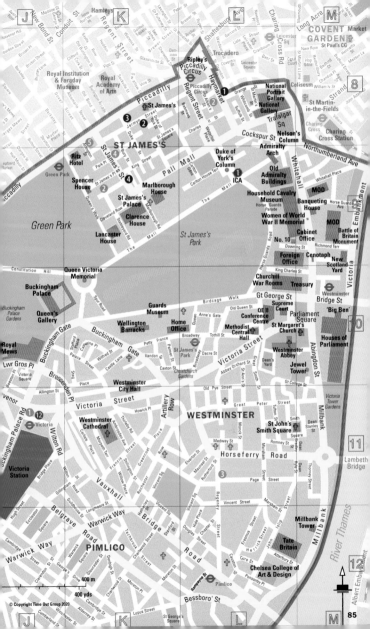

Buckingham Palace & Royal Mews

The Mall, SW1A 1AA (Palace 0303 123 7300, Royal Mews 0303 123 7302, Queen's Gallery 0303 123 7301, www.rct.uk). Green Park tube or Victoria tube/rail. **Open** *admission times & prices vary.* **Map** *p85 J10.*

Constructed as a private house for the Duke of Buckingham in 1703 and converted into a palace by John Nash in 1820, Buckingham Palace has been used as the primary home of every British monarch since Queen Victoria. The palace's State Apartments are open to the public each year while the family are away on their summer hols. At other times of year, visit the Queen's Gallery to see the Queen's personal collection of treasures, including paintings by Rembrandt, Sèvres porcelain and the Diamond Diadem crown.

Further along Buckingham Palace Road, the **Royal Mews** houses the royal fleet of Rolls-Royces, the splendid royal carriages and the horses, individually named by the Queen.

Churchill War Rooms

Clive Steps, King Charles Street, SW1A 2AQ (020 7930 6961, www.iwm.org.uk). St James's Park or Westminster tube. **Open** *9.30am-6pm daily.* **Admission** *£22; £11-17.60 reductions; free under-5s.* **Map** *p85 L10.*

Out of harm's way beneath Whitehall, this cramped and spartan bunker was where Winston Churchill planned the Allied victory in World War II, and the rooms powerfully bring to life the reality of a nation at war. The cabinet rooms were sealed on 16 August 1945, keeping the complex in a state of suspended animation: every pin stuck into the vast charts was placed there in the final days of the conflict. The humble quarters occupied by Churchill and his deputies give a tangible sense of wartime hardship, an effect reinforced by the wailing sirens and wartime speeches on the audio guide (free with admission).

Household Cavalry Museum

Horse Guards, Whitehall, SW1A 2AX (020 7930 3070, www.householdcavalrymuseum.co.uk). Westminster tube or Charing Cross tube/rail. **Open** *Apr-Oct 10am-6pm daily. Nov-Mar 10am-5pm daily.* **Admission** *£8.50; £6.50 reductions; free under-5s.* **Map** *p85 L9.*

Household Cavalry is a fairly workaday name for the military peacocks who make up the Queen's official guard. They tell their stories through video diaries at this small but entertaining museum, which also offers the chance to see medals, uniforms and shiny cuirasses (breastplates) up close. You also get a peek – and sniff – of the magnificent horses that parade just outside every day: the stables are separated from the main museum by no more than a screen of glass. *See also p60 and p62.*

▶ *The smaller Guards Museum (Wellington Barracks, Birdcage Walk, SW1E 6HQ, 020 7414 3428, www.theguardsmuseum.com) provides a similar insight into the history of the Foot Guards.*

♥ National Gallery

Trafalgar Square, WC2N 5DN (020 7747 2885, www.nationalgallery.org.uk). Charing Cross tube/rail. **Open** *10am-6pm Mon-Thur, Sat, Sun; 10am-9pm Fri.* **Tours** *11am Mon-Fri.* **Admission** *free. Special exhibitions vary.* **Map** *p85 L8.*

Founded in 1824, the National Gallery is one of the world's great repositories for art. There are masterpieces from virtually every European school of art, from austere 13th-century religious

💜 Houses of Parliament

*Parliament Square, SW1A 0AA
(Commons information 020 7219
4272, Lords information 020
7219 3107, tickets 020 7219 4114,
www.parliament.uk/visiting).
Westminster tube.* **Tours** *every
Sat plus Mon-Fri when not in
session.* **Public galleries** *Mon-Fri
when in session (check the website
for further details).* **Audio tour**
*£19.50; £8-£17 reductions; free
under-5s.* **Guided tour** *£26.50;
£11.50-£22 reductions; free under-
5s.* **Map** *p85 M10.*

The British Parliament has an
extremely long history, with the
first parliamentary session held
in St Stephen's Chapel in 1275. The
Palace of Westminster, however,
only became the permanent
seat of Parliament in 1532, when
Henry VIII moved to a new
des-res in Whitehall.

The current palace is a
wonderful mish-mash of styles,
dominated by Gothic buttresses,
towers and arches. It looks much
older than it is: the Parliament
buildings were designed in 1860
by Charles Barry (ably assisted
by Augustus Pugin) to replace
the original building, which had

been destroyed by fire in 1834.
Of the original palace, only the
Jewel Tower (020 7222 2219, www.
english-heritage.org.uk) and,
within the Parliament buildings,
Westminster Hall, remain.

Visitors are welcome (subject to
stringent security checks) either
to tour the palace buildings, or
to observe the political debates
in the House of Lords and House
of Commons; Prime Minister's
Question Time at noon on
Wednesday is often sparky.

For more insight into the
history, architecture and arcane
practices of parliament, book an
audio tour or (better) the revealing
90-minute guided tour, which
takes in both Houses, Westminster
Hall, the Queen's Robing Room
and the Royal Gallery. (The
Elizabeth Tower housing Big
Ben is, however, shrouded in
scaffolding and inaccessible until
2021 due to restoration work.)

▶ *More expensive tour tickets
can be bought on the day from the
ticket office at the front of Portcullis
House on Victoria Embankment,
SW1A 2LW (10am-4pm Mon-Fri,
8.45am-4.45pm Sat & tour days).*

paintings to the sensual delights of Titian, Caravaggio and Van Gogh.

The gallery itself is huge; don't try to see everything in one visit. The modern Sainsbury Wing contains the gallery's earliest works: Italian paintings by masters such as Giotto and Piero della Francesca, as well as the medieval 'Wilton Diptych', showing Richard II with the Virgin and Child. In the West Wing are Italian Renaissance masterpieces by Correggio, Titian and Raphael. The North Wing displays 17th-century Dutch, Flemish, Italian and Spanish old masters, including Rembrandt's *A Woman Bathing in a Stream* and Caravaggio's *Supper at Emmaus*. In the East Wing, you'll find works by the French Impressionists and Post-Impressionists, including Monet's *Water-Lilies*, one of Van Gogh's *Sunflowers* and Seurat's *Bathers at Asnières*. Don't miss Renoir's astonishingly lovely *The Skiff* (*La Yole*). Downstairs, the ground-floor galleries host major temporary exhibitions.

National Portrait Gallery

St Martin's Place, WC2H 0HE (020 7306 0055, www.npg.org.uk). Leicester Square tube or Charing Cross tube/rail. Open 10am-6pm Mon-Thur, Sat, Sun; 10am-9pm Fri. Admission free. Special exhibitions vary. Map p85 L8.
Portraits don't have to be stuffy. The NPG has everything from oil paintings of stiff-backed royals to photographs of soccer stars and gloriously unflattering political caricatures. Portraits are arranged in chronological order from the top of the gallery. On the second floor are the earliest works, portraits of Tudor and Stuart royals and notables, including Holbein's 'cartoon' of Henry VIII and the 'Ditchley Portrait' of his daughter, Elizabeth I, her pearly slippers placed firmly on a colourful map of England. On the same floor, the

18th-century collection features Georgian writers and artists (including Congreve, Dryden, Wren and Swift), as well as Regency greats, military men such as Wellington and Nelson, plus Byron, Wordsworth and other Romantics. The first floor is devoted to the Victorians (Dickens, Brunel, Darwin) and to 20th-century luminaries, such as TS Eliot and Ian McKellen.

Trafalgar Square

Leicester Square tube or Charing Cross tube/rail. Map p85 L8.
Trafalgar Square was conceived in the 1820s as a homage to Britain's naval power. Always a natural gathering point, the square now regularly hosts celebrations and even mass protests. The focus is **Nelson's Column**, a Corinthian pillar topped by a statue of the naval hero, supported by four lions, but the changing contemporary sculpture on the **Fourth Plinth** brings fresh colour. On the east side, **St Martin-in the Fields** (020 7766 1100, www.stmartin-in-the-fields.org) is the parish church for Buckingham Palace and hosts delightful lunchtime and evening candlelit concerts. In the south-west corner, the **Admiralty Arch** is the gateway to the Mall, commissioned by Edward VII in memory of his mother, Queen Victoria.

Westminster Cathedral

42 Francis Street, SW1P 1QW (020 7798 9055, www. westminstercathedral.org. uk). Victoria tube/rail. Open 6.30am-7pm Mon-Fri; 7.30am-7.30pm Sat, Sun. Admission free; donations appreciated. Map p85 K11.
With its domes, arches and soaring tower, the most important Catholic church in England looks surprisingly Byzantine. There's a reason: architect John Francis

💙 Tate Britain

*Millbank, SW1P 4RG (020 7887 8888, www.tate.org.uk). Pimlico tube. **Open** 10am-6pm daily. Tours 11am, noon, 2pm, 3pm daily. **Admission** free. Special exhibitions vary. **Map** p85 L12.*

Tate Modern (*see p76*) might get all the attention, but (whisper it) we prefer the original Tate Gallery – or Tate Britain, as it's now known. This isn't nostalgia. Tate Britain was handsomely refurbished a few years ago, has a better organised collection than its illustrious counterpart and is much less busy, which makes viewing art more enjoyable.

Unlike the themed galleries at Tate Modern which can be disorientating, the main floor of the Tate Britain is a logical journey through the history of British art from Holbein in the 1540s. Key artists are given more substantial treatment: William Blake and Henry Moore have their own rooms, while JMW Turner occupies his own extensive Clore Gallery.

Built on the site of the pentagonal Millbank Prison, which held criminals destined for transportation to Botany Bay, the stately riverside gallery was founded by sugar magnate Sir Henry Tate and opened in 1897 with a display of 245 British paintings. Now, the collection is rather more extensive. Constable, Millais, Whistler, Hogarth and Bacon are all represented, and the blockbuster exhibitions – David Hockney, William Blake and Steve McQueen, to name but a few – are increasingly excellent.

A long-term redevelopment plan called the Millbank Project has upgraded the galleries while conserving original features, opening new spaces to the public and adding a new café. The Millbank entrance is lovely these days, with its stained glass and striking spiral staircase; downstairs in the restaurant, a new Alan Johnston ceiling mural complements the restored 1926-27 Rex Whistler wall mural *Pursuit of Rare Meats*.

💙 Westminster Abbey

*20 Dean's Yard, SW1P 3PA (information 020 7222 5152, tours 020 7654 4834, www. westminster-abbey.org). St James's Park or Westminster tube. **Open** 9.30am-3.30pm Mon, Tue, Thur, Fri; 9.30am-3.30pm, 4.30-6pm Wed; 9am-3pm Sat (until 1pm in winter). Abbey Museum, Chapter House, College Gardens & tours times vary; check website for details. **Admission** £24; £10-£21 reductions; £48 family; free under-5s. Tours £7. Map p85 L10.*

The cultural, historic and religious significance of Westminster Abbey is impossible to overstate, but also hard to remember as you're shepherded around, forced to elbow fellow tourists out of the way to read a plaque or see a tomb. The best plan is to get here as early in the day as you can – although it also quietens down towards closing time.

Edward the Confessor commissioned a church dedicated to St Peter on the site of a seventh-century version, but it was only consecrated on 28 December 1065, eight days before he died. William the Conqueror subsequently had himself crowned here on Christmas Day 1066 and, with just two exceptions, every English coronation since has taken place in the Abbey.

Many royal, military and cultural notables are interred here. The most haunting memorial is the **Grave of the Unknown Warrior**, in the nave. In the exquisite **Lady Chapel** are the tombs of Elizabeth I and Mary Queen of Scots. In **Innocents Corner** lie the remains of two lads believed to be Edward V and his brother Richard (their bodies were found at the Tower of London). **Poets' Corner** is the final resting place of Chaucer, who was the first writer to be buried here. The remains of Dryden, Johnson, Browning and Tennyson are also present.

Hidden for over 700 years, the Triforium (the gallery set into the walls above the nave) reopened in 2018 as the **Queen's Diamond Jubilee Galleries**, which tell the long and complex history of this glorious place through a series of symbolic royal documents and historical oddities. Elsewhere, look out for the stained glass **Queen's Window** by David Hockney (2018).

▶ *Even when the abbey is at its most crowded, the 900-year-old College Garden – one of the oldest cultivated spaces in Britain, with some lovely mulberry trees – remains tranquil.*

Bentley, who built it between 1895 and 1903, was heavily influenced by Hagia Sophia in Istanbul. Compared to the candy-cane exterior, the interior is surprisingly restrained (in fact, it's unfinished), but there are still some impressive marble columns and mosaics. Eric Gill's sculptures of the Stations of the Cross (1914-18) were dismissed as 'Babylonian' when they were first installed, but worshippers have come to love them. An upper gallery holds the 'Treasures of the Cathedral' exhibition, where you can see an impressive Arts and Crafts coronet, a Tudor chalice, holy relics and Bentley's amazing architectural model of his cathedral, complete with tiny hawks.

Restaurants

Bleecker £
205 Victoria Street, SW1E 5NE (www.bleeckerburger. co.uk). Victoria tube/rail. **Open** *11am-11pm daily.* **Map** *p85 J11* ❶
Burgers
This popular street-food burger outfit is pure filth... in the best possible way. Made with rare-breed, dry-aged beef, the burgers don't compromise on quality but there's nothing pretentious about them – they're just bun, cheese and killer pucks of meat. Serious carnivores will adore the award-winning 'Bleecker black': two pink patties sandwiching a slice of black pudding. But given the inevitable, crippling post-scoff food coma, be sure to come hungry and eat fast.

Ikoyi £££-£££
1 St James's Market, SW1Y 4AH (020 3583 4660, ikoyilondon. com). Piccadilly Circus tube. **Open** *noon-3pm (last orders 2.30pm), 5.30pm-midnight (last orders 10pm) Mon-Sat.* **Map** *p85 L8* ❷
West African

London may have a trough-load of upscale North African eateries, but there are not so many from the rest of the continent. Hooray, then, for Ikoyi, a hip little joint in an otherwise staid area of town. The menu zips across West Africa, showcasing a host of fusiony flavours that'll be truly new to most foodie Londoners. Heat, it's worth pointing out, is a thing here. Sweltering, face-sweating pepper heat. It's not a place for the faint-hearted.

🖤 Regency Café £
17-19 Regency Street, SW1P 4BY (020 7821 6596, regencycafe. has.restaurant). St James's Park tube or Victoria tube/rail. **Open** *7am-2.30pm, 4-7.15pm Mon-Fri; 7am-noon Sat.* **Map** *p85 L11* ❸ *Café*
This classic caff has been here since 1946. Behind its black-tiled art deco exterior, customers sit on brown plastic chairs at Formica-topped tables, watched over by muscular boxers and Spurs stars of yore, whose photos hang on the tiled walls. Lasagne, omelettes, salads, every conceivable cooked breakfast and mugs of tannin-rich tea are meat and drink to the Regency. Still hungry? The improbably gigantic cinnamon-flavoured bread and butter pud will see you right for the rest of the week.

Sake no Hana ££££
23 St James's Street, SW1A 1HA (020 7925 8988, sakenohana.com/ london). Green Park tube. **Open** *noon-3pm, 6-11pm Mon-Thur; noon-3pm, 5.30-11.30pm Fri; noon-3pm, 5.30-11.30pm Sat; noon-4pm Sun.* **Map** *p85 K9* ❹ *Japanese*
As you'd expect from the Hakkasan restaurant group, Sake no Hana is beautifully designed. That and the fine range of contemporary Japanese dishes and slick service make it a popular place for business lunches and well-heeled families. For a filling meal, the 'Taste of Sake

no Hana' (£31) consists of miso soup, a choice of *sukiyaki*, tempura or grilled dish, a handful of sushi and a dessert. There's also plenty for wine and saké buffs to get stuck into. Don't forget to glance upwards while you're dining: the sculptural wood slatting above your head definitely deserves a look.

♥ Wolseley £££
160 Piccadilly, W1J 9EB (020 7499 6996, www.thewolseley.com). *Green Park tube.* **Open** 7am-11pm (last orders) Mon-Fri; 8am-11pm (last orders) Sat, Sun. **Map** p85 K8 ❺ *Brasserie*

A self-proclaimed 'café-restaurant in the grand European tradition', the Wolseley combines London heritage and Viennese grandeur. The kitchen is much celebrated for its breakfasts, and the scope of the main menu is admirable. From oysters, steak tartare or soufflé suisse, via wiener schnitzel or grilled halibut with wilted spinach and béarnaise, to Portuguese custard tart or apple strudel, there's something for everyone. On Sunday afternoons, three-tiered afternoon tea stands are in abundance.

Pubs & bars

Boisdale of Belgravia
15 Eccleston Street, SW1W 9LX (020 7730 6922, www.boisdale.co.uk). *Victoria tube/rail.* **Open** noon-1am Mon-Fri; 6pm-1am Sat. *Live music starts* 10-9pm. **Admission** £5 Mon-Thur; £7.50 Fri, Sat. *Check the website for ticketed events.* **Map** p85 J11 ❶

There's nowhere quite like this posh, Scottish-themed enterprise, and that includes its sister branches in the City, Mayfair and Canary Wharf. If you're here to drink, there's a terrific choice of single malts. That said, the outstanding wine list is surprisingly affordable, with house selections starting at around £25. Additional appeal comes from live jazz (six nights a week) and a heated cigar terrace.

Dukes Bar
Dukes Hotel, 35 St James's Place, SW1A 1NY (020 7491 4840, www. dukeshotel.com/dukes-bar). Green Park tube. **Open** 2-11pm Mon-Sat; 4-10.30pm Sun. **Map** p85 K9 ❷

If you want to go out for a single cocktail, strong and expensive and very well made, go to Dukes. It's in a luxury hotel, but you're sure to get the warmest of welcomes – as long as you're not wearing trainers. There are three small rooms, all decorated in discreetly opulent style; you feel cocooned. The bar is famous for the theatre of its Martini-making – at the table, from a trolley, using vermouth made exclusively for it at the Sacred distillery in Highgate – but other drinks are just as good.

Shops & services

♥ Dover Street Market
18-22 Haymarket, SW1Y 4DG (020 7518 0680, london.doverstreet market.com). Green Park tube. **Open** 11am-7pm Mon-Sat; noon-6pm Sun. **Map** p85 L8 ❶ *Fashion*

No longer on Dover Street (which gave this globally renowned store its name), DSM now resides in the old Burberry HQ. Rei Kawakubo's ground-breaking multistorey store is a mecca for the fashion obsessed. Housing some of London's brightest stars – Grace Wales Bonner's wonderfully elegant menswear and Molly Goddard's dream dresses woven out of tulle – it's a real champion of the capital's pioneering fashion designers. All 14 of the Comme des Garçons collections are here, alongside exclusive lines from such designers as Valentino, Givenchy and Azzedine Alaïa.

❤ St James's Park

0300 061 2350, www.royalparks. org.uk. St James's Park tube. **Open** *5am-midnight daily.* **Map** *p85 L9.*

There's only one London park where you might spot a pelican swallow a pigeon. St James's Park, a 90-acre wedge of green between Westminster, Trafalgar Square and Buckingham Palace, is the oldest of eight royal parks – those parks that are Crown rather than municipal property. It is also one of London's finest, with narrow lanes meandering round a lake and gorgeous sculpted flower beds, a lakeside café, copious wildfowl and one of the most romantic views in the city. This comes from a bridge across the graceful central lake, which was created from a more formal canal by John Nash in the 1820s. Look east and, above the trees in the near distance, hover the spires, pinnacles and domes of Whitehall – with no square modern towers in sight, it looks like something from Prague or Disneyland; look west and, if the leaves are off the trees, you'll see **Buckingham Palace** (*see p86*).

It's a peaceful place – except when it's used for ceremonial events like **Trooping the Colour** (*see p62*).

It's quite a transformation for a park, formed from a marshy field attached to a leper hospital, that later became a haunt of prostitutes. Henry VIII was the first to use the land for leisure, creating a bowling alley and ground for hunting. James I had more formal gardens laid out and imported a menagerie that included two crocodiles. In the 17th century, Charles II had it redesigned again, by the French landscape gardener from Versailles, adding a pair of pelicans that had been a gift from the Russian ambassador – pelicans have been resident ever since. In fact, wildlife has been a constant theme. Early occupants included deer, leopards and an elk, but by the 18th century the park was being used to graze cows – fresh milk could be bought here until 1905. Now, wildfowl are the draw, with 17 different species splashing about in the central lake. Those bag-jawed pelicans are fed between 2.30pm and 3pm daily.

Fortnum & Mason

Floris

*89 Jermyn Street, SW1Y 6JH
(03301 340180, www.florislondon.
com). Green Park tube.* **Open**
*9.30am-6.30pm Mon,Tue, Fri, Sat;
9.30-7pm Wed; 11.30am-5.30pm
Sun.* **Map** *p85 K8* ❷ *Health &
beauty*

Enterprising young Spaniard Juan
Floris set up his fragrance shop in
1730 and it has been run by the same
family ever since. One imagines not
too much has changed. Everything
is behind glass cabinets and oak-
panelled counters in the manner of
an old-fashioned apothecary, and
smartly dressed men and women
guide you through the selection
process; much more civilised than
a department store.

♥ Fortnum & Mason

*181 Piccadilly, W1A 1ER (020 7734
8040, www.fortnumandmason.
co.uk). Green Park or Piccadilly
Circus tube.* **Open** *10am-9pm
Mon-Sat; noon-6pm Sun (11.30am
for browsing).* **Map** *p85 K8* ❸
Department store

In business for over 300 years,
Fortnum & Mason is as historic as
it is inspiring. A sweeping spiral
staircase soars through the four-
storey building, while light floods
down from a central glass dome.
The iconic eau de nil blue- and
gold- colour scheme, with flashes
of rose pink, abounds on both the
store design and the packaging
of chocolates, biscuits, teas and
preserves. A food hall in the
basement has a good range of fresh
produce, including honey from
beehives on top of the building.
There are various eateries, including
an ice-cream parlour. The famous
hampers start from £60 – though
they rise to a whopping £6,000 for
the most luxurious.

Lock & Co Hatters

*6 St James's Street, SW1A 1EF
(020 7930 8874, www.lockhatters.
co.uk). Green Park tube.* **Open**
*9am-5.30pm Mon-Fri; 9.30am-5pm
Sat.* **Map** *p85 K9* ❹ *Milliners*

Lock & Co is perhaps the most
famous hat shop in the world. It is
certainly one of the oldest, dating
from 1759, and has been frequented
by such names as Charlie Chaplin
and Admiral Lord Nelson. But,
history aside, it is simply very good.
It has one of the most comprehensive
selections of classic hats to be found
anywhere in London: bowlers, top
hats, homburgs, berets, panamas –
all exquisitely made.

Entertainment

Institute of Contemporary Arts

*The Mall, SW1Y 5AH (020 7930
0493 information, 7930 3647
tickets, www.ica.art). Piccadilly
Circus tube or Charing Cross tube/
rail.* **Open** *noon-11pm Tue-Thur,
Sun; noon-midnight Fri, Sat.*
Admission *£5; free Tue.* **Map** *p85
L9* ❶ *Arts venue*

Founded in 1947 by a collective of
poets, artists and critics, the ICA
offers exhibitions, arthouse cinema,
performance art, philosophical
debates, art-themed club nights and
anything else that might challenge
convention – but 'convention' is so
much harder to challenge now that
everyone's doing it.

Kensington & Chelsea

It was Prince Albert who oversaw the inception of **South Kensington's** world-class museums, colleges and concert hall, using the profits of the 1851 Great Exhibition. The area was nicknamed 'Albertopolis' in his honour. Here you'll find the **Natural History Museum**, the **Science Museum** and the **Victoria & Albert Museum** (V&A), plus Imperial College, the Royal College of Art, the Royal College of Music and the **Royal Albert Hall**, variously used for boxing, motor shows, table-tennis tournaments, rock concerts and, most famously, the BBC Proms.

Neighbouring **Knightsbridge**, on the other hand, has no cultural pretensions: a certain type of Londoner comes here to spend, spend, spend in the designer shops

❤ Shortlist

Must-see museum
V&A *p101*

Best for kids
Kensington Gardens *p97*,
Natural History Museum *p97*,
Science Museum *p100*

Best cultural venue
Royal Albert Hall *p102*

Best gourmet experience
Claude Bosi at Bibendum *p105*,
Farmacy *p109*,
The Ledbury *p110*

Best for decadent shopping
Harrods *p104*

Best secret garden
Chelsea Physic Garden *p104*,
Kyoto Garden, Holland Park *p108*

and world-famous department stores. Expensive brands – Gucci, Prada, Chanel – dominate, but for many tourists Knightsbridge means one thing: **Harrods**.

Bordering the area to the north, **Hyde Park** and **Kensington Gardens** form one of London's largest Royal Parks. The land was appropriated in 1536 from the monks of Westminster Abbey by Henry VIII for hunting deer; Kensington Palace remains a royal residence, but Hyde Park is now a hub for large-scale public events and demonstrations. London's oldest boating lake, the **Serpentine**, is here, along with art at the **Serpentine** and **Serpentine Sackler** galleries.

Heading south down Exhibition Road, **Chelsea** has a couple of worthwhile attractions in the mercilessly modern art of the **Saatchi Gallery** and the botanical marvel that is the **Chelsea Physic Garden**. West of Kensington Gardens, meanwhile, is the **Design Museum** and delightful **Holland Park**, with **Portobello Road Market** and **Notting Hill** to the north.

→ Getting around

This is a large district, served by a similarly large number of tube stations. For the Natural History Museum, Science Museum and V&A, take the District, Circle or Piccadilly lines to South Kensington. Buses also run along the main thoroughfares.

Natural History Museum

Kensington

Sights & museums

Kensington Palace & Kensington Gardens

Kensington Gardens, W8 4PX (0333 320 6000, www.hrp.org. uk). High Street Kensington or Queensway tube. **Open** *Palace Mar-Oct 10am-6pm daily. Nov-Feb 10am-4pm daily.* **Admission** *£23.70; £11.80-£19 reductions; free under-5s. Buy online for discounts.* **Map** *p98 D9.*

It was in 1689 that William III – averse to the dank air of Whitehall – relocated here, sectioning off a corner of Hyde Park for his residence. The palace is still occupied by royalty today; William and Kate have a flat here. Kensington Gardens is delineated from Hyde Park (p103) only by the line of the Serpentine and the Long Water. It's lovelier than its easterly neighbour, with gorgeous trees, a bronze Peter Pan statue, the paddling-friendly Diana, Princess of Wales Memorial Fountain and the Diana, Princess of Wales Memorial Playground, with its massive wooden pirate ship in a vast sandpit. On the south side is the extraordinary **Albert Memorial** by Sir George Gilbert Scott.

The palace itself was radically altered first by Sir Christopher Wren and again under George I, when intricate trompe l'oeil ceilings and staircases were added. Visitors follow a whimsical trail focused on four 'stories' of former residents – Diana; William and Mary, and Mary's sister Queen Anne; Georges I and II; Queen Victoria – unearthing the facts through handily placed 'newspapers'. Artefacts include paintings by the likes of Tintoretto, contemporary art and fashion installations, and even Victoria's (tiny) wedding dress.

♥ Natural History Museum

Cromwell Road, SW7 5BD (020 7942 5000, www.nhm.ac.uk). South Kensington tube. **Open** *10am-5.50pm daily.* **Admission** *free. Special exhibitions vary. Tours free.* **Map** *p98 E11.*

Both a research institution and a fabulous museum, the NHM opened in Alfred Waterhouse's purpose-built, Romanesque palazzo on the Cromwell Road in 1881. Now joined by the splendid Darwin Centre extension, the

original building still looks quite magnificent. The pale blue and terracotta façade just about prepares you for the natural wonders within.

The vast entrance hall – previously home to the iconic Diplodocus skeleton, now displays another huge beast: a blue whale. The 82ft- (25m) long, 4.5-tonne skeleton is suspended dramatically from the ceiling, taking centre-stage as part of an exhibition that tells the tale of evolution and of human impact on the natural world.

From the entrance hall, a left turn leads into the west wing, or Blue Zone, where queues form to see animatronic dinosaurs – especially the endlessly popular T rex. Here too, is the Mammals Hall, where you can stare out all manner of stuffed animals from a polar bear to a pygmy shrew.

A right turn from the central hall leads past the Creepy Crawlies exhibition to the Green Zone. Stars include a cross-section through a giant sequoia tree and an amazing array of stuffed birds.

Beyond is the Red Zone, where a Stegosaurus skeleton takes pride of place. Earth's Treasury is a mine of information on a variety of precious metals, gems and crystals; From the Beginning is a brave attempt to give the expanse of geological time a human perspective; Volcanoes and Earthquakes explores the immense energy and power of the natural world through dramatic film footage, interactive games and an earthquake simulator.

Many of the museum's 22 million insect and plant specimens are housed in the Darwin Centre, where they take up nearly 17 miles of shelving. With its eight-storey Cocoon, this is also home to the museum's research scientists, who can be watched at work.

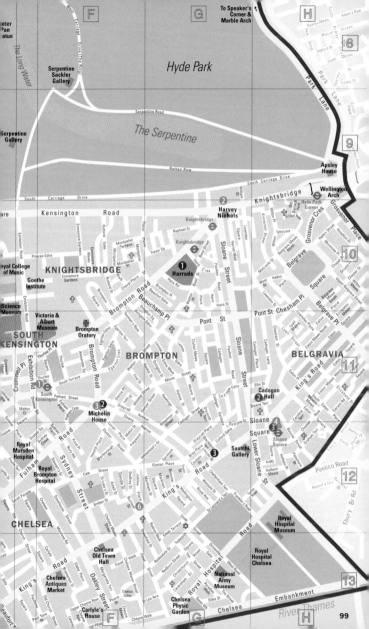

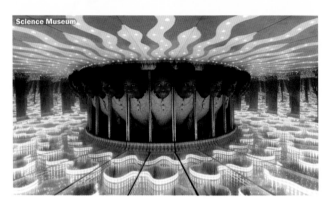

Science Museum

♥ Science Museum

Exhibition Road, SW7 2DD (020 7942 4000, www.sciencemuseum. org.uk). South Kensington tube. **Open** *10am-6pm daily.* **Admission** *free. Special exhibitions vary.* **Map** *p98 E10.*

The Science Museum is a celebration of the wonders of technology in the service of our daily lives. In the ground floor Energy Hall, Making the Modern World is introduced by Puffing Billy, the world's oldest steam locomotive, and contains Stephenson's Rocket, the Apollo 10 command module and an absorbing collection of technological marvels dating back to 1750. Also here, is Exploring Space, where rocket science and the lunar landings are illustrated by dramatically lit mock-ups and full-size models.

On the second floor, Information Age is dedicated to the history of communications technology, from the 19th-century international telegraph network all the way up to the worldwide web. The stunning new Winton Gallery – designed by Zaha Hadid Architects as a wind tunnel for the gallery's centrepiece, a 1929 Handley Page aircraft – reveals how mathematics has shaped the modern world, from foetal monitoring and artificial intelligence to World War II code-breaking and astronomy.

The third floor is dedicated to flight, including the hands-on Launchpad Gallery, which has levers, pulleys, explosions and all manner of experiments. It is also home to Wonderlab: The Statoil Gallery (entry costs from £8), where visitors are encouraged to learn about the physical world through play. Fun mirrors help to explain geometry, plasma globes are effectively bottled lightning, and the chemistry bar is home to live experiments that let you get messy and spectacular with crystals, dry ice, bubble volcanoes and non-Newtonian fluids.

Bathed in an eerie blue light, are the three floors of the Wellcome Wing, where the museum makes sure it stays on the cutting edge of science. Antenna is a web-savvy look at breaking science stories, while the enjoyable and troubling Who Am I? gallery features engaging interactive displays – from a cartoon of ethical dilemmas that introduces you to your dorsolateral prefrontal cortex to a chance to find out what gender your brain is. Compelling objects include a jellyfish that's 'technically immortal', the

💜 Victoria & Albert Museum

Cromwell Road, SW7 2RL (020 7942 2000, www.vam.ac.uk). South Kensington tube. **Open** *10am-5.45pm Mon-Thur, Sat, Sun; 10am-10pm Fri. Tours 10.30am, 12.30pm, 1.30pm, 3.30pm daily.* **Admission** *free. Special exhibitions vary.* **Map** *p98 F11.*

The V&A was opened in 1899 by Queen Victoria in her last public engagement. It has gone on to become one of the world's most magnificent museums.

The details? There are some 150 grand galleries over seven floors. They contain countless pieces of furniture, ceramics, sculpture, paintings, posters, jewellery, metalwork, glass, textiles and dress, spanning several centuries. You could run through the highlights for the rest of this guide, but key artefacts include the seven Raphael Cartoons, painted in 1515 as tapestry designs for the Sistine Chapel; the finest collection of Italian Renaissance sculpture outside Italy; the Ardabil carpet, the world's oldest and arguably most splendid floor covering, in the Jameel Gallery of Islamic Art; and the Luck of Edenhall, a 13th-century glass beaker from Syria. The fashion galleries run from 18th-century court dress right up to contemporary chiffon numbers, while the architecture gallery has videos, models, plans and descriptions of various styles.

The ongoing FuturePlan project has seen more than 85 per cent of the V&A's public spaces transformed, from the stunning Medieval & Renaissance Galleries to the ambitious galleries of Europe 1600-1815. The Toshiba Gallery of Japanese Art includes 550 works running from the sixth century AD to the first Sony Walkman and an origami outfit by Issey Miyake. Recent additions include the museum's 'Rapid Response Collection', which features contemporary design and architecture reflecting important news events, while major temporary exhibitions – Alexander McQueen, Mary Quant, David Bowie – are frequently blockbuster sell-outs.

The entrance on Exhibition Road brings visitors through the porcelain-tiled Sackler Courtyard to the purpose-built Sainsbury Gallery. It's a fitting introduction to a fabulous museum.

▶ *The V&A also runs the Museum of Childhood in Bethnal Green (see p180).*

statistically average British man (he's called Jose), a pound of human fat displayed alongside a gastric band, and half of Charles Babbage's brain (the other half is in the Hunterian Museum).

Serpentine & Serpentine Sackler galleries

Kensington Gardens, near Albert Memorial, W2 3XA (020 7402 6075, www.serpentinegalleries.org). Lancaster Gate or South Kensington tube. **Open** *10am-6pm Tue-Sun.* **Admission** *free; donations appreciated.* **Map** *p98 E9 & F8.*

The Serpentine Gallery – much-loved for its sometimes challenging exhibitions of contemporary art – was originally squeezed into one small 1930s tea house. Here, the rolling two-monthly programme of exhibitions features a mix of up-to-the-minute artists and edgy career retrospectives. But – perhaps symbolic of the gallery's limitations of space – every spring it also commissions a renowned architect, who's never before built in the UK, to build a temporary pavilion outside. The pavilion then hosts a packed programme of cultural events (June to September).

A permanent solution to the issue of space was found in 2013, when the gallery opened a second location, the Serpentine Sackler, just across the bridge from the original. Devoted to emerging art in all forms, the Sackler is a Grade II-listed, Palladian former gunpowder store, with a clean-lined restaurant over which the late architect Zaha Hadid cast a billowing white cape of a roof.

Restaurants

Daquise ££

20 Thurloe Street, SW7 2LT (020 7589 6117, daquise.co.uk). South Kensington tube. **Open** *noon-11pm daily.* **Map** *p98 F11* ➊ *Polish*

This much-loved grande dame of London Polish restaurants (established 1947) offers a home-from-home ambience with a stylish twist. In the shabby-chic, light and airy interior, enlivened with fresh flowers, robust, flavourful, no-nonsense traditional dishes are served with great charm. Classic cold starters of meltingly tender herring with cream, apple, onion and flax oil, or beetroot with subtly warming horseradish, are ladled directly from capacious earthenware bowls, while mains are assembled directly at the table from well-worn saucepans, borne by the chefs who lovingly prepared the dishes.

Shops & services

The **V&A** has a superb gift shop, stuffed with stylish exhibition-related buys; the **Science Museum** has a lively range of geek-free science presents for kids, and the **Natural History Museum** has cute cuddly dinosaurs.

Entertainment

❤ Royal Albert Hall

Kensington Gore, South Kensington, SW7 2AP (020 7589 8212, www.royalalberthall.com). South Kensington tube or bus 9, 10, 52, 360, 452. **Tours** *most days 9.30am-4.30pm; £13.75; £6.75-£11.75 reductions; free under-5s.* **Box office** *9am-9pm daily.* **Tickets** *£15-£275.* **Map** *p98 E10* ➊ *Concert hall*

In constant use since opening in 1871, with boxing matches, motor shows and Allen Ginsberg's 1965 International Poetry Incarnation among the headline events, the Royal Albert Hall continues to host a very broad programme. The classical side is dominated by the superb BBC Proms (*see p62*), which runs every night for two months in summer and sees a huge array of orchestras

Royal Albert Hall

and other ensembles battling the difficult acoustics. It's well worth catching a concert that features the thunderous Grand Organ.

Hyde Park & Knightsbridge

Sights & museums

Hyde Park
0300 061 2000, www.royalparks. gov.uk. Hyde Park Corner, Lancaster Gate or Marble Arch tube. **Map** *p98 FG8*
One of the largest Royal Parks, Hyde Park is one and a half miles long and a mile wide. It was a hotspot for demonstrations in the 19th century and remains so – a 2003 march against the Iraq War that ended in the park was the largest in British history. The legalisation of public assembly here led to the creation of Speakers' Corner in 1872 (near Marble Arch tube), where political and religious ranters still have the floor on Sunday afternoons, and Marx, Orwell and the Pankhursts

once spoke. Rowing boats can be hired on the Serpentine – but adjoining Kensington Gardens (*p97*) is really much prettier.

Wellington Arch
Hyde Park Corner, W1J 7JZ (020 7930 2726, www.english-heritage. org.uk). Hyde Park Corner tube. **Open** *Apr-Sept 10am-6pm daily. Oct 10am-5pm daily. Nov-Mar 10am-4pm daily.* **Admission** *£6.30; £3.80-£5.70 reductions; £16.40 family; free under 5s. Joint ticket with Apsley House £15; £9.10-£13.50 reductions; £39.10 family.* **Map** *p98 H9.*
Built in the late 1820s to mark Britain's triumph over Napoleonic France, Decimus Burton's Wellington Arch was initially topped by an out-of-proportion equestrian statue of Wellington. However, Captain Adrian Jones's 38-ton bronze *Peace Descending on the Quadriga of War* has finished it with a flourish since 1912. The arch has three floors, with an English Heritage bookshop and various displays, covering the history of the arch and the Blue Plaques scheme, and the Quadriga Gallery providing space for excellent temporary exhibitions. There are great views from the balcony in winter (leafy trees obscure the sightlines in spring and summer).

On the opposite side of the roundabout is **Apsley House** (149 Piccadilly, W1J 7NT, 020 7499 5676, www.wellingtoncollection. co.uk, closed Mon, Tue, also Wed-Fri in winter, £11.60, £7-£10.50 reductions, or joint ticket with Wellington Arch). Known as No.1 London, it was built by Robert Adam in the 1770s and was the home of the Duke of Wellington for 35 years. It houses an impressive collection of porcelain and paintings, including a portrait of the Iron Duke by Goya. In winter, twilight tours of the house are especially atmospheric.

Restaurants

Bar Boulud £££
Mandarin Oriental Hyde Park, 66 Knightsbridge, SW1X 7LA (020 7201 3899, www.barboulud. com). Knightsbridge tube. **Open** *noon-10.30pm Mon-Wed, Sun; noon-11.30pm Thur-Sat.* **Map** *p98 G10* ❷ *French*

Overseen by renowned chef Daniel Boulud, the restaurant has an eye-catching view of the open-plan kitchen, where chefs work in meditative calm. Charcuterie from Gilles Verot is a big draw, as are the elegant French brasserie options and finger-licking American staples. We've had burgers here and loved every bite – try a beef patty topped with pulled pork and green chilli mayonnaise – but other culinary gems might include a robust French onion soup, resplendent with caramelised onions and topped with molten gruyère.

Shops & services

The other landmark department store here is **Harvey Nichols** (109-125 Knightsbridge, SW1X 7RJ, 020 7235 5000, www. harveynichols.com).

♥ Harrods
87-135 Brompton Road, SW1X 7XL (020 7730 1234, www.harrods. com). Knightsbridge tube. **Open** *10am-9pm Mon-Sat; noon-6pm Sun (browsing from 11.30am).* **Map** *p98 G10* ❶ *Department store*

It might be unashamedly ostentatious, stuffed with tourists and in possession of the world's most vulgar statue (Dodi and Diana in bronze by the Egyptian escalators), but Harrods – London's most famous department store – is still spectacular. Serious shoppers browse the elegantly tiled and fragrant food halls on the ground floor or the wealth of exclusives in the beauty halls. But indulge

Harrods

the excesses too: Harrods has an art gallery, a stunning interiors department and a kitchenware floor that hosts live cooking lessons from household names. Got kids? Head straight to Toy Kingdom on the fourth floor, with its enchanted forest, intergalactic science lab and bespoke sweets-maker. Elsewhere, Harrods excels at shoes – with a gargantuan footwear department stocking labels such as Ferragamo, Charlotte Olympia and Giuseppe Zanotti – while the Fashion Lab is dedicated to young designer labels such as Zadig & Voltaire, Wildfox and the Kooples.

Chelsea

Sights & museums

♥ Chelsea Physic Garden
66 Royal Hospital Road, SW3 4HS (020 7352 5646, www. chelseaphysicgarden.co.uk). Sloane Square tube or bus 11, 19, 22. **Open** *Apr-Oct 11am-6pm Mon-Fri, Sun. Nov, Dec, Feb, Mar 11am-4pm Mon-Fri. Closed late Dec, Jan. Tours times vary; phone to check.* **Admission** *£9.50; £5 reductions; free under-5s. Tours free.* **Map** *p98 G13.*

Passing through these modest red-brick walls is like stepping into a secret garden: a place by the Thames but with its own microclimate, where rare plants from Britain and across the globe have been collected – and now thrive. Set up by apothecaries in 1673, Chelsea Physic Garden contains the world's oldest rock garden, created in 1773 from black Icelandic basalt imported by Joseph Banks (the most-famous plant hunter of all) and decorated with masonry from the Tower of London. Today, the garden is also home to Britain's first garden of ethnobotany (the study of the botany of different ethnic groups and indigenous peoples), and a Garden of Medicinal Plants, tracing the chronology of plant remedies over almost an acre, from ancient Greek herbs to plants that are likely to be used in future medicine. There's also a shop where visitors can buy unusual plants, and a café serving very good homemade cakes.

National Army Museum

Royal Hospital Road, SW3 4HT (020 7730 0717, www.nam. ac.uk). Sloane Square tube or bus 170. **Open** *10am-5.30pm daily; until 8pm 1st Wed of the mth.* **Admission** *free.* **Map** *p98 G13.*
Thanks to a £24m redesign, which saw a huge atrium carved out of the middle of the building, the National Army Museum is a bright, modern space. Its five new galleries represent different aspects of the armed forces, with a much keener focus on social history and diversity. Some old-fashioned models of battles (notably Waterloo) and uniforms remain, of course, along with favourite exhibits such as Major Michael 'Bronco' Lane's frost-bitten fingertips and the skeleton of Napoleon's horse Marengo. In Play Base, under-eights can take on an assault course, climb aboard

a command liaison vehicle or develop their fieldcraft skills.

Next door, the Grade I-listed **Royal Hospital Chelsea** (020 7881 5200, www.chelsea-pensioners. co.uk, tours £13.50) is a fitting place of retirement for 300 former British soldiers, known as Chelsea Pensioners. Recognisable by their scarlet uniform and tricorn hats, veterans offer tours around the 66-acre site. The lovely gardens host the Chelsea Flower Show (*see p61*) each spring.

Saatchi Gallery

Duke of York's HQ, King's Road, SW3 4RY (020 7811 3070, www. saatchigallery.com). Sloane Square tube. **Open** *10am-6pm daily.* **Admission** *free.* **Map** *p98 G12.*
Charles Saatchi's gallery offers 50,000sq ft (4,645sq m) of space for temporary exhibitions. Given his fame as a promoter in the 1990s of what became known as the Young British Artists – Damien Hirst, Tracey Emin, Gavin Turk, Sarah Lucas et al – it will surprise many that the focus of exhibitions here has been internationalist in outlook, with China, Africa and India all featuring, including sell-out exhibition *Tutankhamun: Treasures of the Golden Pharaoh*. Still, Richard Wilson's superb oil-sump installation *20:50* has survived from the Saatchi Gallery's previous incarnations and remains here as the only permanently displayed artwork.

Restaurants

♥ Claude Bosi at Bibendum
£££
Michelin House, 81 Fulham Road, SW3 6RD (020 7581 5817, bibendum.co.uk). South Kensington tube. **Open** *6.30-9.45pm Wed; noon-2.15pm, 6.30-9.45pm Thur, Fri; noon-2.15pm, 6.30-10pm Sat; noon-2.15pm, 6.30-9pm Sun.* **Map** *p98 F11* **3** *French*

First opened more than 30 years ago, Bibendum is a bona fide London institution. For a start, the building (the massive old Michelin House) is a spectacular art deco pile and one of the city's most striking bits of architecture. Wander through the cavernous former garage forecourt (now Bibendum's Oyster Bar, 020 7589 1480) and up to London's nattiest dining room. With grey leather banquettes, fine art and those awesome Michelin Man-stained glass windows, it's an absolute picture. Gawp all you want, but you come here to eat. Bibendum is home to French fine-dining powerhouse Claude Bosi. The food is overwhelmingly excellent and meticulous: from the delicate choux pastry amuse-bouches through mains of seabass *à la Grenobloise* or tripe and cuttlefish gratin to exquisite desserts such as black fig millefeuille. Blow the budget and be blown away.

Colbert £££

50-52 Sloane Square, SW1W 8AX (020 7730 2804, www. colbertchelsea.com). Sloane Square tube. **Open** *8am-11pm Mon-Sat; 8am-10pm Sun.* **Map** *p98 H12* **4**
Brasserie

Paying homage to Continental grand cafés with marble, linen napkins and mirrors aplenty, Colbert feels more casual and local than its siblings – the Wolseley (see *p92*), the Delaunay and Brasserie Zédel – and the posters in the booth-lined bar area advertising performances by Olivier and Vivien Leigh at the Royal Court Theatre next door (see *p107*) lend a sense of history. It also trumps the others with pavement tables from which to admire the beautiful people. More importantly, it serves the best lunch in the area: perhaps a deliciously decadent smoked haddock florentine with spinach, poached egg and a buttery cream

sauce; or a croque madame – brioche filled with comté cheese, *jambon blanc* and béchamel sauce, topped with a fried egg.

Medlar £££

438 King's Road, SW10 0LJ (020 7349 1900, www. medlarrestaurant.co.uk). Fulham Broadway tube or bus 11, 22. **Open** *noon-3pm, 6.30-10.30pm Mon-Fri; noon-3pm, 6-10.30pm Sat; noon-3pm, 6-9.30pm Sun.* **Map** *p98 E13* **5** *Modern European*

The decor here is understated: a soothing grey-green colour scheme and unobtrusive artwork. The real artistry arrives on the plates, dishes of astounding excellence. Assemblies are complex and have lengthy names: rump of Belted Galloway with café de paris snails, stuffed portobello, shallot purée and béarnaise, for example. But every ingredient justifies its place in entirely natural-seeming juxtapositions of flavour, texture and colour. And the execution is nearly flawless. Save room for wonderful (and relatively simple) puddings, such as poached quince with buttermilk pannacotta and pistachio cake.

Rabbit £££

172 King's Road, SW3 4UP (020 3750 0172, www.rabbit-restaurant. com). Sloane Square tube. **Open** *6-11pm (last orders 10.30pm) Mon; noon-midnight (last orders 10.30pm) Tue-Sat; noon-5pm (last orders 4pm) Sun.* **Map** *p98 F12* **6** *British*

More than a restaurant, Rabbit feels a bit like a theme bar that does food, right down to a 'stable door' entrance. But to see it as a party venue does the cooking a disservice: the Gladwin brothers dish up inventive mouthfuls of joy that warm you up for heavy, slow-cooked mains (perhaps pigs' cheeks with malt, stout, garlic and pennywort) and lighter, faster-cooked dishes (such as tempura duck liver). However, the 'British with a twist' ethos is best summed up by the desserts: try a Viennetta parfait made of Magnum ice-cream lollies, or an intriguing cep and white-chocolate bourbon.

Shops & services

No longer the haunt of 1960s Mary Quant-wannabes or 1970s punks, the **King's Road** now teems with pricey fashion houses and air-conditioned poodle parlours. Yet on a sunny day, it still makes for a vivid stroll.

Conran Shop

*Michelin House, 81 Fulham Road, SW3 6RP (020 7589 7401, www.conranshop.co.uk). South Kensington tube. **Open** 10am-6pm Mon, Tue, Fri; 10am-7pm Wed, Thur; 10am-6.30pm Sat; noon-6pm Sun. **Map** p98 F11* ❷ *Homewares*
Sir Terence Conran's flagship store in the Fulham Road's beautiful 1909 Michelin Building showcases furniture and design for every room in the house as well as the garden. In addition to design classics, such as the Eames DAR chair, there are plenty of portable accessories, gadgets, books, stationery items and toiletries that make great gifts or souvenirs. **Other location** 55 Marylebone High Street, W1U 5HS (020 7723 2223).

John Sandoe

*10-12 Blacklands Terrace, SW3 2SR (020 7589 9473, johnsandoe. com). Sloane Square tube. **Open** 9.30am-6.30pm Mon-Sat; 11am-5pm Sun. **Map** p98 G12* ❸ *Books & music*
Tucked away on a side street, this 50-year-old independent has always looked just as a bookshop should, with stock literally packed to the rafters. The enthusiasm and knowledge of the staff can be taken

as, forgive us, read – several have worked here for decades, their passion for books undimmed.

Entertainment

Cadogan Hall

*5 Sloane Terrace, off Sloane Street, SW1X 9DQ (020 7730 4500, cadoganhall.com). Sloane Square tube. **Box office** 10am-6pm Mon-Sat; noon-6pm Sun (performance days only). **Map** p98 H11* ❷ *Concert hall*
Jazz groups and rock bands have been attracted by the acoustics in this renovated former Christian Science church, but the programming at the austere yet comfortable 950-seat hall is dominated by classical. The Royal Philharmonic is resident; other orchestras also perform, and there's regular chamber music.

Royal Court Theatre

*Sloane Square, SW1W 8AS (020 7565 5000, royalcourttheatre.com). Sloane Square tube. **Box office** 10am-6pm Mon Fri; 11am-6pm Sat (performance days only). **Tickets** £12-£40. **Map** p98 H12* ❸ *Theatre*
From John Osborne's *Look Back in Anger*, staged in the theatre's opening year of 1956, to the more recent likes of Jez Butterworth, Simon Stephens and debbie tucker green, the emphasis at the Royal Court has always been on new voices in British and international theatre. Since Vicky Featherstone took over as artistic director (the first woman in the role) in 2013, the shows have got artier, though there's still room for established names, including the legendary Caryl Churchill. Expect to find punchy, socially engaged new work by first-time and international playwrights upstairs, and bigger, state-of-the-nation works by household names downstairs.

Holland Park & Notting Hill

Sights & museums

Design Museum

224-238 Kensington High Street, W8 6AG (020 3862 5900, designmuseum. org). High Street Kensington tube. **Open** *10am-6pm (last admission 5pm) daily.* **Admission** *free; temporary exhibitions vary.*

Dating to 1962, the Grade II*-listed former Commonwealth Institute building on Kensington High Street is itself a classic piece of modern architecture, with a pioneering hyperboloid roof (effectively a series of undulating arches) made of copper-clad concrete. There's plenty of room for temporary exhibitions, the archive, a library, two shops, a ground-floor café and impressive mezzanine restaurant, as well as the permanent collection.

Called 'Designer Maker User', the collection traces the development of 20th- and 21st-century design, starting with a supremely detailed timeline at the entrance. Thereafter there are plenty of artefacts to satisfy visitors who are just looking for a bit of fuzzy hey-wow tech nostalgia – Sony Walkmans, Xbox controllers and early iPhones. The ticketed temporary exhibitions are always worth a look: some focus on particular designers, including Cartier and Camper; some explore broader themes, such as cycling or recycling; and some do a bit of both, as at the necessarily loose but always compelling annual Designs of the Year awards exhibition.

♥ Holland Park

Ilchester Place, W8 6LU (020 7602 2226, www.rbkc.gov.uk). Holland Park/Kensington High Street tube. **Open** *7.30am-30mins before dusk daily.*

Holland Park, whose 55 acres add up to one of London's finest green spaces, was formerly the grounds of Jacobean mansion Holland House, named after its second owner, the Earl of Holland, whose wife was the first person in England to successfully grow dahlias. In the 19th century, Holland House was a hub of political and literary activity, visited by Disraeli and Lord Byron among others, but it was largely destroyed by the Blitz during World War II – though enough of it remains to have been Grade I-listed and for a fancy-pants youth hostel, **Safestay Holland Park** (020 7870 9629, www.safestay. com/ss-london-holland-park), to move in. These days, dahlias are still grown, but there are also the Japanese-style Kyoto Gardens, with their koi carp and bridge at the foot of a waterfall. Holland Walk, along the park's eastern edge, is one of the most pleasant paths in central London, and there's a fine café and adventure playground. In summer, open-air theatre and opera are staged (operahollandpark.com).

Leighton House

12 Holland Park Road, W14 8LZ (020 7602 3316, www. leightonhouse.co.uk). High Street Kensington tube. **Open** *10am-5.30pm Sat, Sun.* **Admission** *£9; £7 reductions.*

In the 1860s, artist Frederic Leighton commissioned a showpiece house. He ensured that, behind the sternly Victorian red-brick façade, it was full of treasures from all over the world, as well as his own works and those of his contemporaries. The house is decorated in high style: magnificent downstairs reception rooms designed for lavish entertaining; a dramatic staircase leading to a light-filled studio that takes up most of the first floor; and, above all, the Arab Hall, which showcases Leighton's huge collection of 16th-century Middle Eastern tiles. The only private space in the whole house is a tiny single bedroom. Visiting hours are limited until 2021 to allow for ongoing renovation work to restore original architecture and improve visitor facilities. Nearby, **18 Stafford Terrace** (W8 7BH, www.rbkc.gov.uk), former home of cartoonist Edward Linley Sambourne, is also worth a visit.

Museum of Brands, Packaging & Advertising

*111-117 Lancaster Road, W11 1QT (020 7243 9611, www. museumofbrands.com). Notting Hill Gate tube. **Open** 10am-6pm Mon-Sat; 11am-5pm Sun. **Admission** £9; £5-£7 reductions; £24 family; free under-7s.*

A fascinating exploration of how brands have evolved from the Victorian era to modern day, the museum is a seemingly endless collection of wrappers, posters, toys, boxes and general collectibles. The main part of the display is the 'time tunnel', a winding corridor of dark cabinets stuffed with colourful curios arranged chronologically. With the arrival of each new decade an information panel helps to put the changing designs and new fashions into context. A separate gallery functions as a sort of shrine to a few favourite brands: one cabinet holds every iteration of can and bottle produced by Guinness; another is packed with Kellogg's cereal boxes. We'd prefer a bit more analysis of the social trends that created all these designs – but as a nostalgia-stuffed tribute to the many, many things we buy, the museum is unparalleled.

Farmacy

Restaurants

Farmacy ££

*74 Westbourne Grove, W2 5SH (020 7221 0705, farmacylondon.co.uk). Bayswater or Royal Oak tube. **Open** 9am-5pm, 6-10pm Mon-Fri; 9am-4pm, 6-10pm Sat; 9am-4pm, 6-9.30pm Sun. Vegetarian*

Farmacy (as in health from the farm, geddit?) is free from most things – dairy, refined sugars, meat, additives and chemical nasties – but fortunately, it's not lacking in taste. From the food coming out of the kitchen to the ultra-sleek decor, it's smart, but relaxed and friendly. The menu is 'clean indulgence', which means that it has lots of naughty-sounding but actually super-healthy things to choose from: mushroom tagliatelle made with spelt flour; a nut-based burger loaded with avocado pickle; zingy lemon cheesecake. The weekend High Tea menu is a plant-based, treat-filled extravaganza (*see p29*).

❤ The Ledbury £££

127 Ledbury Road, W11 2AQ (020 7792 9090, www.theledbury.com). Westbourne Park tube. **Open** *6.30-9.45pm Mon, Tue; noon-2pm, 6.30-9.45pm Wed-Sun. Modern European*

Few haute establishments have the hospitable hum of the Ledbury, and even fewer boast two Michelin stars. But this former pub remains top-tier for gustatory good times. British ingredients – smoked eel, Cumbrian lamb – line up alongside delicacies such as Tokyo turnips, Bresse chicken and black truffle, but it's chef Brett Graham's clever contemporary treatment of them that sets the place apart. Ledbury signatures are consistently thrilling – particularly the flame-grilled mackerel with pickled cucumber, celtic mustard and shiso; and, well, all the desserts.

Snaps & Rye £

93 Golborne Road, W10 5NL (020 8964 3004, snapsandrye.com). Westbourne Park tube. **Open** *9am-5pm Tue-Sat; 9.30am-3.30pm Sun. Danish*

Snaps (alcohol infusions) & Rye (the accompanying food) embodies all that's best about Scandinavian design: simple and functional, but every detail designed or chosen with aesthetic pleasure in mind. The owners have also taken great pains to make their food, prepared by British chef Tania Steytler, as good as it can possibly be. While Denmark's famous open-faced sandwiches (*smørrebrød*) are simple in concept, Steytler raises them to great heights through the use of superb ingredients, masterly cooking skills and attention to detail. Other options are meatballs, herring, cured salmon and apple cake. Feeling the cold but don't fancy snaps? Try *cocio*, a Nordic hot chocolate.

Yashin £££

1A Argyll Road, W8 7DB (020 7938 1536, www.yashinsushi.com). High Street Kensington tube. **Open** *noon-3pm, 6-11pm daily. Sushi*

The centrepiece sushi counter gives the game away: set on the dark green tiles behind the team of *itamae* (sushi chefs), a neon sign reads 'without soy sauce'. This is how the chefs ask you to eat your artfully crafted sushi. In place of a dunking, each piece is finished with its own flavourings or even a quick blast from a blowtorch.

Shops & services

Portobello Road Market

Portobello Road, W10 (www. portobelloroad.co.uk). Ladbroke Grove or Notting Hill Gate tube. **Open** *9am-6pm Mon-Wed; 9am-1pm Thur; 9am-7pm Fri, Sat. Market*

Best known for antiques and collectibles, the markets around Portobello Road now encompass everything from fashion to food. Antiques start at the Notting Hill end, with more than 2,000 specialist antiques dealers squeezed tightly into any available space, and bargain-hunters jostle with camera-laden tourists to the soundtrack of live jazz. There are food stalls to sustain you as you push on to explore the fashion market under the Westway flyover. Best visited on a less-frantic Friday morning, it's here you'll find fashionistas and trendy teens delving through troves of prized vintage, boutique fashion and retro memorabilia. And don't stop there: continue up to Golborne Road for bargains away from the masses, helped by the presence of eccentric second-hand interiors stalls. The main Antiques Arcade is only open on Saturday.

West End

Oxford Street is working hard to stay top of London's shopping destinations, with wider pavements, a revamped roundabout at Marble Arch and a shiny new super-station at Tottenham Court Road. North of Oxford Street, the luxury cafés and boutiques of **Marylebone** lead to graceful Regent's Park, while in **Fitzrovia** the days of post-war drunken poets have given way to an era of new-media offices. South of Oxford Street, **Mayfair** oozes wealth, while neon-lit **Piccadilly Circus** is a bit of town every Londoner does their best to avoid.

    Soho – once notorious as the West End's sleazy late-night party zone is still a lively bohemian area with an almost inconceivable number of bars, restaurants and shops. To the east, crowds flock to the shops and attractions of **Covent Garden**.

Best small plates
10 Greek Street *p125*,
Barrafina *p137*,
Zoilo *p118*

Best high-end dining
Kitty Fisher's *p121*,
Roka *p117*,
Social Eating House *p126*

Best cocktails
Bar Américain *p127*,
The Connaught Bar *p121*,
Friendly Society *p128*,
Swift *p129*

Best cultural venue
Donmar Warehouse *p142*,

Royal Academy of Arts *p120*,
Royal Opera House *p142*,
Wigmore Hall *p119*,

Best gigs and giggles
Comedy Store *p131*,
Ronnie Scott's *p133*

Best for kids
Hamleys *p122*,
London Transport Museum *p135*

Best shops
Browns *p122*,
Liberty *p123*,
Machine-A *p135*,
The Shop at Bluebird *p140*

Oxford Street & north

There is relentless trade on
Oxford Street, but few locals
esteem the historic thoroughfare:
clogged pavements make for
unpleasant shopping. Escape
the crowds among the pretty
boutiques around **Marylebone
High Street**, or dip into the oft-
overlooked **Wallace Collection**.
To the north, on busy Marylebone
Road, is the inexplicably popular
Madame Tussauds and the
York Gate entrance to **Regent's
Park** (*see p172*).

Heading east, **Fitzrovia** –
once home to radicals, writers
and boozers, mostly in reverse
order – retains sufficient traces
of bohemianism to appeal to the
media types that now frequent it.
Fine hotels and restaurants cluster
on Charlotte Street.

Sights & museums

Cartoon Museum

*63 Wells Street, W1A 3AE (www.
cartoonmuseum.org). Oxford
Circus or Tottenham Court Road
tube.* **Open** *10.30am-5.30pm Tue,
Wed, Fri, Sat; 10.30am-8pm Thur;
noon-4pm Sun.* **Admission** *£8.50;
£3-5 reductions; free under-18s.*
Map *p114 K6.*

The best of British cartoon art is
on show here. The displays start in
the early 18th century, when high-
society types back from the Grand
Tour introduced the Italian practice
of *caricatura* to polite company.
From Hogarth, they move through
Britain's cartooning 'golden age'
(1770-1830) to examples of wartime
cartoons, ending up with modern
satirists such as Gerald Scarfe
and the wonderfully loopy Ralph
Steadman. There's also original

→ **Getting around**

London's West End is a large area so you'll need to use public transport to
get around. The main tube stations include Oxford Circus, Covent Garden,
Piccadilly Circus and Leicester Square. It's worth noting that it only takes
ten minutes to walk from Piccadilly Circus to Covent Garden or Oxford
Circus, and a similar time from Tottenham Court Road to Leicester Square.

1921 Rupert Bear artwork by Mary Tourtel, Frank Hampson's Dan Dare, Leo Baxendale's Bash Street Kids and a painted Asterix cover by that well-known Briton, Albert Uderzo. The museum hosts numerous events and workshops throughout the year; check the website for details.

Madame Tussauds

Marylebone Road, NW1 5LR (www. madametussauds.com/london). Baker Street tube. **Open** *Times vary; see website. Timed tickets available online.* **Admission** *£35; £30 reductions; free under-3s. Cheaper tickets available online in advance.* **Map** *p114 H5.*

Madame Tussaud brought her show to London in 1802, 32 years after it was founded in Paris, and it's been expanding ever since. There are now some 300 wax figures in the collection: current movie A-listers who require no more than a first name (Angelina, Brad), a bevy of royals (not least Wills and Kate, and Harry and Meghan), and sundry sports stars including Bobby Moore and Mo Farah. Rihanna and One Direction can be found hanging out among the Music Megastars, while Dickens, Einstein and Madame Tussaud herself kick back in the Culture section. There's a section dedicated to YouTube stars Zoe and Alfie, as well as a Donald Trump alongside political luminaries such as Nelson Mandela, Martin Luther King and Barack Obama.

Kids love the Marvel Super Heroes section, where waxworks of Iron Man, Spider-Man and an 18ft Hulk are accompanied by a '4D' film with 'real' effects. The Star Wars area and King Kong experience are also popular.

Sherlock Holmes Museum

221b Baker Street, NW1 6XE (020 7224 3688, www.sherlock-holmes. co.uk). Baker Street tube. **Open** *9.30am-6pm daily.* **Admission** *£15; £10 reductions.* **Map** *p114 G5.*

The four storeys of this famous address are dedicated to Conan Doyle's literary detective (as opposed to the TV version). Visitors are greeted by a respectable-looking chap in a bowler hat and whiskers; this, you will deduce is Doctor Watson. And every lovingly recreated detail – including murder weapons and waxwork scenes – feels like

Sherlock Holmes Museum

WEST END

a fragment of historical reality. A fair percentage of visitors believe that the whole set-up is real, and upstairs in Mrs Hudson's room there is a folder of letters addressed to Holmes from fans all over the world. It's fairly pricey for what it is, but there's plenty of fun on display – elementary and otherwise.

Wallace Collection

Hertford House, Manchester Square, W1U 3BN (020 7563 9500, www.wallacecollection.org). Bond Street tube. **Open** *10am-5pm daily. Free tours at 2.30pm Mon-Thur; 11.30am, 2.30pm Fri-Sun.* **Admission** *free.* **Map** *p114 H6.*
Built in 1776 and tucked away on a quiet square, the Wallace is looking particularly lovely after extensive refurbishment. This handsome house contains an exceptional collection of 18th-century French furniture, paintings and *objets d'art*, as well as an amazing array of medieval armour and weaponry taking up much of the ground floor. It all belonged to Sir Richard Wallace, who, as the illegitimate offspring of the fourth Marquess of Hertford, inherited in 1870 the treasures his father had amassed in the last 30 years of his life. Room after grand room contains Louis XIV and XV furnishings and Sèvres porcelain; the galleries are hung with paintings by heavyweights including Titian, Gainsborough, Canaletto, Rembrandt, Velázquez and Rubens.

Restaurants

♥ Chiltern Firehouse £££££
1 Chiltern Street, W1U 7PA (020 7073 7676, www.chilternfirehouse. com). Baker Street tube. **Open** *7-10.30am, noon-3pm, 5.30-10.30pm Mon-Fri; 8-10am, 11am-3pm, 6-10.30pm Sat, Sun.* **Map** *p114 H6* ❶ *Modern European*
This lovely 1889 Grade II-listed Victorian Gothic fire brigade building was rebuilt from the inside out to create one of London's most hyped hotels, but the discreetly gated garden is also the entrance to one of London's finest restaurants. The kitchen can do fiddly and pretty, exemplified by appetisers such as the tiny, slider-like 'doughnuts' filled with crab meat, but pretty is only part of the story. The restaurant's success is built on its reputation as a celeb-magnet but when that fades, the flavour combinations and exemplary modern cooking techniques, as 'curated' by Portuguese superchef Nuno Mendes, will remain. The

Wallace Collection

best seats are at the kitchen counter, from which you can watch the chefs work their magic.

Fischer's £££

50 Marylebone High Street, W1U 5HN (020 7466 5501, www.fischers. co.uk). Baker Street or Regent's Park tube. **Open** *7.30am-10.30pm Mon; 7.30am-11pm Tue-Sat; 8am-10.30pm Sun.* **Map** *p114 H5* ❷ *Austrian*

Chris Corbin and Jeremy King have made a habit of producing destination restaurants that don't feel stand-offish. This revival of the Mittel-European grand café is no exception. It's another celebrity hotspot – they love both Fischer's ageless elegance and its two-track booking system (fast-track for slebs; sidings for the hoi polloi) – but the prices here, in a setting where the monthly bill for wood polish might cause a Habsburg lip to tremble, are not as inflated as you'd expect. The main menu would be familiar to someone touring the Austro-Hungarian Empire in their charabanc, but there is fabulous sachertorte and strudel for those who can't manage a full meal.

Honey & Co £

25A Warren Street, W1T 5LZ (020 7388 6175, honeyandco. co.uk). Warren Street tube. **Open** *8am-10.30pm Mon-Fri; 9.30am-10.30pm Sat.* **Map** *p114 K5* ❸ *Middle Eastern*

A bijou delight, with small tables and chairs packed closely together. The kitchen is run by an accomplished Israeli husband-and-wife team. This pedigree shines in a daily-changing menu that draws influences from across the Middle East. The meze selection includes fabulously spongy, oily bread, *sumac*-spiked tahini, smoky taramasalata, crisp courgette croquettes with *labneh*, pan-fried feta and a bright salad with lemon and radishes. A main might be a

whole baby chicken with lemon and a chilli and walnut *muhamara* paste. It's imaginative home-style cooking, and service is charming.

Portland £££

113 Great Portland Street, W1W 6QQ (020 7436 3261, portlandrestaurant.co.uk). Oxford Circus tube. **Open** *6-10pm Mon, Tue; noon-2.30pm, 6-10pm Wed-Sat.* **Map** *p114 J6* ❹ *Contemporary European*

It's rare to go to a restaurant and be astonished, but chef Merlin Labron-Johnson cooks like a wizard. Favourite dishes include pig's head croquettes, aged mimolet cheese and granola, or pickled shiitake mushrooms. Desserts – such as 'chocolate bar, peanut butter praline, peanut ice-cream' – are skilfully executed and the wine list is short but imaginative. It's a small, bare-wood, no-frills kind of place, but it's very attractive and the flavours are sensational.

♥ Roka ££££

37 Charlotte Street, W1T 1RR (020 7580 6464, www.rokarestaurant. com). Goodge Street or Tottenham Court Road tube. **Open** *noon-3.30pm, 5.30-11.30pm Mon-Fri; 12.30-4pm, 5.30-11.30pm Sat; 12.30-4pm, 5.30-10.30pm Sun.* **Map** *p114 K6* ❺ *Japanese*

Roka gets top marks for glitz and glamour. Much of the action takes place at the central *robata* grill, where a repertoire of contemporary *izakaya*-inspired food is created in full view. The 13-course tasting menu is popular with first-time diners, taking them on a spin of the best Roka has to offer: elegant dishes such as hand-made *kimchi*, sashimi and sticky skewers of *tebasaki* (chicken wings) are finished off with a trio of desserts, featuring delights such as Pocky-style chocolate and sesame biscuit sticks. It isn't cheap, but each dish is impeccable.

Roti Chai £££

3 Portman Mews South, W1H 6AY (020 7408 0101, www.rotichai. com). Marble Arch tube. **Dining room** *noon-2.30pm, 5-10.30pm Mon-Fri; 5-10.30pm Sat; 5-9pm Sun.* **Street kitchen** *noon-10.30pm Mon-Sat; 12.30-9pm Sun.* **Map** *p114 H7* ❻ *Pan-Indian*

The ground-floor 'street kitchen', with its utilitarian furniture and canteen vibe, is ideal for a swift midday feed – and the alert young staff keep things pacy. The menu is modelled on those of urban India's snack shacks, so you'll find food such as *bhel pooris*, chilli *paneer* and *pani puri*. Larger dishes include 'railway lamb curry' (tender meat and potato in a rich gravy spiced with star anise and cinnamon bark). In the basement, the 'dining room' is a darker, sexier (and pricier) space.

❤ Zoilo £££

9 Duke Street, W1U 3EG (020 7486 9699, www.zoilo.co.uk). Bond Street tube. **Open** *5.30-10pm Mon; noon-2.30pm, 5.30-10pm Tue-Sat.* **Map** *p114 H7* ❼ *Argentinian*

If the idea of deconstructed, small-plates Argentinian cooking seems a contradiction in terms, pull up a counter seat and prepare to be amazed. With few actual tables, most of the seating is around the ground-floor bar or the downstairs kitchen – it shouts 'watch us work, look how good we are!'. Diners can witness the creation of dazzling offerings like octopus cooked *sous vide*, fried *queso de chancho* ('head cheese'), or miniature steak, each rustled up with flair and a feel for authenticity. Desserts run from a traditional, ultra-sweet '*tres leches*' milk cake to a tart passionfruit sorbet, and most of the all-Argentinian wine list is available by the glass or small carafe. Plates might be small, but when flavours

Oxford Street

are as compelling as these, you want as many different dishes as you can get.

Shops & services

Major department stores hold sway over much of Oxford Street, home to **Selfridges** (no.400), **John Lewis** (no.300) and chain flagships for **Uniqlo** (no.311), **Primark** (no.499-517) and **Topshop** (no.214). Fab Four fans head to the **London Beatles Store** (231 Baker Street, 020 7935 4464, www.beatlesstorelondon.co.uk).

Daunt Books

83-84 Marylebone High Street, W1U 4QW (020 7224 2295, www. dauntbooks.co.uk). Baker Street tube. **Open** *9am-7.30pm Mon-Sat; 11am-6pm Sun.* **Map** *p114 H6* ❶ *Books & music*

This beautiful Edwardian shop's elegant three-level back room – complete with oak balconies, viridian-green walls and stained-glass window – houses a much-praised travel section (guidebooks, maps, travelogues) and is a first-rate stop for literary fiction, biography, gardening and more. There's a good range of author readings to boot.

Gallery of Everything

4 Chiltern Street, W1U 7PS (020 7486 8908, shop.musevery.

com). Baker Street tube. **Open**
11am-6.30pm Tue-Sat; 2-6pm Sun.
Map *p114 H6* ❷ *Art & merchandise*
It all started in a former dairy
in Camden – or perhaps in
Duchamp's urinal. The former
was, in 2009, the site of the hugely
popular Museum of Everything
exhibition of outsider or non-
academic or naïve or private or...
well, of art you don't usually see
in galleries. Further exhibitions
followed, here and in other cities,
all delivered with a winning pop
sensibility and a shrewd eye
for artistry and interest. This
gallery-shop continues the good
work – even if you're not in the
hunt for original art, the excellent
merchandise makes winningly
idiosyncratic souvenirs.

Selfridges

*400 Oxford Street, W1A 1AB (0800
123400, www.selfridges.com). Bond
Street or Marble Arch tube.* **Open**
*10am-10pm Mon-Fri; 9.30am-9pm
Sat; noon-6pm Sun (browsing
from 11.30am).* **Map** *p114 H7* ❸
Department store
With its plethora of concession
boutiques, store-wide themed
events and collections from all
the hottest brands, Selfridges is
as dynamic as a department store
can be. While the basement is
chock-full of hip home accessories
and stylish kitchen equipment,
it's Selfridges' fashion floors that
really get hearts racing. With a

winning combination of new
talent, hip and edgy labels, high-
street brands and luxury high-end
designers, the store stays ahead of
the pack. Highlights include the
huge denim section, the extensive
Shoe Galleries and, on the third
floor, the 37,000sq ft (3,437m sq)
Body Studio, a temple of top-notch
activewear that aims to kit out
people of all shapes and sizes. Level
4 hosts the predictably excellent
Toy Shop. There are always new
excitements in the food hall,
ranging from great deli and bakery
produce to classy packaged goods,
while regularly changing pop-ups
and special events keep customers
on their toes.

Entertainment

100 Club
*100 Oxford Street, W1D 1LL (020
7636 0933, www.the100club.co.uk).
Oxford Circus or Tottenham Court
Road tube.* **Tickets** *£10-£25.* **Map**
p114 K7 ❶ *Live music*
The 100 Club began life in 1942
hosting the Feldman Club, but
over the decades jazz would give
way to punk: one historic show,
in September 1976, featured the
Sex Pistols, the Clash and the
Damned. These days the famous,
350-capacity basement room is
more of a hub for pub rockers,
blues rockers and, in a return to
its roots, trad jazzers. The space
comes into its own for the odd
secret gig by A-list bands such as
Primal Scream and Oasis.

♥ Wigmore Hall
*36 Wigmore Street, W1U 2BP
(information 020 7258 8200, tickets
020 7935 2141, wigmore-hall.org.
uk). Bond Street tube.* **Box office**
*Non-performance days 10am-7pm
Mon-Sat; 10am-2pm Sun.
Performance days 10am-7pm daily.*
Tickets *free-£35.* **Map** *p114 J6* ❷
Concert hall

Built in 1901 as the display hall for Bechstein pianos, this world-renowned, 550-seat concert venue has perfect acoustics for the 460 concerts that take place each year. Music from the classical and romantic periods are mainstays, usually performed by major classical stars to an intense audience, but under artistic director John Gilhooly there has been a broadening in the remit: more Baroque and jazz (with heavyweights like Brad Mehldau), including late-night gigs. Monday lunchtime recitals are broadcast live on BBC Radio 3.

Mayfair

The broad curve of **Regent's Street** connects Oxford Circus to **Piccadilly Circus**, famous for its Eros statue and illuminated advertising panels. To the west, Mayfair has long meant money, but these days not necessarily stuffy exclusivity, with even the tailors of **Savile Row** loosening their ties.

Sights & museums

Body Worlds
*London Pavilion, 1 Piccadilly Circus, W1J 0DA (0330 223 3233, bodyworlds.co.uk). Piccadilly Circus tube. **Open** 10am-7pm daily (last entry 6pm). **Admission** prices from £22.50; £16-20 reductions; book online. **Map** p142 L8.*
Gunther von Hagens' famous collection of human bodies preserved via his own 'plastination' technique has found a permanent home at Piccadilly Circus. It's unsettling to move from the throngs of people outside into an exhibition that lays humanity bare in such a stark way. Visitors report finding the skinless cadavers sincerely life-affirming, sometimes even spurring them on to give up the booze and start exercising.

Handel & Hendrix in London
*25 Brook Street, W1K 4HB (020 7495 1685, handelhendrix.org). Bond Street tube. **Open** 11am-6pm Mon-Sat (last entry 5pm). **Admission** £10; £5 reductions; free under-5s. **Map** p114 J7.*
Separated by just a brick wall are the former homes of two of history's most innovative and influential musicians – George Frideric Handel (1685-1759) and Jimi Hendrix (1942-1970). Handel moved to Britain from Germany aged 25 and settled in this house 12 years later, remaining here until his death. The house – where he composed his *Messiah* and *Music for the Royal Fireworks* – has been faithfully restored, with furnishings, paintings and some of the composer's scores.

The upstairs flat at no.23, where Jimi lived with his girlfriend in 1968, has also been painstakingly recreated, right down to the discarded fag butts. As well as the period bedroom, there's a timeline room with a few artefacts and plenty of audio and film, and a brilliant annex where Jimi's record collection is itemised and explored.

♥ Royal Academy of Arts
*Burlington House, W1J 0BD (020 7300 8000, www.royalacademy. org.uk). Green Park or Piccadilly Circus tube. **Open** 10am-6pm Mon-Thur, Sat, Sun; 10am-10pm Fri (last admission 30mins before closing time). **Admission** free. Exhibitions vary. **Map** p114 K8.*
Britain's first art school was founded in 1768 and moved to the extravagantly Palladian Burlington House a century later, but it's now best known not for education but for exhibitions. Ticketed blockbusters are generally held in the Sackler Wing or the main galleries; shows in the John Madejski Fine Rooms are drawn from the RA's holdings, which

range from Constable to Hockney, and are free. The biggest event here is the annual Summer Exhibition, which for more than two centuries has drawn from works entered by the public.

The RA also occupies a 19th-century building at 6 Burlington Gardens, which exhibits unabashedly contemporary art, from Tracey Emin and David Hockney to lightworks by Mariko Mori. It's linked to the original building thanks to a £56 million redevelopment by architect David Chipperfield. The new expanded campus includes gallery spaces, cafés, a lecture theatre and learning centre.

Restaurants

♥ Kitty Fisher's ££££

10 Shepherd Market, W1J 7QF (020 3302 1661, www.kittyfishers. com). Green Park tube. **Open** *noon-2.30pm, 6-9.30pm Mon-Sat.* **Map** *p114 J9* ⑧ *Modern European*

Named after an 18th-century courtesan known for her wit and extravagance, Kitty Fisher's will leave you with a big smile on your face – if you don't mind paying for the privilege. The signature dish is beef cut from a ten- to 12-year-old Galician milking cow, chargrilled and served with cheese-stuffed salad potatoes and blackened onion (£80, serves two). To cut your bill in half, stick to small plates (£6-£12.50) such as melted taleggio with London honey, wholegrain mustard and loads of shaved truffle, or whipped cod's roe on dainty soldiers. The basement dining room is intimate and hugely atmospheric, but tables do get booked up well in advance.

Pubs & bars

♥ Connaught Bar

The Connaught, Carlos Place, W1K 2AL (020 7499 7070, www.the-connaught.co.uk). Bond Street or Green Park tube. **Open** *11am-1am Mon-Sat; 11am-midnight Sun.* **Map** *p114 J8* ①

Inside one of the more discreet of London's mega-expensive hotels, the Connaught Bar is all about old-school style and glamour. Designed by David Collins, its mirrors, low lighting, silver leaf and tasteful palette will put you in mind of a deco steamship. Even if you can only stretch to a single drink, it's worth it, especially if you order a martini – a trolley is wheeled up beside you and the drink mixed on top.

Royal Academy of Arts

Mr Fogg's Residence

15 Bruton Lane, W1J 6JD (020 7036 0608, www.mr-foggs.com). Green Park tube. **Open** *4.01pm-2.01am Mon-Fri; 1.31pm-2.01am Sat; 3.01pm-12.01am Sun.* **Map** p114 J8 ❷

For sheer spectacle, Mr Fogg's is hard to beat. The place is stuffed with the detritus left by the titular Victorian explorer: every wall is covered with hunting rifles, stuffed animals, weathered flags and maps – all imaginary souvenirs of course, but that doesn't make the profusion of clutter any less fun. With an interior like this, it would be easy for cocktails to take second place, but seriously knowledgeable bar staff make sure the drinks are punchy and altogether sensational.

Shops & services

Mayfair is a focal area for British designer showcases, but there isn't much to see if you're not getting a suit made.

♥ Browns

23-27 South Molton Street, W1K 5RD (020 7514 0016, www. brownsfashion.com). Bond Street tube. **Open** *10am-7pm Mon-Wed, Sat; 10am-8pm Thur, Fri; noon-6pm Sun.* **Map** p114 J7 ❹ *Fashion*

The buying team at Browns are magicians, with an uncanny ability to pull in the most interesting, talking-point pieces of a designer's collection. Having been owned by Joan Burnstein and her family for four decades, fashion store Farfetch has now taken the reins, bringing technological innovation to its offerings. Among the 100-odd designers jostling for attention across five interconnecting shops are fashion heavyweights Chloé, Dries Van Noten and Balenciaga. You'll also find designs from rising stars, and shop exclusives are common. No.24 now houses Browns Focus, a younger and more casual look; while Labels for Less is loaded with last season's leftovers.

Burlington Arcade

51 Piccadilly, W1J 0QJ (020 7493 1764, www.burlingtonarcade. com). Green Park tube. **Open** *9am-7.30pm Mon-Sat; 11am-6pm Sun.* **Map** p114 K8 ❺ *Mall*

In 1819, Lord Cavendish commissioned Britain's very first shopping arcade. Nearly two centuries later, the Burlington is still one of London's most prestigious shopping 'streets', patrolled by 'beadles' decked out in top hats and tailcoats. Highlights include collections of classic watches at David Duggan, established British fragrance house Penhaligon's, and Sermoneta, selling Italian leather gloves in a range of bright colours. High-end food shops come in the form of Luponde Tea and Ladurée; head to the latter for exquisite Parisian macaroons. Burlington also houses a proper shoe-shine boy working with waxes and creams. This may not offer the best shopping in London, but it's certainly one of the best shopping experiences.

♥ Hamleys

188-196 Regent Street, W1B 5BT (0371 704 1977, www.hamleys. com). Oxford Circus tube. **Open** *10am-9pm Mon-Fri; 9.30am-9pm Sat; noon-6pm Sun.* **Map** p114 K7 ❻ *Toys*

Visiting Hamleys is certainly an experience – whether a good one or not will depend on your tolerance for noisy, over-excited children, especially during school holidays and the run-up to Christmas, when the store runs special kids' events. As you doubtless know, Hamleys is a ginormous toy shop, with attractive displays of all this season's must-have toys across five crazed floors, and perky demonstrators ramping up the temptation levels.

💜 Liberty

Regent Street, W1B 5AH (020 7734 1234, www.liberty.co.uk). Oxford Circus tube. **Open** *10am-8pm Mon-Sat; noon-6pm Sun (browsing from 11.30am).* **Map** *p114 K7* **❼**
Department store

Founded in 1875, Liberty's current premises were built in 1925 – the distinctive half-timbered frontage constructed from the remains of a couple of decommissioned warships, HMS *Hindustan* and HMS *Impregnable*. Which goes a good way to summarising the place: it's a superbly loveable mix of tradition and fashion. The store's interconnecting jumble of rooms, with the odd fireplace and cushioned window seat, have an intimate feel – as if you've strayed into a private room in a stately home.

At the main entrance is Wild at Heart's exuberant floral concession and a room devoted to the store's own label. Fashion brands focus on high-end British designers, such as Vivienne Westwood and Christopher Kane. The Paper Room is the place to find Liberty's micro-floral print stationery and gifts, while the Dining Room offers quirky cookware and gadgetry. In the Literary Lounge, opened by French publishing powerhouse Assouline, you can flick through fashion, art and photography coffee-table books. The Beauty Hall stocks cult brands such as Aesop, Le Labo, Byredo and celebrated skin products from Egyptian Magic. Despite being up with the latest fashions, Liberty respects its dressmaking heritage

in its third-floor haberdashery department and extensive men's tailoring chamber. For all its pomp and fizz, the store doesn't take itself too seriously – there's a genuine sense of whimsy in its approach to retail. Collaborations with brands such as Puma and Nike produce floral sneakers (that instantly sell out) and, via its Art Fabrics project, Liberty has worked with babydoll-dress fancier Grayson Perry and even Hello Kitty to create exclusive fabrics. The store still has a little sewing school, with crafty classes for aspiring seamstresses. Visitors can also have their moustache expertly trimmed and waxed at Murdock barbers or their barnacles plucked off by expert chiropodists in the Margaret Dabbs Sole Spa.

Postcard Teas

9 Dering Street, W1S 1AG (020 7629 3654, www.postcardteas.com). Bond Street or Oxford Circus tube. **Open** *10.30am-6.30pm Mon-Sat. Tastings £20; £15 reductions.* **Map** *p114 J7* **8** *Food & drink*

The range in this exquisite little shop is not huge, but it is selected with great care, and all teas are sourced from small cooperatives. There's a central table for those who want to try a pot; or book in for one of the tasting sessions held on Saturdays between 10am and 11am. Stunning tea-ware and accessories are also sold.

Soho & around

For more than two centuries, poseurs, spivs, tarts, toffs, drunks and divas have gathered in Soho. But the district's time as the focus of all that's benevolently naughty – and a proportion of the truly wicked too – has gone. Today, PRs, shoppers and tourists mingle with sundry party-people. Still, if you want to drink or eat, you could hardly find a better part of town in which to do so. And a wander along **Old Compton Street**, Soho's main artery, should show you a bit of mischief.

From here, two classic Soho streets – **Greek Street** and **Frith Street** – lead north to **Soho Square**, the only breathing space in a maze of old alleyways. Running parallel is **Dean Street**, once home to Karl Marx, lined with old-school pubs and cosy restaurants.

'West Soho' (the area west of Berwick Street) has been reborn as the epicentre of street fashion, with shops on **Carnaby Street** and **Kingly Street** recapturing something of the spirit of what made them famous in the 1960s.

Just to the south of Soho is London's bustling **Chinatown**. The ersatz oriental gates, stone

Kingly Street

lions and pagoda-topped phone boxes around Gerrard Street suggest a Chinese theme park, but this remains a genuine focal point for London's Chinese community. Nearby, **Leicester Square** – known for cinemas and, for many years, drunk out-of-towners – is inching towards a classier reputation.

Sights & museums

Photographers' Gallery

16-18 Ramillies Street, W1F 7LW (020 7087 9300, thephotographersgallery.org. uk). Oxford Circus tube. **Open** *10am-6pm Mon-Wed, Fri, Sat; 10am-8pm Thur; 11am-6pm Sun.* **Admission** *£5; £2.50 reductions; free under-18s; free after 5pm. Temporary exhibitions vary.* **Map** *p114 K7.*

Given a handsome refit by Irish architects O'Donnell+ Tuomey, this old, brick corner building is home to London's only gallery dedicated solely to the photographic arts. The upper floors have two airy exhibition spaces, while a bookshop, print sales room and café are tucked into the ground floor and basement. The exhibitions are varied, and enhanced by quirky details such as the camera obscura in the third-floor Eranda Studio and a projection wall in the café.

Restaurants

❤ 10 Greek Street £££

10 Greek Street, W1D 4DH (020 7734 4677, www.10greekstreet. com). **Tottenham Court Road tube. Open** *noon-11pm Mon-Sat; noon-10pm Sun.* **Map** *p114 L7* ⑨ *Modern European*

This small, unshowy restaurant has made a name for itself with a short but perfectly formed menu and an easygoing conviviality. Dishes are seasonal and the kitchen produces lots of interesting but ungimmicky combinations – such as a special of halibut fillet with yellow beans, chilli and garlic, on a vivid romesco sauce. It's good value too. Tables are closely packed, and in the evening it can get noisy.

Bao £

53 Lexington Street, W1F 9AS (baolondon.com). **Oxford Circus or Piccadilly Circus tube. Open** *noon-3pm, 5.30-10pm Mon-Thur; noon-10.30pm Sat; noon-5pm Sun. No reservations.* **Map** *p114 K7* ⑩ *Taiwanese*

This slick Taiwanese operation has successfully made the journey from market pop-up to permanent Soho establishment. The tantalising menu is fresh and innovative, based on Taiwanese street food dishes, with *xiao chi* (small eats) and of course *bao* (fluffy white steamed buns) stuffed with braised pork, soy-milk-marinated chicken, or even Horlicks ice-cream. Complementing the moreish food is the drinks list. Sakés, artisanal ciders, well-matched beers and hot oolong teas vie for attention alongside creations such as foam tea – a chilled light oolong artistically topped with foamed cream. Arrive hungry, leave happy.

Ceviche ££

17 Frith Street, W1D 4RG (020 7292 2040, www.cevichefamily.com/ ceviche). **Leicester Square tube. Open** *5-11pm Mon, Tue; noon-3pm, 5-11pm Wed, Thur; noon-3pm, 5-11.30pm Fri; noon-11.30pm Sat; noon-10pm Sun.* **Map** *p114 L7* ⑪ *Peruvian*

Ceviche showcases citrus-cured fish. It is available in half a dozen different forms, though the menu also includes everything from terrific chargrilled meat and fish skewers (*anticuchos*) to a simple but perfectly executed corn cake. Factor in the seating options (trendy at the steel counter-bar, more comfortable in the rear dining area), the charismatic, attentive staff and the party atmosphere, and it's no wonder this place has been such a huge hit.

Hoppers £

49 Frith Street, W1D 4SG (www. hopperslondon.com). **Tottenham Court Road or Leicester Square tube. Open** *noon-2.30pm, 5.30-10.30pm Mon-Thur; noon-10.30pm Fri, Sat. No reservations.* **Map** *p114 L7* ⑫ *Sri Lankan*

For those not familiar with Sri Lankan cuisine, a hopper is a bowl-shaped savoury crêpe, usually eaten at breakfast, and this small stylish joint has them down to a T. Decor is an effortless mix of old and new; exposed brick meets wood panelling; pretty patterned tiles meet carved-wood devil masks. The menu, likewise, gives traditional Sri

Lankan street food a fashionable lift: slender breaded and deep-fried mutton rolls come with a ginger, garlic and chilli 'ketchup'; a dinky dish of roast bone marrow is treated to a fiery 'dry' sauce, and the guinea fowl curry is unapologetically spicy.

Polpo Soho ££

*41 Beak Street, W1F 9SB (020 7734 4479, polpo.co.uk). Piccadilly Circus tube. **Open** 11.30am-11pm Mon-Sat; 11.30am-10pm Sun. **Map** p114 K7* ⑬ *Italian*

This Italian restaurant pioneered both London's small plates trend and its no-bookings culture. With peeling paint and battered wooden panelling, the decor may not look like much, but you won't find better Venetian food anywhere in W1. Brown paper menus and chunky tumblers for wine glasses underline the sense of squatter chic, as does sharing small plates of unfussy food. These stretch from humble plates of olives to tasty crab *arancini*, sirloin steak and calf's liver, or spinach and egg *pizzette*.

Quo Vadis £££

*26-29 Dean Street, W1D 3LL (020 7437 9585, www.quovadissoho. co.uk). Tottenham Court Road tube. **Open** 8-10.30am, noon-2.30pm, 5.30-10.30pm Mon-Fri; noon-2.30pm, 5.30-10.30pm Sat. **Map** p114 L7* ⑭ *Modern British*

This bona-fide Soho institution is rapidly approaching its centenary. It continues to fill up at peak times with the same old confidence and old-school Soho characters. The familiar stained-glass windows – a QV calling card – maintain the chic levels, and service is as sharp as ever, if perhaps a little impersonal. British standards are given modern flourishes by the QV kitchen: a gamey pheasant pie with lashings of silky mash on the side is perfect comfort food and plenty to share between two; for lunch, try the classic smoked eel sarnie.

❤ Social Eating House £££

*58 Poland Street, W1F 7NR (020 7993 3251, www.socialeatinghouse. com). Oxford Circus tube. **Open** noon-2.30pm, 6-10.30pm Mon-Sat. **Map** p114 K7* ⑮ *British*

Chef-patron Jason Atherton, once sorcerer's apprentice to Gordon Ramsey, has the golden touch. In 2013, he opened his Little Social deluxe bistro right opposite his Michelin-starred Pollen Street Social in Mayfair. Just weeks later, chef role delegated to Paul Hood, Atherton opened Social Eating House – still our favourite of his stable. The ground-floor dining room has a mirrored ceiling to create the impression of space in a small room; upstairs is a smart cocktail bar, called the Blind Pig, which also has a separate entrance. But most of the action is in the dining room, with a kitchen brigade who are clearly at the top of their game: stunning presentation and amazing flavour combinations, with great service.

Xu ££

*30 Rupert Street, W1D 6DL (020 3319 8147, xulondon.com). Piccadilly Circus tube. **Restaurant** 5-11pm Mon-Wed; noon-3pm, 5-11pm Thur, Fri; noon-4pm, 5-11pm Sat; noon-4pm, 5-10pm Sun. **Teahouse** noon-5pm Sat, Sun. **Map** p114 L8* ⑯ *Taiwanese*

Vintage is the vibe at Xu (pronounced 'Shu'. Not 'Joo'. Not 'Sue'.) The first 'smart' restaurant from the crew behind cult hit Bao (*see p125*), it's a love letter to 1930s Taipei. The narrow, potentially awkward two-floor space has been reformatted as a bundle of mini dining spots, each with its own air of intimacy. The upstairs room even has a teeny bar at its centre. As for the food, it's magnificent, layered with the full spectrum of sweet, sour and spice. First up, a pancake filled not with duck but tender short rib, enriched with bone marrow and served in the hollowed-out canoe of a calf shin with a potato 'crumb' on top. Then, a stunning cold tomato and smoked eel soup-of-sorts, oscillating between sweet and salty, smoky and tangy. And chilli egg drop crab: a creamy curry, full of crabby flavour and punchy chilli, with the odd blob of wibbly egg and delicious briny accents, when the salmon roe pops on your tongue.

Wun's Tearoom & Bar £

28 Greek Street, W1D 4DZ (020 8017 9888, tearoom.bar). Leicester Square or Tottenham Court Road tube. **Open** *noon-midnight Mon-Wed; noon-late Thur, Fri; 11am-late Sat; 11am-midnight Sun.* **Map** *p114 L7* **⑰**

The team behind Bun House have converted their flagship site into a tearoom that captures the spirit of 1960s Hong Kong. Authentic Cantonese cuisine (think claypot dishes and XO roasted bone marrow), served against a backdrop of exposed brickwork and cracked plaster, feels like a retro street café. Downstairs, the neon-lit cocktail bar with jade green walls and velvet seating, is a sultry late-night den serving Chinese cocktails.

Pubs & bars

♥ Bar Américain

Brasserie Zédel, 20 Sherwood Street, W1F 7ED (020 7734 4888, www.brasseriezedel.com/bar-americain). Piccadilly Circus tube. **Open** *4pm-midnight Mon-Wed; 4pm-1am Thur, Fri; 1pm-1am Sat; 4-11pm Sun.* **Map** *p114 K8* **❸**

We love the simplicity of the cocktail list here: around 20 drinks, most of them tried and tested classics. Expertly rendered martinis and manhattans and daiquiris sit alongside inventive house specialities like the Danse Banane,

which includes ginger liqueur, pickled banana, pineapple and lemon. Fancy a quiet drink in the West End without having to pay through the nose? You can't do much better than the Américain's beautiful art deco interior.

Bar Termini

7 Old Compton Street, W1D 5JE (07860 945018, bar-termini-soho.com). Leicester Square or Tottenham Court Road tube. **Open** *10am-11.30pm Mon-Thur; 10am-1am Fri, Sat; 11am-10.30pm Sun. Booking necessary after 5pm, when 60min time limit applies.* **Map** *p114 L7* **❹**

Bar Termini does two things: coffee and cocktails, in a room for 25, with seated service only, though you may stand if you order a single 'espresso al bar' (£1) – then drink and run in the Italian style. The coffee list has three signature brews, all of them classics but with a twist. The alcohol list has four negronis, a selection of *aperitivi*, four wines and one bottled beer. There are also baked goods by day, and charcuterie and cheese in the evening. If you're arriving after 5pm, not only will you need to book, but your visit will be strictly limited to one hour.

Blind Pig

Social Eating House, 58 Poland Street, W1F 7NR (020 7993 3251, www.socialeatinghouse. com). Oxford Circus tube. **Open** *3pm-midnight Mon-Thur; 1pm-midnight Fri, Sat.* **Map** *p114 K7* **❺**

If you fancy getting straight to the booze, Social Eating House's excellent cocktail bar isn't immediately obvious at street level: look under the vintage 'Optician' sign and you'll find a door knocker marked with a blindfolded hog. Once inside, you can get stuck into mighty fine cocktails with mighty silly names: who could resist a

Slap 'n' Pickle (gin, brandy and pickle brine), Kindergarten Cup (incorporating 'Skittles-washed Ketel One'), or a Robin Hood, Quince of Thieves (brandy, quince liqueur, mead)?

French House

49 Dean Street, W1D 5BG (020 7437 2799, www.frenchhousesoho.com). Leicester Square tube. **Open** *noon-11pm Mon-Sat; noon-10.30pm Sun. Food served noon-3pm Mon, Fri; noon-3pm, 6.30-9.30pm Tue-Thur.* **Map** *p165 L7* ❻

Through the door of this venerable establishment have passed many titanic drinkers of the pre- and post-war eras. The venue's French heritage enticed de Gaulle to run a Resistance operation from upstairs – it's now a tiny restaurant. De Gaulle's image survives behind the bar, where beer is served in half pints, and litre bottles of Breton cider are still plonked on the famed back alcove table. Be aware of the strict 'no phones' policy.

♥ Friendly Society

79 Wardour Street, W1D 6QB (020 7434 3805). Leicester Square tube. **Open** *4-11.30pm Mon-Fri; 2-11.30pm Sat; 2-10.30pm Sun.* **Map** *p114 L7* ❼

Friendly Society benefits from the power of surprise: after entering through a bland back-alley doorway, you're greeted at the bottom of the stairs by Soho's most idiosyncratic drinking den. Barbie dolls hang from the ceiling, there's a big fishbowl in the middle and old movies are projected on to a back wall. Although the short cocktail menu has been the same for ever, the staff always seem perplexed when you order one, though that's definitely part of the charm. The crowd here is gay in the broadest sense – anyone with a sense of fun will feel at home, whatever their gender and sexuality. Come here when you fancy dancing to Donna Summer while sipping (relatively) inexpensive prosecco.

Lyric

37 Great Windmill Street, W1D 7LT (020 7434 0604, www.lyricsoho.co.uk). Piccadilly Circus tube. **Open** *11am-11.30pm Mon-Thur; 11am-midnight Fri, Sat; noon-10.30pm Sun. Food served noon-10pm daily.* **Map** *p114 L8* ❽

Small, slightly shambolic and with a jovial share-a-table vibe, the Lyric is a longstanding favourite, not least because of its location near a fantastically crowded part

Soho Square

of London where disappointing, pricey tourist traps are the norm. The Victorian pub's 18 taps pour out reliable pints, including Camden Hells and Brooklyn Lager, as well as more unusual guests – perhaps the hyper-citrussy High Wire Grapefruit brew from Magic Rock.

♥ Swift

12 Old Compton Street, W1D 4TQ (020 7437 7820, www.barswift. com). Tottenham Court Road tube. Open 3pm-midnight Mon-Sat; 3-10.30pm Sun. Map p114 L7 ⑨

Swift is the third fabulous bar from the couple who brought us cult faves Nightjar and Oriole. On the former site of ground-breaking Lab Bar, Swift is split in two: a buzzy, casual-yet-sparkling bar on the ground level and a dark lounge below. Upstairs, the look is faintly Italian, mirrored by a menu of affordable *aperitivi*, while the basement is lit for romantic trysts. The staff are attentive, guiding you through a menu of great originality that edges towards nightcaps; try the powerful Amber Cane, a reinvented manhattan with rum in place of bourbon.

Shops & services

You can shop in Soho for everything from cheap street fashion to upscale designer garb and stylish items from home-decor stores. Buzzy **Berwick Street** market is the place for street-food stalls, vintage shops and indie vinyl. **Denmark Street** has become a hub for music shops. **Carnaby Street** has long been a favourite among fans of music and fashion, while the three-tiered **Kingly Court** complex contains a funky mix of established chains and hip boutiques. Quaint **Cecil Court** is known for its antiquarian book, map and print dealers,

housed in premises that haven't changed in a hundred years.

Algerian Coffee Stores

52 Old Compton Street, W1D 4PB (020 7437 2480, algeriancoffeestores.com). Leicester Square tube. Open 9am-7pm Mon-Wed; 9am-9pm Thur, Fri; 9am-8pm Sat. Map p114 L7 ⑨ *Food & drink*

For more than 125 years, this unassuming little shop has been trading over the same wooden counter. The range of coffees is broad, with house blends sold alongside single-origin beans; some serious teas and brewing hardware are also available. If you're just passing, pick up an espresso or latte to go.

Axel Arigato

19-23 Broadwick Street, W1F 0DF (020 7494 1728, axelarigato.com). Piccadilly Circus tube. Open 11am-7pm Mon-Wed; 11am-8pm Thur-Sat; noon-6pm Sun. Map p114 K7 ⑩ *Shoes*

After successfully building a fan base online, Swedish footwear brand Alex Arigato chose Soho for its flagship store. The handcrafted designer trainers are meticulously displayed on marbled pedestals and stone podiums, while the white colour scheme, concrete and mirrored surfaces of the shop's interior reflect its minimalist aesthetic. There are accessories and clothing too, as well as a selection of Japanese literature and objects that inspired the collection.

Foyles

107 Charing Cross Road, WC2H 0DT (020 7437 5660, www.foyles. co.uk). Tottenham Court Road tube. Open 9am-9pm Mon-Sat; noon-6pm Sun (browsing from 11.30am). Map p114 L7 ⑪ *Books*

With 37,000sq ft (3,437sq m) of floorspace laid out around an impressive central atrium, Foyles' eight levels are packed with more than 200,000 books, as well as CDs and literary gifts. The shop's focus is on the social aspect of reading. A whole floor is dedicated to events, from readings by Michael Palin and Jarvis Cocker, to themed book groups or literary tours, and there's a space dedicated to contemporary art.

Gosh!

1 Berwick Street, W1F 0DR (020 7437 0187, www.goshlondon. com). Oxford Circus tube. **Open** *10.30am-7pm daily.* **Map** *p114 L7* ⓬ *Books*

There's nowhere better to bolster your comics collection. There's a huge selection of manga, but graphic novels take centre stage, from early classics such as *Krazy Kat* to Alan Moore's erotic Peter Pan adaptation *Lost Girls*. Classic children's books, of the *This is London* vein, are another strong point. First port of call? The central table, where you'll find new releases – sometimes even before official publication.

Japan Centre

35B Panton Street, SW1Y 4EA (020 3405 1246, www.japancentre. com). Piccadilly Circus tube. **Open** *10am-9.30pm Mon-Sat; 11am-8pm Sun.* **Map** *p114 L8* ⓭ *Food & homewares*

This well-regarded centre offers all things Japanese, from specialist food ingredients to kitchenware and homewares. In the basement food hall, specialist rooms for tea, saké and miso are set around open kitchens and a central dining area.

MAC Carnaby

30 Great Marlborough Street, W1F 7JA (0370 192 5555, www. maccosmetics.co.uk). Oxford Circus tube. **Open** *10am-9pm Mon-Sat; 11.30am-6pm Sun.* **Map** *p114 K7* ⓮ *Cosmetics*

This impressive outpost of beauty heavyweight MAC features the brand's ever-popular collaborations and tongue-in-cheek limited edition lines – Haute Dogs, for instance, whose lipsticks were inspired by pedigree pooches. There are also nine kaleidoscopic make-up stations, for quick drop-in demos or longer, bookable lessons. Upstairs is dedicated to Mac's Pro line, beloved of make-up artists and drag queens alike. With an exhaustive selection of products, it's shopping nirvana for slaphappy amateurs and studious pros.

♥ Machine-A

13 Brewer Street, W1F 0RH (020 7734 4334, www.machine-a. com). Oxford Circus tube. **Open** *11am-7pm Mon-Wed; 11am-8pm Thur-Sat; noon-6pm Sun.* **Map** *p114 L7* ⓯ *Fashion*

Hats off (make it an Alex Mattsson baseball cap) to Machine-A for championing London's most exciting emerging designers at this Soho concept store. It's the natural habitat for the young, bold and brave, a small space full of pieces that practically sizzle with energy. Outside, the neon signage is a cheeky nod to its massage-parlour neighbours on Brewer Street.

Monki

37 Carnaby Street, W1V 1PD (020 8018 7400, www.monki.com/ gb). Oxford Circus tube. **Open** *10am-8pm Mon-Sat; noon-6pm Sun.* **Map** *p114 K7* ⓰ *Fashion*

Hailing from Sweden, Monki's aesthetic is a bold urban one featuring cute animal prints, oddly shaped sweater dresses and eccentric accessories – current hits include the animal-print backpacks, chunky leather ankle boots and cute woolly mittens emblazoned with big logos for less than a fiver.

Sounds of the Universe

7 Broadwick Street, W1F 0DA (020 7734 3430, soundsoftheuniverse. com). Tottenham Court Road tube. **Open** *10am-7.30pm Mon-Sat; 11.30am-5.30pm Sun.* **Map** *p114 L7* **17** *Music*

SOTU's remit is broad. This is especially true on the ground floor (new vinyl and CDs), where grime and dubstep 12-inches jostle for space alongside new wave cosmic disco, electro-indie re-rubs and Nigerian compilations. The second-hand vinyl basement is big on soul, jazz, Brazilian and alt-rock.

We Built This City

57 Carnaby Street, W1F 9QF (020 3642 9650, www.webuilt-thiscity. com). Oxford Circus tube. **Open** *10am-7pm Mon-Wed; 10am-8pm Thur-Sat; 11am-6.30pm Sun.* **Map** *p114 K7* **18** *Gifts*

Tired of all the tourist tat? If you're after funky souvenirs, We Built This City is the place for you. It sells a selection of pieces by London artists inspired by the city around them from premises given a supercool graphic look, inside and out, by east London artist Camille Walala.

We Built This City

YMC

11 Poland Street, W1F 8QA (020 7494 1619, www.youmustcreate. com). Oxford Circus tube. **Open** *11am-7pm Mon-Sat; noon-6pm Sun.* **Map** *p114 K7* **19** *Fashion*

Impeccably designed staples are the forte of this London label. It's the place to head to for simple vest tops and T-shirts, stylish macs, tasteful knits and chino-style trousers, for both men and women.

Entertainment

Shaftesbury Avenue is the very heart of Theatreland. The Victorians built seven grand theatres here, six of which still stand. The most impressive is the gorgeous **Palace Theatre** on Cambridge Circus, currently home to *Harry Potter & the Cursed Child* (*see p134*). Those looking for late-night partying will find plenty of lively bars and pubs, though decent club options are increasingly thin on the ground. For details of Soho's gay scene, *see p45*.

♥ Comedy Store

1A Oxendon Street, SW1Y 4EE (020 7024 2060, thecomedystore. co.uk/london). Leicester Square or Piccadilly Circus tube. **Open** *11am-9.30pm Mon-Thur; 11am-midnight Fri; 3pm-midnight Sat; 3-9pm Sun.* **Admission** *£5-£23.50.* **Map** *p114 L8* **3** *Comedy*

The Comedy Store is still the daddy of all the laff clubs. Seemingly as old as London itself (it actually started in 1979, above a strip club), the Store has been instrumental in the growth of alternative comedy, and still to this day hosts stunning shows most nights of the week. The live room was created specifically for stand-up and it shows, with 400 chairs hugging the stage to keep each show intimate. Veteran improvisers the Comedy Store Players perform every Wednesday and Sunday. Don't miss the raucous King Gong open-mic night on the last Monday of the month.

Curzon

99 Shaftesbury Avenue, W1D 5DY (0333 321 0104, www. curzoncinemas.com/soho). **Tickets** *£26.90; £15.40 reductions. Leicester Square tube. Screens 3.* **Map** *p114 L7* **4** *Cinema*

Arthouse film fans have been known to go weak at the knees at the mention of the Soho Curzon, which has some of the best programming in London – a mix of arty new releases and documentaries, often introduced by the filmmakers themselves. Watching a film at the Curzon always feels special, surrounded by film lovers without it being pretentious. The coffee is good, the bar relaxed, and if you're watching a British film, you'll likely be seeing the finished product a stone's throw from where it was edited in Soho. Perfect for whiling away a rainy afternoon.

Odeon Leicester Square

24-26 Leicester Square, WC2H 7JY (0333 006 7777, www.odeon.co.uk). Leicester Square tube. **Tickets** *£18.75-£40.75; £13.25-£15.75 reductions. Screens 5.* **Map** *p114 L8* **5** *Cinema*

This freshly revamped cinema is London's number-one destination for red carpet premières. Not only do you get blockbuster bangs in the ultra-modern 800-seat auditorium with Dolby Screen; you get them in splendour: there are some gorgeous 1930s art deco features, and it's one of the few remaining cinemas to retain its circle – from which the view (at extra cost) is pretty spectacular.

Picturehouse Central

Trocadero, Shaftesbury Avenue, Piccadilly, W1D 7DH (0871 902 5747, www.picturehouses.com). Piccadilly Circus tube. **Tickets** *£13.90-£16.90; £7.90-£14.90 reductions. Screens 7.* **Map** *p114 L8* **6** *Cinema*

On the corner of Shaftesbury Avenue, this central London cinema is an absolute gem. It's

Ronnie Scott's

the antidote to Piccadilly Circus's rage-inducing pavements, with three floors of beautifully designed space. Before you even get anywhere near the plush screening rooms, a hundred hanging lightbulbs lead you up a grand terracotta-tiled staircase past a mural inspired by a century of cinema.

Prince Charles
7 Leicester Place, off Leicester Square, WC2H 7BY (020 7494 3654, www.princecharlescinema.com). Leicester Square tube. **Tickets** *£9-£14.50. Screens 2.* **Map** *p114 K8* ❼ *Cinema*
This is the only time you'll spend in a cinema when no one's going to shush you. Singalong screenings at the Prince Charles are all about audience participation: whether your movie is *Frozen*, *Rocky Horror* or *The Sound of Music*. You can even settle in for a marathon all-night pyjama party. Having started life screening porn, the Prince Charles is central London's wildcard cinema, providing a fantastic blend of new-ish blockbusters and arthouse titles, with heaps of horror, sci-fi and teen-flick all-nighters, double bills and short seasons. It's comfy, cheap and cheerful.

♥ Ronnie Scott's
47 Frith Street, W1D 4HT (020 7439 0747, www.ronniescotts. co.uk). Leicester Square or Tottenham Court Road tube. **Open** *6pm-3am Mon-Sat; noon-4pm, 6.30pm-midnight Sun.* **Admission** *free-£50.* **Map** *p114 L7* ❽ *Jazz*
Opened (on a different site) by the British saxophonist Ronnie Scott in 1959, this jazz institution was the setting for Jimi Hendrix's final UK performance, among many other distinctions. It continues to attract jazz heavyweights such as well-established talents such as Chick Corea to hotly tipped purists

such as Kurt Elling to futuristic mavericks such as Robert Glasper. Perch by the rear bar, or get table service at the crammed side-seating or at the more spacious (but noisier) central tables in front of the stage.

SHE Soho
23A Old Compton Street, W1D 5JL (020 7437 4303, she-soho. com). Leicester Square tube. **Open** *4-11.30pm Mon-Thur; 4pm-midnight Fri, Sat; 4-10.30pm Sun.* **Map** *p114 L7* ❾ *Lesbian venue*
Shockingly, this Soho basement bar is London's only exclusively lesbian venue, and it takes this responsibility seriously. Run by the team behind Ku Bar, SHE has a comparable flair for laying on entertainment: as well as club nights, it regularly offers comedy, cabaret, karaoke and quiz evenings. Open Box, a monthly drag king talent contest hosted by scene heroes Adam All and Apple Derrières, is definitely worth popping in your Google Calendar.

Soho Theatre
21 Dean Street, W1D 3NE (020 7478 0100, sohotheatre.com). Tottenham Court Road tube. **Box office** *9am-9pm Mon-Sat.* **Tickets** *£11-£35.* **Map** *p114 L7* ❿ *Theatre*
Since it opened in 2000, Soho has built a reputation for excellence across cabaret, comedy and, yes, theatre. With its cool blue neon lights, ever-buzzing café and late-night shows it attracts a younger, hipper crowd than most London spaces. Across three studio spaces it puts on an eclectic line-up of aspiring writers and youth theatre (many of whom go on to the Edinburgh Fringe) as well as a host of household names (Phoebe Waller-Bridge, Michael McIntyre, David Hoyle...) and international stars.

Best of the West End

The show must go on...and on...

The Book of Mormon

Prince of Wales Theatre, Coventry Street, Soho, W1D 6AS (0844 482 5110, www.bookofmormonlondon. com). Piccadilly Circus tube. **Box office** *10am-8pm Mon-Sat.* **Tickets** *£20-£150.* **Map** *p114 L8* ⑪
South Park creators Trey Parker and Matt Stone's smash musical about the absurdities of Mormonism is not as shocking as you might expect. There's lots of swearing and close-to-the-bone jokes, but this is a big-hearted affair about the spirit and sounds of Broadway's golden age. And it's very, very funny.

Hamilton

Victoria Palace Theatre, 126 Victoria Street, Victoria, SW1E 5EA (0844 482 5151, www. hamiltonmusical.com/london). Victoria tube. **Box office** *10am-5.30pm Mon-Wed, Fri; 10am-12.30pm, 2.30-5.15pm Thur, Sat.* **Tickets** *£37.50-£190.* **Map** *p85 J11* ⑫
From the moment it opened in 2017, Lin-Manuel Miranda's Broadway-devouring rap musical about Alexander Hamilton, the first secretary of the US Treasury, has dominated the West End. Much has been made of its diverse casting and sociological import, but the fact is that *Hamilton* is, first and foremost, a ferociously enjoyable show. Miranda – who wrote everything – understands what mainstream audiences like about musical theatre and hip hop, and he has managed to craft a brilliant hybrid that combines big emotions and big melodies with funny, technically virtuoso storytelling. The best musical of our generation.

Harry Potter and the Cursed Child

Palace Theatre, 113 Shaftesbury Avenue, Soho, W1D 5AY (0330 333 4813, www.harrypottertheplay. com/uk). Leicester Square tube. **Box office** *In person 10am-7pm Mon-Sat.* **Tickets** *£15-£65 (1 part); £30-£130 (both parts).* **Map** *p114 L7* ⑬
The final adventure in JK Rowling's Harry Potter series isn't a book or a film, but a monumentally ambitious two-part London stage play, written by Jack Thorne. The production is phenomenal and as close as you'll ever get to stepping into Harry's magical world – small wonder it won a record nine Olivier Awards. It's booked up well in advance but there's a weekly online sale at 1pm on Fridays and the returns queue is worth a shot.

Matilda the Musical

Cambridge Theatre, 32-34 Earlham Street, Covent Garden, WC2H 9HU (020 7087 7745, www. matildathemusical.com). Covent Garden tube or Charing Cross tube/rail. **Box office** *In person 10am-7.30pm Mon-Sat; 10am-3pm Sun. By phone 10am-6pm Mon-Sat.* **Tickets** *£20-£122.50.* **Map** *p114 M7* ⑭
Adapted from Roald Dahl's riotous children's novel, with songs by superstar Aussie comedian Tim Minchin, this RSC transfer received rapturous reviews on its first outing in Stratford-upon-Avon and has been going strong ever since, winning multiple Olivier awards.

Les Misérables

Sondheim Theatre, 51 Shaftesbury Avenue, Soho, W1D 6BA (0844 482 5151, www.lesmis.com). Leicester

Covent Garden & around

Londoners may bemoan the crowds, but it should come as no surprise that Covent Garden is so popular with visitors. A traffic-free oasis in the heart of the city, it centres on the restored 19th-century covered market of Covent Garden Piazza. Shoppers flock here to wander the Italian-style arcades and surrounding streets, which are packed with upmarket chain stores (including the world's largest Apple Store), dainty boutiques and gentrified cafés – a far cry from the gambling dens and brothels of the past.

On the west side, **St Paul's Church** is known as the 'Actor's Church' for its long association with Covent Garden's theatres. It was designed by Inigo Jones in 1631 and features memorial plaques of famous thespians including Vivien Leigh and Charlie Chaplin. Its portico is a favourite haunt of busking musicians, artists, jugglers and escapologists.

The real attractions, however, are the reinvigorated **Royal Opera House** and the family-friendly **London Transport Museum**. There are some good restaurants to discover too.

Square or Piccadilly Circus tube. **Box office** *In person 10am-7.45pm Mon-Sat. By phone 10am-8pm Mon-Sat.* **Tickets** *£12.50-£97.25.* **Map** *p114 L8* ⓯
The RSC's version of Boublil and Schönberg's musical first came to the London stage in 1985. It's not the freshest show in town, but the voices remain lush, the revolutionary sets are film-fabulous, and the lyrics and score (based on Victor Hugo's novel) will be considerably less trivial than whatever's on next door.

The Play that Goes Wrong
Duchess Theatre, 3-5 Catherine Street, Covent Garden, WC2B 5LA (0330 333 4810, www. theplaythatgoeswrong.com). Charing Cross tube/rail. **Box office** *10am-6pm Mon, 10am-8pm Tue-Sun.* **Tickets** *£20-£65.* **Map** *p114 N7* ⓰
It's impossible not to be delighted by the success of this play, which began life at the tiny Old Red Lion theatre pub and has now been sitting pretty in the West End since 2014. It even has its own seasonal spin-off, *Peter Pan Goes Wrong.*

Sights & museums

♥ London Transport Museum
Covent Garden Piazza, WC2E 7BB (020 7379 6344, www.ltmuseum. co.uk). Covent Garden tube. **Open** *10am-6pm daily.* **Admission** *£18; £17 reductions; free under-18s. Discounts available online.* **Map** *p114 M7.*
London's prodigious growth in Victorian times into the biggest, most flabbergastingly exciting and frankly unpleasant city the world

Harry Potter and the Cursed Child

had ever known was largely down to transport infrastructure, which supported an unprecedented population explosion.

It is this story that the London Transport Museum tells so well, tracing the city's transport history from the horse age to the present day. The museum also raises some interesting and important questions about the future of public transport in the city, even offering a fanciful imagining of London's travel network in the years ahead.

Engaging and inspiring, the collections are in broadly chronological order, beginning with the Victorian gallery, where a replica of Shillibeer's first horse-drawn bus service from 1829 takes pride of place. Along the way there is a Northern Line simulator to drive, and train carriages and buses to jump on and climb up.

London by Design explores how, under the leadership of Frank Pick in the early 20th century, London Transport developed one of the most coherent brand identities in the world with arresting poster art from the likes of Abram Games, Graham Sutherland and Ivon Hitchens.

Hidden London is a recreation of a disused tube station, complete with blackened walls, peeling posters and exposed wiring. Fully immersive and packed with trivia, it brings together the stories of the city's forgotten spaces.

Younger children will love the small but terrific play zone, All Aboard, where they can repair a mini Tube train, make passenger announcements and operate the Emirates Air Line cable car.

Restaurants

The Barbary ££
16 Neal's Yard, WC2H 9DP (thebarbary.co.uk). Covent Garden tube. **Open** *noon-2.30pm, 5-10pm Mon-Wed; noon-3pm, 5-10pm Thur, Fri; noon-10pm Sat; noon-9.30pm Sun.* **Map** *p114 M7* ⓲
North African
The Barbary takes everything that's good about its sister restaurant Palomar and reinvents it. Seating is on 24 stools arranged at a horseshoe-shaped counter bar. Down one wall, there's a standing counter, where they'll feed you snacks like deep-fried pastry

London Transport Museum *p135*

'cigars' filled with cod, lemon and Moroccan spices while you wait for a seat. And the food – inspired by the eponymous Barbary coast, which stretches from Morocco to Egypt – is heady with smoke and North African spices. The signature *naan e beber*, made to an ancient recipe, emerges from the fiercely hot tandoor deliciously fluffy and blistered. Main courses such as slow-braised octopus with oranges cooked over a coal-fired *robata* are impossibly tender; while *knafeh* (filo pastry filled with goat's cheese and pan-fried until it's crispy on the outside, chewy on the inside, and sprinkled with roasted pistachio nuts) is dessert heaven.

♥ Barrafina ££
10 Adelaide Street, WC2N 4HZ (020 7440 1456, www.barrafina. co.uk). Charing Cross or Leicester Square tube. Open noon-3pm, 5-11pm Mon-Sat; 1-3.30pm, 5.30-10pm Sun. No reservations. Map p114 M8 ⑲ Tapas
Like its predecessor in Soho, Barrafina Covent Garden takes no reservations, so arrive early – or late – if you don't want to queue at this perennially popular tapas

restaurant. The menu is studded with tempting Mallorcan and Catalan dishes, but watch out if you're properly hungry: the bill adds up fast. Despite the fancy prices, remember that Barrafina is a modern Spanish tapas bar rather than a restaurant per se – this means that the list of sherries, cavas and other wines by the glass are as much a part of the appeal as the food, and perfect for experimenting with as you nibble.

Chick'n'Sours £
1A Earlham Street, WC2H 9LL (020 3198 4814, chicknsours.co.uk). Open noon-10pm Mon-Wed; noon-10.30pm Thur-Sat; noon-8pm Sun. Map p114 L7 ⑳ Korean
Combining KFC (that's Korean Fried Chicken, food fans) with cocktails has proved to be a winning formula. Set in a basement, the vibe is somewhere between house party and Prohibition speakeasy. There's a bar in the middle, a playlist of feel-good tunes and the food comes served on granny's best china plates. The speciality K-Pop burger is impossibly juicy and over four inches tall; it's double-fried

The Barbary

for crunchiness and served with *gochujang* (an umami-tastic red chilli paste) mayo, fiery *sriracha*, kimchi, chilli vinegar and Asian slaw. Follow it up with sweet-sticky disco wings and a peanut and pickled watermelon salad. Or go for an Asian mash-up of Shin Cup fries (with *sriracha* sour cream and spring onions) and Seoul Destroyer burger (with Korean schmaltz, nacho cheese and kimchi).

❤ J Sheekey £££

28-32 St Martin's Court, WC2N 4AL (020 7240 2565, j-sheekey.co.uk). Leicester Square tube. **Open** *noon-3pm, 5pm-midnight Mon-Sat; noon-3.30pm, 5.30-10.30pm Sun.* **Map** *p114 L8* ㉑ *Fish & seafood*
After well over a century of service, Sheekey's status as a West End institution is assured. With its monochrome photos of stars of stage and screen, wooden panelling and cream crackle walls, and array of silver dishes atop thick white tablecloths, it oozes old-fashioned glamour. The menu runs from super-fresh oysters and shellfish via old-fashioned snacks (herring roe on toast) to upmarket classics (dover sole, lobster thermidor). The fish pie – a rich, comforting treat – is acclaimed, but we feel the shrimp and scallop burger merits similar status.

Adjoining Sheekey restaurant, **J Sheekey Atlantic Bar** (nos.28-32, jsheekeyatlanticbar.co.uk) serves a similar menu – with an expanded range of oysters – to customers sitting at the counter.

Kanada-Ya £

64 St Giles High Street, WC2H 8LE (020 7240 0232, www.kanada-ya.com). Tottenham Court Road tube. **Open** *noon-3pm, 5-10.30pm Mon-Sat; noon-8.30pm Sun. No reservations.* **Map** *p114 L7* ㉒
Japanese
Small, brightly lit and minimal, this is not the place for a leisurely

meal: there are always lengthy mealtime queues outside its doors. But there's a reason for Kanada-Ya's already-large fan base: exceptional ramen. If you don't eat pork, forget it; but those pork bones are simmered for 18 hours to create the smooth, rich, seriously savoury *tonkotsu* broth – one of the best in London. If you don't have much time, the wait at Ippudo, just opposite, is always more bearable than that at Kanada-Ya.

Tandoor Chop House ££

8 Adelaide Street, WC2N 4HZ (020 3096 0359, tandoorchophouse.com). Charing Cross tube. **Open** *noon-11pm Mon-Thur; noon-11.30pm Fri, Sat; noon-10pm Sun.* **Map** *p114 M8* ㉓ *Indian*
TCH is slightly less hectic and slightly more refined than **Dishoom** (*see p170*). With cheerfully attentive service and a bustling Bombay vibe, it's a twist on what you'd get in an old-fashioned Brit 'chop house', only using Indo-Punjabi spices and swapping the grill for the tandoor. Plates are small and meant for sharing. Start with the pistachio-studded seekh kebab strewn with pomegranate seeds and coriander, or the 'beef dripping' *keema naan*. For mains, be sure to try the thickly marinated, fatty-edged lamb chops, all soot and spice, or the juicy spice-rubbed rib-eye. But don't stop there: the malted kulfi ice cream is silky smooth and intense, served with chunks of caramelised banana and salted peanuts.

Terroirs ££

5 William IV Street, WC2N 4DW (020 7036 0660, www.terroirswinebar.com). Charing Cross tube/rail. **Open** *noon-11pm Mon-Sat.* **Map** *p114 M8* ㉔
Terroirs – a wine bar with excellent food – is really two places under one roof. The always-crowded ground floor has a casual feel

and a menu to match, focused on small plates for sharing. You can sample some of the same dishes in the atmospheric and surprisingly roomy basement, which feels more like a restaurant: the menu here, with its focus on rustic French dishes, seems designed to guide diners more towards a traditional starter-main-dessert approach. The wine list is an encyclopaedia of organic and biodynamic bottles.

Pubs & bars

Beaufort Bar at the Savoy

*The Savoy, Strand, WC2R 0EZ (020 7420 2111, www.thesavoylondon. com/restaurant/beaufort-bar). Charing Cross tube/rail or Embankment tube. **Open** 5pm-1am Mon-Sat. **Map** p114 M8* ⑩
Set in London's most famous hotel, the ultra-suave Beaufort Bar is quite possibly the most attractive space to sip a drink in the city. Just off the busy lobby, it's a hideaway of supreme style and opulence, with jet-black walls, theatrical lighting and enough discreet touches of gold to remind you you're somewhere special. The drinks live up to the ambience, pushing the boundaries of mixology and incorporating fizz to great effect.

Cross Keys

*31 Endell Street, WC2H 9BA (020 7836 5185, www.crosskeys coventgarden.com). Covent Garden tube. **Open** 11am-11pm Mon-Sat; noon-10.30pm Sun. **Map** p114 M7* ⑪
Central London pubs with a local vibe are the rarest of things, but the Cross Keys is precisely that. With its canopy of copper implements, garish carpet and walls covered in vintage beeraphernalia, it feels like it hasn't changed for 30 years. Despite the local competition, it makes zero effort to appeal to tourists, which is ironic, since sipping a pint in the failing sunlight amid wafts from the nearby chippie is one of the most perfectly London experiences you'll get in the West End.

Shops & services

James Smith & Sons

*Hazelwood House, 53 New Oxford Street, WC1A 1BL (020 7836 4731, www.james-smith.co.uk). Holborn or Tottenham Court Road tube. **Open** 10am-5.45pm Mon, Tue, Thur, Fri; 10.30am-5.45pm Wed; 10am-5.15pm Sat. **Map** p114 M7* ⑳
Accessories
Nearly 190 years after it was established, this charming shop,

Neal's Yard

with Victorian fittings still intact, is holding its own in the niche market of umbrellas and walking sticks. The stock here isn't the throwaway type of brolly that breaks at the first sign of a breeze. The lovingly crafted brollies – perhaps a classic City umbrella with a malacca cane handle at £225 – are built to last. A repair service is also offered.

Neal's Yard Dairy

17 Shorts Gardens, WC2H 9AT (020 7500 7520, www.nealsyarddairy. co.uk). Covent Garden tube. **Open** *10am-7pm Mon-Sat.* **Map** *p114 M7* ㉑ *Food & drink*

Neal's Yard buys from small farms and creameries and matures the cheeses in its own cellars until they're ready to sell in peak condition. Names such as Stinking Bishop and Lincolnshire Poacher are as evocative as the aromas in the shop. It's best to walk in and ask what's good today: you'll be given tasters by the well-trained staff. **Other location** Borough Market, 6 Park Street, SE1 9AB.

The Shop at Bluebird

Nigel Cabourn Army Gym

28 Henrietta Street, WC2E 8NA (020 7240 1005, www.cabourn. com/about/the-army-gym). Covent Garden tube. **Open** *11am-6.30pm Mon-Wed, Fri, Sat; 11am-7pm Thur; noon-5pm Sun.* **Map** *p114 M8* ㉒ *Menswear*

This is the only Cabourn shop outside Japan, selling the hallowed designer's vintage-inspired collections, dreamed to life by consulting his vast personal archive of over 4,000 pieces. As the name might suggest, you're guaranteed to be able to get hold of some camo here, but there's also a solid amount of smart tailoring and shirting, all drawing on the best of British design.

❤ The Shop at Bluebird

Carriage Hall, 29 Floral Street, WC2E 9DP (7351 3873, theshopatbluebird.com). Covent Garden tube. **Open** *10am-7pm Mon-Sat; noon-6pm Sun.* **Map** *p114 M7* ㉓ *Fashion & homewares*

This chic lifestyle boutique relocated from the King's Road to Covent Garden. Inside you'll find a broad selection of designer clothing, shoes, accessories, books, music (both CDs and vinyl) and the odd piece of furniture. There's also a slew of hard-to-find niche skincare brands, including New York's Bigelow, Ole Henriksen, DCL and Kaeline. Fashion is wide-ranging; London-based designers Emma Cook and Peter Jensen are to be found here, as are US faves Alexander Wang and Marc by Marc Jacobs, and Japanese heavyweights Junya Watanabe and Comme des Garçons. Look out for lesser-known labels as well, such as the rock-inspired Rika and Isabel Marant, and vintage-inspired eyewear from hip label Prism.

Vintage Showroom

14 Earlham Street, WC2H 9LN (7836 3964, www.

thevintageshowroom.com). *Covent Garden tube.* **Open** *11am-7pm Mon-Sat; noon-6pm Sun.* **Map** *p114 L7* 24 *Vintage menswear*

In the old FW Collins & Sons ironmongery, Roy Luckett and Doug Gunn show a tiny selection of their famous west London menswear archive, which they routinely loan out to big-name designers, denim brands and vintage obsessives. With stock sourced from around the world (Roy and Doug have some hair-raising stories of dealings with collectors and hoarders in obscure locations), it follows that the pair occasionally find it hard to part with an item, and they've been known to try to dissuade shoppers from buying the rarer pieces on display. But the shop has London's best men's vintage collection, with an emphasis on Americana (denim, sweats, a few choice tees) and classic military and British pieces.

Entertainment

Coliseum

St Martin's Lane, WC2N 4ES (7845 9300, londoncoliseum.org). Leicester Square tube or Charing Cross tube/rail. **Box office** *Non-performance days 10am-6pm Mon-Sat. Performance days 10am-8pm Mon-Sat.* **Tickets** *£12-£155.* **Map** *p114 M8* 17 *Opera*

It's been a tough few years for the **English National Opera** (ENO). Notionally the hipper and more accessible of London's two principal opera companies (with all works performed in English), it has seriously struggled with its finances, partly as a result of a reduction in subsidy while trying to lower ticket prices. But things are looking up: a willingness to open the doors of the London Coliseum – London's biggest theatre – to musicals seems to have paid off and it's no longer

Don Quixote, Royal Ballet *p142*

Romeo & Juliet, Royal Ballet

Katye Kabanova, Royal Opera *p142*

Covent Garden

It may be central London's smallest major theatre, but the Donmar's influence outstrips its size many times over. Following on from Sam Mendes and Michael Grandage, Josie Rourke made it her mission to steer the Donmar away from boutique productions of classics with big-name celebrities and aim for a livelier, younger programme that is orientated more towards new writing. Having taken over as artistic director in 2019, Michael Longhurst's debut season focused on performances that 'interrogate the world we live in' including the revival of David Greig's *Europe*.

♥ Royal Opera House

Bow Street, WC2E 9DD (7304 4000, www.roh.org.uk). Covent Garden tube. **Box office** *10am-8pm Mon-Sat.* **Tickets** *£4-£200.* **Map** *p114 M7* ⑲ *Opera*

Home to both the Royal Opera and the Royal Ballet, the ROH was founded in 1732 by John Rich on the profits of his production of John Gay's *Beggar's Opera*. The current Grade-1 listed building, built roughly 150 years ago, has undergone several major refurbs, including the £27-million 'Open Up' redevelopment in 2018 which aimed to combat opera's eternally stuffy image by inviting the public to hang out in the building's enhanced spaces (including a new bar, restaurant and café) and to enjoy free taster performances. Under the youthful head of opera, Oliver Mears, the programme has been financially cautious. Still, it pretty much does what you expect a nation's flagship opera company to do: famous shows, big name performers and an admirable focus on opening up the building to new audiences. There's more intimate, experimental work on offer in the basement **Linbury Theatre**.

in special funding measures. Typically there's now an ENO-produced revival with a starry cast running for a few weeks in the spring, and an outside production in the summer. These run during dark periods, rather than replacing the usual programming, which has remained largely exemplary despite the money woes. Appointed to the artistic directorship in 2017, American Daniel Kramer has kept the ship steady, with a mix of non-traditional takes on the canon and more overtly challenging works. Keeping the prices down has remained a priority, and plans have been announced to diversify the opera's overwhelmingly white chorus.

♥ Donmar Warehouse

41 Earlham Street, WC2H 9LX (3282 3808, www.donmarwarehouse.com). Covent Garden or Leicester Square tube. **Box office** *10am-6pm Mon-Sat.* **Tickets** *£7.50-£35.* **Map** *p114 M7* ⑱ *Theatre*

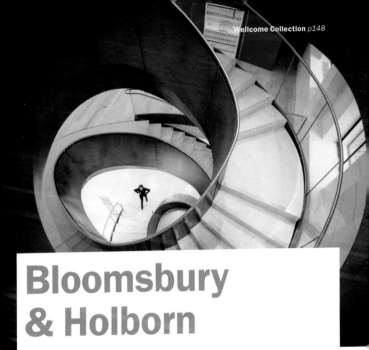

Bloomsbury & Holborn

Developed in the 18th and 19th centuries around a series of elegant squares, **Bloomsbury** is best known for its literary credentials and as the home of the superb **British Museum**. It also hosts the University of London and an appealing collection of smaller museums, bookshops and pubs. To the east is **Clerkenwell**, with its concentration of restaurants and gastropubs. South-east of Bloomsbury, **Holborn** is the heart of legal London and straddles the boundary between the West End and the City.

Best Moorish menu
Moro *p149*

Best boozer
Princess Louise *p152*

Best for bookworms
London Review Bookshop *p150*

Best museums
British Museum *p147*,
Sir John Soane's Museum *p151*,
Wellcome Collection *p148*

Best for kids
Great Court at Somerset house *p151*,
Postal Museum *p146*

Bloomsbury

In bookish circles, Bloomsbury is a name to conjure with, forever associated with a group of early 20th-century writers and intellectuals (Virginia Woolf among them). Beyond the cultural behemoth that is the **British Museum**, the surrounding green squares are perfect for an afternoon stroll.

Sights & museums

Charles Dickens Museum
48 Doughty Street, WC1N 2LX (020 7405 2127, dickensmuseum. com). Chancery Lane or Russell Square tube. **Open** *10am-5pm Tue-Sat.* **Admission** *£9.50; £4.50-£7.50 reductions; free under-6s.* **Map** *p145 N5.*

London is scattered with plaques marking addresses where Dickens lived, but this is the only one to have been preserved as a museum. He lived here from 1837 to 1840, writing *Nicholas Nickleby* and *Oliver Twist* while in residence. Ring the doorbell to gain access to four floors of Dickensiana, collected over the years from various former residences. Some rooms are arranged as they might have been when he lived here (especially atmospheric during the occasional candlelit openings); others deal with different aspects of his life, from struggling hack to famous performer. But the study has the key artefact: the chair and desk at which Dickens wrote *Great Expectations*.

Foundling Museum
40 Brunswick Square, WC1N 1AZ (020 7841 3600, foundlingmuseum. org.uk). Russell Square tube. **Open** *10am-5pm Tue-Sat; 11am-5pm Sun.* **Admission** *£13.20; £9.90 reductions; free under-22s.* **Map** *p145 M5.*

This museum recalls the social history of the Foundling Hospital, set up in 1739 by shipwright and sailor Thomas Coram. Returning to England from America in 1720, Coram was appalled by the number of abandoned children he saw. Securing royal patronage, he persuaded Hogarth and Handel to become governors; it was Hogarth who made the building Britain's first public art gallery, with works from notable artists such as Gainsborough and Reynolds. The most heart-rending display is a tiny case of mementoes that were left by mothers to identify the child in case they could one day come back for them.

→ **Getting around**

Bloomsbury is served by Russell Square tube station, although Tottenham Court Road tube is also handy for the British Museum. Use Holborn or Chancery Lane stations for Gray's Inn and Lincoln's Inn, and Temple tube for Somerset House.

BLOOMSBURY & HOLBORN

Mail Rail

University College London museums

www.ucl.ac.uk/culture. Goodge Street or Warren Street tube. **Map** *p145 L5.*

UCL manages a number of excellent collections, developed since the 1820s to help academic staff in their teaching and research. Many of them are open to the public and free to visit. Housed in a former Edwardian library, the **Grant Museum of Zoology** (Rockefeller Building, 21 University Street, WC1E 6DE, 020 3108 2052, closed Sun) retains the air of a Victorian collector's house. The 67,000 specimens include the remains of many rare and extinct creatures, with skeletons of the dodo and the zebra-like quagga (hunted to extinction in the 1880s), as well as pure oddities, not least the jar of moles. Don't miss the Micrarium – a kind of booth walled with little illuminated microscope slides.

Across the road, the **Petrie Museum of Egyptian Archaeology** (Malet Place, WC1E 6BT, 020 7679 2884, closed Mon, Sun) is named after Flinders Petrie, tireless excavator of ancient Egypt. Where the British Museum is strong on the big stuff, the Petrie is an extraordinary selection of minutiae, which reveal how people lived and died in the Nile Valley. Highlights include colourful tiles, carvings and frescoes from heretic pharaoh Akhenaten's capital, Tell el Amarna, and the world's largest collection of mummy portraits from the Roman period.

♥ Postal Museum & Mail Rail

15-20 Phoenix Place, WC1X 0DA (0300 0300 700, www. postalmuseum.org). Russell Square tube or Farringdon tube/rail. **Open** *10am-5pm daily.* **Admission** *£17; £8-13 reductions; free under-3s. Family play area (45min session) £5; £1.50 with Mail Rail ticket.* **Map** *p145 N5.*

One hundred years ago, the Post Office built a secret railway under central London. Stretching six-and-a-half miles from Paddington to Whitechapel and linking post offices across the city, the driverless electric line carried up to four million letters a day. But in 2003, after 75 years of service, this wonder of engineering was shut

🖤 British Museum

Great Russell Street, WC1B 3DG (020 7323 8000, www. britishmuseum.org). Russell Square or Tottenham Court Road tube. **Open** *10am-5.30pm Mon-Thur, Sat, Sun; 10am-8.30pm Fri. The Great Court is accessible from 9am.* **Admission** *free; donations appreciated. Temporary exhibitions vary. Audio guides £7; £6 reductions.* **Map** *p145 L6.*

With more than six million visitors a year, the British Museum is officially the country's most popular tourist attraction. When it opened in 1759 it was the first national public museum anywhere in the world. The current building is a neoclassical marvel built in 1847 by Robert Smirke, one of the pioneers of the Greek Revival style. In 2000, Lord Foster added a glass roof to the Great Court, now claimed to be 'the largest covered public square in Europe' and a popular public space ever since. This £100-million landmark surrounds the domed Reading Room, where Marx, Lenin, Dickens, Darwin, Hardy and Yeats once worked. The Sainsbury Exhibitions Gallery is dedicated to blockbuster shows, including 'Rodin & the Art of Ancient Greece' in 2019. Previous exhibitions included a rare visit from China's Terracotta Army and an eye-opening tour of Ice Age art.

In the museum proper, star exhibits include ancient Egyptian artefacts – the Rosetta Stone on the ground floor, mummies upstairs – and Greek antiquities, including the marble friezes from the Parthenon known as the Elgin Marbles. Room 41 displays Anglo-Saxon artefacts, including the famous Sutton Hoo treasure. Also upstairs, the Celts gallery has Lindow Man, killed in 300 BC and so well preserved in peat you can see his beard, while the ground-floor Wellcome Gallery of Ethnography holds an Easter Island statue and regalia collected during Captain Cook's travels. The King's Library is home to a permanent exhibition entitled 'Enlightenment: Discovering the World in the 18th Century', which covers archaeology, science and the natural world.

Time won't permit you to see everything in one day, so concentrate on a particular area or plan on making several visits.

▶ *The daily Eye Opener tours are free. From Friday to Sunday there are also 'Around the World in 90 Minutes' tours (£14).*

down and the tunnels fell silent. The Mail Rail is now back in service – but this time two battery-powered trains take passengers rather than letters through the tunnels. The museum charts 500 years of the pioneering British postal service. It's got original Penny Black stamps, pneumatic tubes, a superb kids' play area (called Sorted!) and a 5-wheeled post bike that wouldn't look out of place on the streets of Shoreditch. But the main event is across the street at the old Mail Rail engineering depot, where you can hop on board for a 15-minute journey that's deeper than the Tube.

♥ Wellcome Collection

183 Euston Road, NW1 2BE (020 7611 2222, wellcomecollection. org). Euston Square tube or Euston tube/Overground. **Galleries** *10am-6pm Tue, Wed, Fri-Sun.* **Library** *10am-6pm Mon-Wed, Fri; 10am-8pm Thur; 10am-4pm Sat.* **Admission** *free.* **Map** *p145 L5.*

Sir Henry Wellcome, a pioneering 19th-century pharmacist, amassed a vast and idiosyncratic collection of implements and curios relating to the medical trade, now displayed here. In addition to these fascinating and often grisly items (ivory carvings of pregnant women, used guillotine blades, Napoleon's toothbrush) there are several serious works of modern and historic art – some of it in boxes that must be opened with protective white gloves. The temporary exhibitions are often brilliant and come with all manner of associated events, from talks to walks. A £17.5 million development project opened up more areas to the public, including the beautiful Reading Room, which is a combination of library, gallery and event space. Fascinating interactives include the 'Virtual Autopsy' table – effectively a giant tablet where you can swipe cuts through 3D cadavers – and a replica of Freud's couch.

Restaurants

The best eats are to be found west and east of Bloomsbury in Fitzrovia (*see p112*) and Clerkenwell.

The Coach ££-£££

26-28 Ray Street, EC1R 3DJ (020 3954 1595, thecoachclerkenwell. co.uk). Farringdon tube/rail. **Open** *7.30am-11pm Mon-Fri; 11am-11pm Sat; noon-10pm Sun.* **Map** *p145 O5* **①** *Gastropub*

This former Victorian pub still has a bar area, albeit one decked out like the lounge of a gentlemen's club, but the focus here is on eating, rather than boozing. The elegant dining room is the perfect backdrop for a menu created by the mighty Henry Harris, formerly of upmarket Knightsbridge bistro Racine. It's a line-up of rustic Gallic food plus a few trad Brit faves, including rare carnivore treats such as buttery calves' brains, served with vinegary capers and flecks of fresh parsley. A leg of rabbit is accompanied by brittle rashers of smoked bacon and a wee jug of creamy, mustard-spiked sauce. This is timeless food, for a chilled-out crowd, in a lovely spot.

The Eagle ££

159 Farringdon Road, EC1R 3AL (020 7837 1353, www.theeaglefarringdon. co.uk). Farringdon tube/rail. **Open** *noon-11pm Mon-Sat; noon-5pm Sun. Food served noon-3pm, 6.30-10.30pm Mon-Fri; 12.30-3.30pm, 6.30-10.30pm Sat; 12.30-4pm Sun.* **Map** *p145 O5* **②** *Gastropub*

Widely credited with launching the revolutionary notion of serving restaurant-quality food in a boozer when it opened in its current form in 1991, the Eagle has long since passed into both legend and middle age. But this high-ceilinged corner room remains a cut above the gastropub competition. Globetrotting mains are chalked twice daily above the bar/open

Moro

kitchen. You can just drink but few do, aware they're missing the big-flavoured likes of moreish tomato and bread soup; a classic steak sandwich; and succulent leg of lamb with jansson's temptation (a potato gratin-style Swedish dish).

♥ Moro ££

34-36 Exmouth Market, EC1R 4QE (020 7833 8336, moro.co.uk). Farringdon tube/rail or bus 19, 38, 341. **Open** *noon-2.30pm, 5.15-10.45pm Mon-Sat; noon-3.30pm, 5-10.30pm Sun. Tapas available all day Mon-Sat from the bar.* **Map** *p145 O5* ❸ *North African/Spanish*

Back in 1997, in a former supermarket on Exmouth Market, Sam(antha) and Sam Clark set the benchmark for a distinctly British style of Mediterranean cooking that puts a North African twist on Iberian food. Their restaurant (accompanied by a range of beautifully produced cookbooks) is still in London's culinary front rank some 20 years later. Moro provides a spectacular showcase for modern Spanish and Portuguese wines, and vibrantly fresh food that throws out surprising and pleasurable flavours at every turn.

Next door to Moro is its offshoot **Morito** (no.32, EC1R 4QE, 020 7278 7007, www.morito.co.uk), a fine no-bookings tapas bar.

Pubs & bars

All Star Lanes

Victoria House, Bloomsbury Place, WC1B 4DA (020 7025 2676, www. allstarlanes.co.uk). Holborn tube. **Open** *3-11pm Mon-Wed; 3pm-midnight Thur; noon-2am Fri; 11am-2am Sat; 11am-10.30pm Sun.* **Map** *p145 M6* ❶

Of Bloomsbury's two subterranean bowling dens, this is the one with aspirations. Walk past the lanes and smart, diner-style seating, and you'll find yourself in a comfortable, subdued side bar with chilled glasses, classy red furnishings, an unusual mix of bottled lagers and some impressive cocktails. There's an American menu and, at weekends, DJs.

149

Museum Tavern

49 Great Russell Street, WC1B 3BA (020 7242 8987, www.greeneking-pubs.co.uk/pubs/greater-london/museum-tavern). Holborn or Tottenham Court Road tube. **Open** *11am-11.30pm Mon-Thur; 11am-midnight Fri, Sat; noon-10pm Sun. Food served noon-9.30pm Mon-Sat; noon-9pm Sun.* **Map** *p145 M6* ❷

Inevitably pandering to tourists who flock to the British Museum opposite, this attractive, traditional hostelry also appeals to Londoners with a taste for decent ales and homely food. Dating back to 1700s (when it was surrounded by marshes and called the Dog & Duck), it boasts some famous patrons including Karl Marx, George Orwell and Sir Arthur Conan Doyle.

Shops & services

Bibliophiles should also check out **Persephone Books** (59 Lamb's Conduit Street, 020 7242 9292, www.persephonebooks.co.uk, ❶) for 20th-century women's writing and **Skoob** (Unit 66, The Brunswick Centre, 020 7278 8760, www.skoob.com, ❷) for second-hand titles.

♥ London Review Bookshop

14 Bury Place, WC1A 2JL (020 7269 9030, www.londonreviewbookshop.co.uk). Holborn or Tottenham Court Road tube. **Open** *10am-6.30pm Mon-Sat; noon-6pm Sun.* **Map** *p145 M6* ❸ *Books*

From the inviting and stimulating presentation to the quality of the books selected, this is an inspiring bookshop. Politics, current affairs and history are well represented on the ground floor; downstairs, audio books lead on to exciting poetry and philosophy sections, everything you'd expect from a shop owned by the purveyor of long-form critical writing that is the *London Review of Books*. Browse through your purchases in the adjoining London Review Cake Shop.

Entertainment

The Place

17 Duke's Road, WC1H 9PY (020 7121 1100, www.theplace.org.uk). Euston tube/Overground/rail. **Box office** *10.30am-5pm Mon-Sat. Performance days 10.30am-7pm.* **Tickets** *£10-£17; £7-£13 reductions.* **Map** *p145 L4* ❶ *Dance*

For genuinely emerging dance, look to the Place, which is home to the London Contemporary Dance School and the Richard Alston Dance Company. The theatre is behind the biennial Place Prize for choreography (next in 2020), which rewards the best in British contemporary dance, as well as regular seasons showcasing new work, among them Resolution! (Jan/Feb) and Spring Loaded (Apr/May).

Holborn & around

The City of London collides with the West End around Holborn. The area is the location of London's four picturesque **Inns of Court** (Gray's Inn, Lincoln's Inn, Middle Temple and Inner Temple), which provided training and lodging for the city's medieval lawyers. Today, anybody may visit the grounds, but access to the grand, collegiate buildings is for lawyers and barristers only. Middle Temple was the HQ for the crusading Knights Templar, who built the **Temple Church** (EC4Y 7BB, www.templechurch.com) in 1185. Nearby are the splendid neo-Gothic **Royal Courts of Justice**, while to the west, the Strand provides access to the cultural institutions of **Somerset House**.

Sights & museums

💜 Sir John Soane's Museum

13 Lincoln's Inn Fields, WC2A 3BP (020 7440 4257, www.soane.org). Holborn tube. **Open** *10am-5pm Wed-Sun.* **Admission** *free; donations appreciated. Tours £15.* **Map** *p145 N6.*

When he wasn't designing notable buildings (among them the original Bank of England), Sir John Soane (1753-1837) obsessively collected art, furniture and architectural ornamentation. In the 19th century, he turned his house into a museum to which, he said, 'amateurs and students' should have access. The result is this perfectly amazing place.

The modest rooms were modified by Soane with ingenious devices to channel and direct daylight, and to expand space, including walls that fold out to display paintings by Canaletto, Turner and Hogarth. The Tivoli Recess – the city's first gallery of contemporary sculpture, with a stained-glass window and plaster sunbursts – has been restored, and further stained glass illuminates a bust of Shakespeare. The Breakfast Room has a beautiful domed ceiling, inset with convex mirrors, while the Monument Court contains a sarcophagus of alabaster, so fine that it's almost translucent, that was carved for the pharaoh Seti I (1291-78 BC) and discovered in the Valley of the Kings. There are also numerous examples of Soane's eccentricity, not least the cell for his imaginary monk 'Padre Giovanni'.

A recent £7-million restoration project has opened up previously unseen parts of the building. The second-floor Model Room holds Britain's largest collection of historical architectural models.

💜 Somerset House & the Embankment Galleries

Strand, WC2R 1LA (020 7845 4600, www.somersethouse.org. uk). Temple tube. **Open** *10am-6pm Mon, Tue, Sat, Sun; 11am-8pm Wed-Fri. Tours Tue, Thur, Sat; see website for details.* **Admission** *free; exhibition prices vary.* **Map** *p145 N8.*

Somerset House

The original Somerset House was a Tudor palace commissioned by the Duke of Somerset. In 1775, it was demolished to make way for the first purpose-built office block in the world. Architect Sir William Chambers spent the last 20 years of his life working on this neoclassical edifice overlooking the Thames, built to accommodate learned societies such as the Royal Academy and government departments. The taxmen are still here, but the rest of the building is open to the public. The **Courtauld Gallery** (courtauld.ac.uk; closed for refurbishment until 2021) is home to a wealth of art from the Renaissance through to the 20th century. Downstairs on the Thames side of the building, the **Embankment Galleries** house exhibitions on a grander scale. But perhaps the most appealing part of the complex is the huge courtyard, where choreographed fountains lure children in the summer, while parents watch idly from café tables. In winter, an ice rink takes over the space (bookings 0333 320 2836, £11, £8.50 reductions), ringed by festive shopping and food stalls.

Two Temple Place

2 Temple Place, WC2R 3BD (020 7836 3715, twotempleplace.org). Temple tube. **Open** *Exhibitions late Jan-mid Apr 10am-4.30pm Mon, Thur-Sat; 10am-9pm Wed; 11am-4.30pm Sun. Private tours only mid Apr-late Jan.* **Admission** *free. Tours free but must be booked in advance.* **Map** *p145 N8.*
The pale Portland stone exterior and oriel windows here are handsome – but the interior is extraordinary. You get a hint about what's to come before you open the door: look right and there's a cherub holding an old-fashioned telephone to his ear. Built as an estate office in 1895 to the close specifications of William Waldorf Astor, Two Temple Place now opens to the public for three months a year with immensely popular exhibitions of 'publicly-owned art from around the UK', arranged by an up-and-coming curator. Ring the bell and you're warmly welcomed by volunteers into a house with decor that combines sublime, extravagant craftsmanship with a thorough lack of interest in coherence: above porphyry tiles, the Three Musketeers adorn the banisters of a staircase; intricately carved literary characters crowd the first floor, mixing Shakespeare with Fenimore Cooper; the medieval-style Great Hall, with lovely stained glass, crams together 54 random busts – Voltaire, Marlborough and Anne Boleyn enjoying the company of Mary Queen of Scots.

Pubs & bars

♥ Princess Louise

208 High Holborn, WC1V 7EP (020 7405 8816, princesslouisepub.co.uk). Holborn tube. **Open** *11am-11pm Mon-Fri; noon-11pm Sat; noon-6.45pm Sun. Food served noon-2.30pm, 6-8.30pm Mon-Thur; noon-2.30pm Fri.* **Map** *p145 M6* ③
With its magnificent Victorian interior restored to its former glory by the Sam Smith's Brewery, the old Louise oozes charm. The ground-floor saloon is spectacularly ornate with etched glass, mirrors, buffed wood panelling and a warren of Victorian frosted-glass booths, each with direct access to the bar. An open fire completes the atmosphere. While the pub is busiest at weekends, a preponderance of stools and bright lighting give the Princess a post-work rather than pre-night-out vibe.

The City

The City's current role as the financial heart of London does no justice to its 2,000-year history. Here, on top of a much more ancient ritual landscape, the Romans founded the city they called Londinium. Within the defensive wall that defines the Square Mile (1.21 square miles, to be exact) were a forum-basilica, an amphitheatre and public baths.

Parts of the Roman city can still be seen (*see p158 Roman Remains*), yet today the area is dominated by the high-rise offices of legal and financial institutions. Fewer than 10,000 souls are resident within the City, but every working day the population increases tenfold, as bankers, brokers, lawyers and traders flood into the area. To understand the City properly, it's best to visit on a weekday when the commuter is king; at weekends many streets feel eerily quiet.

Best sights
St Paul's Cathedral *p160*,
Tower of London *p162*

Best restaurant
Duck and Waffle *p163*,
Modern Pantry *p163*,
St John *p164*

Best bar
Black Rock *p165*,
ZTH Cocktail Lounge *p166*,

Best cultural venue
Barbican Centre *p155*

Best nightlife venue
Fabric *p166*

Best view
Monument *p159*,
Sky Garden *p161*

Must-see museum
Museum of London *p159*

An exception to this is **St Paul's Cathedral**, whose vast stone interior echoes constantly with the voices of worshippers and sightseers. Rising from the ashes of the Great Fire of 1666, Sir Christopher Wren's masterpiece lords it over the many pretty medieval churches dotted around the City.

To get a grasp of London's social history from prehistoric times to the present, don't miss the **Museum of London**. Here, reconstructions of interiors and street scenes, alongside artefacts found during the museum's archaeological digs, offer a fascinating insight.

At the City's eastern edge, the **Tower of London** remains one of the best-preserved medieval fortresses in Europe. Tourists come from far and wide to get a glimpse of the Crown Jewels, Royal Armouries and 13th-century White Tower where traitors to the monarchy came to a sticky end.

→ Getting around

Tube and bus transport in the Square Mile is supplemented by commuter rail services through London Bridge and Blackfriars. Avoid travelling at peak times Monday to Friday when all transport options are filled to bursting.

Newcomers to the City are advised to head to the spiky-roofed **City of London Information Centre** (020 7332 3456, www.cityoflondon.gov.uk), near St Paul's Cathedral. Open daily (9.30am-5.30pm Mon-Sat; 10am-4pm Sun), it has information on sights, events, walks and talks, as well as offering tours with specialist guides, and has free Wi-Fi.

Sights & museums

Bank of England Museum

Entrance on Bartholomew Lane, EC2R 8AH (020 3461 4878, www. bankofengland.co.uk/museum). Bank tube/DLR. **Open** *10am-5pm Mon-Fri.* **Admission** *free.* **Map** *p156 R7.*

Housed inside the former Stock Offices of the Bank of England (there's a full-size recreation of architect Sir John Soane's Bank Stock Office from 1693), this surprisingly lively museum explores the history of the national bank. Founded in 1694 to fund William III's war against the French, today the bank is responsible for printing the nation's banknotes and setting the base interest rate. The building is an impressive fortress with no accessible windows and only one public entrance (to the museum itself). Millions have been stolen from its depots elsewhere in London but the bank itself has never been robbed. As well as ancient coins and original artwork for British banknotes, the museum offers a rare chance to lift nearly 30lbs (14kg) of gold bar (you reach into a secure box, closely monitored by CCTV) and displays Kenneth Grahame's resignation letter – the *Wind in the Willows* author worked here for three decades.

💜 Barbican Centre

Beech Street, EC2Y 8DS (020 7638 8891, www.barbican.org.uk). Barbican tube. **Open** *9am-11pm Mon-Sat; 11am-11pm Sun.* **Box office** *10am-8pm Mon-Sat; noon -8pm Sun.* **Map** *p156 Q6.*

The Barbican Centre lures fans of serious culture into a labyrinthine arts complex, part of a vast estate that includes unnumerable concrete walkways and 2,000 highly coveted flats, built after heavy bombing during World War II. It's a prime example of brutalist architecture, softened a little by time and some central rectangular pools, popular with ducks. The focus is on world-class arts programming with a library, a state-of-the-art cinema, a theatre, a concert hall and two well-regarded art galleries. The resident orchestra is the **London Symphony Orchestra**, with Sir Simon Rattle as music director. The **BBC Symphony Orchestra** also performs here, and there's a laudable amount of contemporary and world music, too. Performances by the **Royal Shakespeare Company** are a regular feature during the winter. The Barbican is also home to London's second-largest conservatory, stuffed with 2,000 tropical plants and trees, plus some ponds filled with fish and turtles.

Dr Johnson's House

17 Gough Square, off Fleet Street, EC4A 3DE (020 7353 3745, www. drjohnsonshouse.org). Chancery Lane tube or Blackfriars tube/ rail. **Open** *May-Sept 11am-5.30pm Mon-Sat. Oct-Apr 11am-5pm Mon-Sat.* **Admission** *£7; £3.50- £6 reductions; £15 family; free under-5s.* **Map** *p156 O7.*

Famed as the author of one of the first – as well as the most significant and unquestionably the wittiest – dictionaries of the English language, Dr Samuel Johnson (1709-84) also wrote poems, essays, literary criticism, a novel and an early travelogue, an acerbic account of a tour of the Western Isles with his biographer James Boswell. You can tour the stately Georgian townhouse where he came up with his inspired definitions – 'to make dictionaries is dull work' was his definition of the word 'dull', while 'oats' is a 'grain, which in England is generally given to horses, but in Scotland supports the people'.

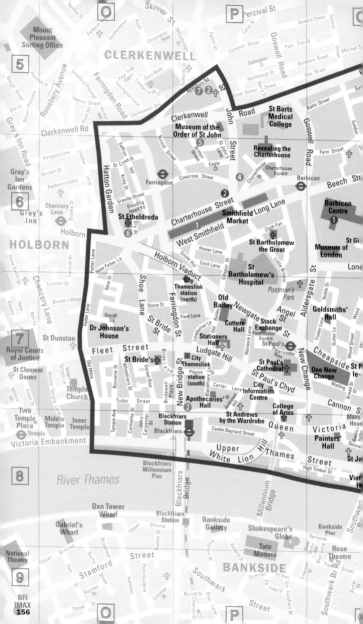

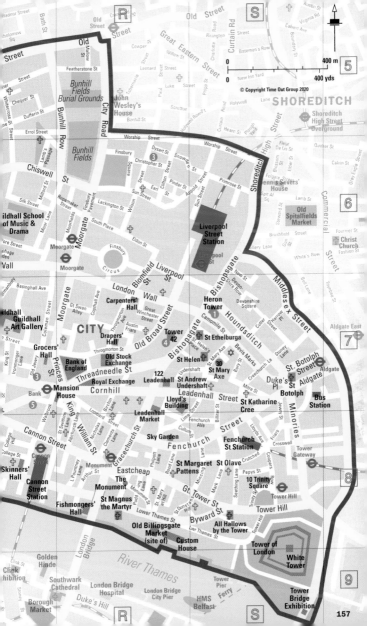

Roman Remains

Discover the foundations of Londinium

Founded in AD 50, 'Londinium' was the heart of Roman Britain. A solid stone and red-tile wall enclosed the city, stretching for two whole miles – a sort of Roman equivalent to the M25. You can still spy small sections of the original wall by the Museum of London and the Tower of London, and along the road known as 'London Wall'.

At the Bloomberg HQ (12 Walbrook, EC4N 8AA), you can sneak past suited City workers to visit the **London Mithraeum** (www.londonmithraeum. com), an underground temple used by a men-only Roman cult, who worshipped the god Mithras.

The space was discovered in 1954 at a World War II bomb site, and the ruins have recently been reconstructed for public display.

The key exhibit at the **Guildhall Art Gallery** (see p158) isn't art at all. The sub-basement contains the scant remains of London's 6,000-seat Roman amphitheatre, built around AD 70. There, Tron-like figures and crowd sound effects give a quaint inkling of scale. Outside in the courtyard again, there's a long, curved line in the paving: this indicates the perimeter of the amphitheatre, 20ft beneath where you stand, through 2,000 years of rubbish and rubble.

Fleet Street

Chancery Lane or Temple tube. **Map** *p156 O7.*

At the eastern end of the arterial Strand a wyvern-topped monument marks **Temple Bar**, the boundary between Westminster and the City of London. During the Middle Ages, the monarch was allowed to pass through the Temple Bar into the City only with the approval of the Lord Mayor of London. Running east, Fleet Street was the location of the country's first printing press, which was installed behind **St Bride's Church** (020 7427 0133, www.stbrides. com) in 1500. London's first daily newspaper, the *Daily Courant*, rolled off the presses in 1702. Fleet Street remained synonymous with the newspapers until the 1980s, when Rupert Murdoch won his bitter war with the print unions. A few grand buildings remain from the heyday of the press, including Reuters (no.85), the Daily Telegraph (no.135) and the jet-black art deco classic Daily Express (nos.121-128).

Guildhall Art Gallery

Guildhall Yard, off Gresham Street, EC2V 5AE (020 7332 3700, www. cityoflondon.org.uk). St Paul's tube or Bank tube/DLR. **Open** *10am-5pm Mon-Sat; noon-4pm Sun.* **Admission** *free. Temporary exhibitions vary.* **Map** *p156 Q7.*

The Guildhall is the headquarters of the City of London. Its focal point is the original banqueting hall, where extravagant receptions have been held for eight centuries, but the picture gallery is also well worth a look. Upstairs is the entertaining and informative thematic Victorian Collection, where you'll find paintings by Constable, Leighton, Millais, Rossetti, Holman Hunt and others. Downstairs, there are absorbing paintings of London from the 1660s to the present, from moving depictions of war and melancholy working streets to the likes of the grandiloquent (and never-enacted) George Dance plan for a new London Bridge. The collection's centrepiece is the massive *Siege of Gibraltar* by John

City Limits

Skyscrapers vie for attention in the Square Mile

The area of the City east of Bank contains many of London's most distinctive skyscrapers. At 1 Lime Street is Richard Rogers' **Lloyd's of London** building, constructed in 1986, with all its ducts, vents, stairwells and lift shafts on the outside. Rogers was also responsible for the 738-foot (225-metre) **Cheesegrater** at 122 Leadenhall. On Fenchurch Street is Rafael Viñoly's 20 Fenchurch Street, nicknamed the **Walkie Talkie** due to its distinctive top-heavy shape, which provides wonderful views from the Sky Garden (see *p161*).

Topping out at 755 feet (230 metres, including a radio mast), **Heron Tower** (110 Bishopsgate, www.herontower.com) became the City's tallest building at the end of 2009, but has since been overtaken by **22 Bishopsgate**, which will reach 912 feet (278 metres) when completed. A block south, Lord Foster's **Gherkin** (30 St Mary Axe) is one of London's finest modern buildings, with a restaurant and bar on its top floors (searcysatthegherkin.co.uk). None of these, however, reach the lofty heights of the **Shard** at 1,016 feet (310 metres; *see p75*).

THE CITY

Copley, which spans two entire storeys of the purpose-built gallery.

♥ Monument
Monument Street, EC3R 8AH (020 7626 2717, www.themonument. info). Monument tube. **Open** *Apr-Sept 9.30am-6pm daily. Oct-Mar 9.30am-5.30pm daily.* **Admission** *£4.50; £2.30-£3 reductions; free under-5s.* **Map** *p156 R8.*

One of 17th-century London's most important landmarks, the Monument is a magnificent Portland stone column, topped by a landmark golden orb with more than 30,000 fiery leaves of gold. The Monument was designed by Sir Christopher Wren and his (often overlooked) associate Robert Hooke as a memorial to the Great Fire. The world's tallest free-standing stone column, it measures 202ft (62m) from the ground to the tip of its golden flames, exactly the distance east to Farriner's bakery in Pudding Lane, where the fire is supposed to have begun on 2 September 1666. The viewing platform is surrounded

by a lightweight mesh cage, but the views are great – you have to walk 311 steps up the internal spiral staircase to enjoy them, though.

♥ Museum of London
150 London Wall, EC2Y 5HN (020 7001 9844, www.museumoflondon. org.uk). Barbican or St Paul's tube. **Open** *10am-6pm daily.* **Admission** *free; suggested donation £5.* **Map** *p156 Q6.*

One of the original settlements established by the Romans after their first invasion in AD43, Londinium survived war, plague and fire to become the bustling metropolis it is today. This journey, from ancient marshland to one of the greatest cities on earth, is documented through a mind-boggling array of exhibits alongside innovative interactive displays.

On the entrance floor, the social history of London is told in chronological displays that begin with 'London Before London', where artefacts include flint axes from 300,000 BC,

❤ St Paul's Cathedral

St Paul's Churchyard, EC4M 8AD (020 7246 8348, www. st pauls.co.uk). St Paul's tube. **Open** *8.30am-4.30pm Mon-Sat. Galleries, crypt & ambulatory 9.30am-4.15pm Mon-Sat. Tours of cathedral & crypt 10am, 11am, 1pm, 2pm Mon-Sat. Special events may cause closure; check before visiting.* **Admission** *Cathedral, crypt & gallery (incl tour) £20; £8.50-£17.50 reductions; £48.50 family; free under-6s. Book online for reductions.* **Map** *p156 P7.*

St Paul's Cathedral hasn't been lucky through most of its history, but it has been at the centre of some of London's most momentous events. The first cathedral to St Paul was built on this site in 604, but fell to Viking marauders. Its Norman replacement, a magnificent Gothic structure with a 490ft (149m) spire (taller than any London building until the 1960s), burned in the Great Fire. The current church was commissioned in 1673 from Sir Christopher Wren, as the centrepiece of London's resurgence from the ashes, and though modern buildings now encroach on the cathedral from all sides, the passing of three centuries has done nothing to diminish the appeal of the master architect's finest work. After a £40-million restoration removed most of the Victorian grime from the outside walls, the extravagant main façade looks as brilliant today as it must have when the last stone was placed in 1708.

The vast open spaces of the interior contain memorials to national heroes such as Wellington and Lawrence of Arabia. The statue of John Donne, metaphysical poet and former Dean of St Paul's, is often overlooked, but it's the only monument to have been saved from old St Paul's. There are also more modern works, including a Henry Moore sculpture and Bill Viola's video installation *Martyrs (Earth, Air, Fire, Water)*.

The Whispering Gallery, inside the dome, is reached by 259 steps from the main hall; the acoustics here are so good that a whisper can be bounced clearly to the other

THE CITY

side of the dome. Steps continue up to first the Stone Gallery (119 tighter, steeper steps), with its high external balustrades, then outside to the Golden Gallery (152 steps), with its giddying views.

Before leaving, head down to the maze-like crypt, where, alongside memorials to such dignitaries as Alexander Fleming, William Blake and Admiral Nelson, you'll find the small, plain tomb of Christopher Wren himself. At their request, Millais and Turner were buried nearby.

found near Piccadilly. 'Roman London' includes an impressive reconstructed dining room complete with mosaic floor. Sound effects and audio-visual displays illustrate the medieval, Elizabethan and Jacobean city, with particular focus on the plague and the Great Fire of 1666.

Downstairs, the lower-ground-floor gallery tells the story of the city from 1666 to the present day. This newer space features everything from an unexploded World War II bomb to the impressive golden Lord Mayor's coach (it dates from 1757). There are displays and brilliant interactives on poverty (an actual debtor's cell has been reconstructed, complete with graffiti), finance, shopping and 20th-century fashion, including a recreated Georgian pleasure garden.

The museum's biggest obstacle had always been its location: the entrance is two floors above street level, and hidden behind a dark and rather featureless brick wall. With visitor numbers higher than ever, the museum is set to move half a mile from its current location to take up residence in the abandoned Victorian market at Smithfield in 2022.

▶ *The Museum of London has a number of excellent free apps, including Streetmuseum and Streetmuseum Londinium, which offer information about historic sites, geolocated to where you're standing.*

💙 Sky Garden

*20 Fenchurch Street (entrance via Philpot Lane), EC3M 8AF (020 7337 2344, skygarden.london). Monument tube. **Open** 10am-6pm Mon-Fri; 11am-9pm Sat, Sun. Advance booking required. **Admission** free. Photo ID required. **Map** p156 R8.*
The distinctive but not widely admired skyscraper, 20 Fenchurch Street (better known as the Walkie

❤ Tower of London

*Tower Hill, EC3N 4AB (033 3320 6000, www.hrp.org.uk /tower-of-london). Tower Hill tube or Tower Gateway DLR. **Open** Mar-Oct 10am-5.30pm Mon, Sun; 9am-5.30pm Tue-Sat. Nov-Feb 10am-4.30pm Mon, Sun; 9am-4.30pm Tue-Sat. **Admission** £30.30; £14.50-£23.70 reductions; £54.50-£76.90 family; free under-5s. Book online for reductions. **Map** p156 S8.*

If you haven't been to the Tower of London before, you should go now. Despite the exhausting crowds, this is one of Britain's finest historical attractions. Who wouldn't be fascinated by a close-up look at the crown of Queen Victoria or the armour (and prodigious codpiece) of King Henry VIII? The buildings of the Tower span 900 years of – mostly violent – history, and the bastions and battlements house a series of interactive displays on the lives of British monarchs, and the often excruciatingly painful deaths of traitors. There's easily enough to do here to fill a whole day, and it's worth joining one of the entertaining free tours led by the Yeoman Warders (or Beefeaters).

Make the **Crown Jewels** your first stop. Beyond satisfyingly solid vault doors are such treasures of state as the Monarch's Sceptre, mounted with the Cullinan I diamond, and the Imperial State Crown, which is worn by the Queen each year for the opening of Parliament.

The other big draw is the Royal Armoury in the central **White Tower**, with its swords, armour, poleaxes, morning stars (spiky maces) and other gruesome tools for separating human beings from their body parts. Kids are entertained by swordsmanship games, coin-minting activities and even a child-sized longbow. The garderobes (medieval toilets) also seem to appeal.

Back outside is **Tower Green**, where executions of prisoners of noble birth were carried out (the last execution, of World War II German spy Joseph Jakobs, was in 1941). Overlooking the green, **Beauchamp Tower**, dating from 1280, has intriguing graffiti by the prisoners who were held here. The Tower only ceased functioning as a prison in 1952 and over the years counted Anne Boleyn, Rudolf Hess and the Krays among its inmates.

Towards the river, the 13th-century **Bloody Tower** is another must-see. The ground floor is a reconstruction of Sir Walter Raleigh's study; the upper floor details the fate of the Princes in the Tower.

Talkie), has a major calling card: a free public space with spectacular views of London. After passing through airport-style security, a lift zips you up 35 floors to the soaring space on the top floors. Flights of steps rise through lush, leafy plants to a series of terraces and an open-air piazza.

Visitors must book a 90-minute timeslot on the Sky Garden website at least three days in advance. If no slots are available, try booking a table at the **Sky Pod Bar** (cocktails there cost around a tenner) or at one of the two restaurants (the **Darwin Brasserie** is cheaper than the **Fenchurch Restaurant**): all three also give access to the viewing floors.

Tower Bridge Exhibition
Tower Bridge Road, SE1 2UP (020 7403 3761, www.towerbridge.org. uk). Tower Hill tube or Tower Gateway DLR. **Open** *Apr-Sept 10am-5.30pm daily. Oct-Mar 9.30am-5pm daily.* **Admission** *£9.80; £4.20-£6.80 reductions; £15.30-£27 family; free under-5s.* **Map** *p156 S9.*
Opened in 1894, this is the 'London Bridge' that wasn't sold to America. Originally powered by steam, the drawbridge is now opened by electric rams when big ships need to venture upstream (check when the bridge is next due to be raised on the website or follow the Twitter feed). An entertaining exhibition on its history is displayed in the old steamrooms and the west walkway, which provides a crow's-nest view along the Thames. Glass panels on the walkways mean you can look directly down past your own feet at the river below – assuming you're not prone to vertigo.

Restaurants

Bordering the City to the north, Clerkenwell has been one of London's prime foodie areas since the 1990s, thanks to gastropub pioneer the **Eagle** (*see p148*), the eclectic eateries of Exmouth Market (including **Moro**; *see p149*) and Modern British powerhouse **St John**.

♥ Duck & Waffle £££
Floor 40, Heron Tower, 110 Bishopsgate, EC2N 4AY (020 3640 7310, duckandwaffle.com). Liverpool Street tube/rail. **Open** *24hrs daily.* **Map** *p156 S7* ❶
Modern European
There's a dedicated entrance in Heron Tower from which a glass lift whizzes you up to the Duck & Waffle on the 40th floor. The views are stunning – if you're facing the right way and, preferably, sitting at a window table (many of which are for couples). Food is an on-trend mix of pricey small plates, raw offerings (oysters, ceviche) and a few main courses (including the namesake duck confit and waffle), as well as sensational barbecue-spiced crispy pigs' ears. Service wavers between keen and offhand, and the acoustics are terrible. But Duck & Waffle is open 24/7 – all-night dining is pretty much unheard of in London, though bear in mind that a limited menu is served between midnight and 5am.

▶ *One floor below Duck & Waffle, Sushisamba (020 3640 7330, www.sushisamba.com) has two small bars and an outdoor roof terrace with arguably better views; sushi and saké are the best things on the fusion menu.*

♥ Modern Pantry £££
47-48 St John's Square, EC1V 4JJ (020 7553 9210, www. themodernpantry.co.uk). Farringdon tube/rail. **Open** *8-11am, noon-9pm Mon; 8-11am, noon-10pm Tue-Fri; 9am-4pm, 6-10pm Sat; 10am-4pm Sun.* **Map** *p156 P5* ❷ *International*

Duck & Waffle p163

This townhouse eatery offers enticing fusion dishes that make the most of unusual ingredients sourced from around the globe. Antipodean and Asian flavours (yuzu, tamarind) pop up frequently, alongside plenty of seasonal British fare (wild garlic, purple sprouting broccoli); the combinations can seem bewildering on the page, but rarely falter in execution, and the signature dish of sugar-cured prawn omelette with chilli, coriander and spring onion is always a winner. The stylish ground-floor café is quite feminine in feel, with soothing white and grey paintwork, white furniture and burnished copper light fittings; there's a more formal restaurant upstairs.

The Ned £££-£££
27 Poultry, EC2R 8AJ (020 3828 2000, www.thened.com/ restaurants). Bank tube/DLR. **Open** see website for individual opening hours and reservations. **Map** p156 Q7 ❸ Various

Set amid The Ned's historic 32,290sq ft former banking hall, are nine restaurants and bars (though not all are open to the public). Imagine a giant food court with different restaurant zones under one ridiculously high roof, each serving a different menu: sort of Harrods Food Hall meets the Wolseley. If you like to sit at a table, head to the more intimate spaces like **Malibu Kitchen** (Californian raw food and grills), **Café Sou** (Parisian brasserie grub), **Millie's Lounge** (classic British dishes) or **Cecconi's** (handmade pasta, seafood). Otherwise perch at **Zobler's** (for kosher-style deli food), **Kaia** (for poké-plus-robata) or order a cocktail from the **Nickel Bar**. For details of the hotel see p194.

♥ **St John** £££
26 St John Street, EC1M 4AY (020 7251 0848, stjohnrestaurant.com). Barbican tube or Farringdon tube/ rail. **Restaurant** noon-3pm, 6-11pm Mon-Fri; 6-11pm Sat; 12.30-4pm Sun. **Bar** 11am-11pm Mon-Fri; 6-11pm Sat; noon-5pm Sun. **Map** p156 P6 ❹ British
Fergus Henderson and Trevor Gulliver's restaurant has been praised to the skies for reacquainting the British with the full possibilities of native produce, and especially anything gutsy and offal-ish. Perhaps as influential, however, has been its almost defiantly casual style. The mezzanine dining room in the former Smithfield smokehouse has bare white walls, battered floorboards and tables lined up canteen-style. St John's cooking is famously full-on, but also sophisticated, concocting flavours that are delicate as well as rich, as in black cuttlefish and onions, with a deep-flavoured ink-based sauce with a hint of mint. The airy bar here is a great place for a drink and a no-fuss snack.

Sweetings £££
39 Queen Victoria Street, EC4N 4SA (020 7248 3062, www. sweetingsrestaurant.co.uk). Mansion House tube. **Open** *11.30am-3pm Mon-Fri.* **Map** *p156 Q7* **5** *Fish & seafood*

Things don't change much at this enduring City classic, and that's the way everyone likes it. The walls remain covered with photos of old sports teams, and many of the staff have been here for years. Lobster and crab bisques preface a choice of fish and seafood dishes that read and taste like upmarket versions of a pub-side stall – smoked fish, whitebait, trout and so forth. Top-quality fish are then served fried, grilled or poached to order. The handful of more elaborate dishes includes an excellent fish pie.

Pubs & bars

For cocktails, book ahead to visit **Oriole** (East Poultry Avenue, Smithfield Markets, EC1A 9LH, 020 3457 8099, www.oriolebar.com **1**).

Blackfriar
174 Queen Victoria Street, EC4V 4EG (020 7236 5474, www. nicholsonspubs.co.uk). Blackfriars tube/rail. **Open** *10am-11pm Mon-Fri; 9am-11pm Sat; noon-10.30pm Sun.* **Map** *p156 P7* **2**

Built in 1875 on the site of a medieval Dominican friary, the Blackfriar had its interior completely remodelled in the Arts and Crafts style. Decent real ales aside, come here for the intricate friezes and carved slogans ('Industry is Ale', 'Haste is Slow') of the main saloon bar. You're basically sinking an ale in the middle of a stunning work of art. Admittedly, there's a far more prosaic bar adjoining it, but this remains one of London's most interesting pub interiors.

❤ Black Rock
9 Christopher Street, EC2A 2BS (020 7247 4580, blackrock.bar). Liverpool Street tube/rail. **Open** *5pm-midnight Mon-Wed; 5am-1am Thur; 5pm-2am Fri, Sat.* **Map** *p156 R6* **3**

Tucked away in the maze-like streets behind Liverpool Street station, this dimly lit subterranean whisky lounge is the place for connoisseurs to blow a hole in their bank accounts. One side of the room is lined with cabinets filled with over 250 bottles, while down the middle a table made from half of an English oak tree has two booze-filled channels hewn in the wood. Choose from the Cherry River – bourbon and morello with spices – or the Table Whisky, an ever-evolving house blend.

City Social Bar
Tower 42, 25 Old Broad Street, EC2N 1HQ (020 7877 7703, citysociallondon.com). Liverpool Street tube/rail. **Open** *noon-late Mon-Fri; 4pm-late Sat.* **Map** *p156 R7* **4**

Chef-about-town Jason Atherton (*see p126*) took over what had been a pretty run-of-the-mill City restaurant on the 24th floor of Tower 42– and made it pretty terrific. It is mighty expensive, however, so we recommend the attached bar, which anyone can just show up to – having negotiated two lots of security, an escalator and at least one lift. The cocktails are great, with just enough invention to make them worth the lofty prices, while the snacks give you a sense of Atherton's culinary prowess.

Jerusalem Tavern
55 Britton Street, EC1M 5UQ (020 7490 4281, www.stpetersbrewery. co.uk/london-pub). Farringdon tube/rail. **Open** *noon-11pm Mon-Fri.* **Map** *p156 P6* **5**

Despite the carefully scuffed wooden floors, peeling paint and tables that look as if they've had centuries-worth of pints spilled on them, the Jerusalem Tavern has actually only been a pub since 1990 – it was originally a coffeehouse. Still, the place feels embedded in the history of the area, notwithstanding nods to modernity from the poshed-up bar snacks, taxidermy cabinets and beer from the excellent St Peter's Brewery in Suffolk.

Ye Olde Mitre

1 Ely Court, Ely Place, EC1N 6SJ (020 7405 4751, www.yeoldemitreholborn.co.uk). Farringdon tube/rail. **Open** *11am-11pm Mon-Fri. Food served 11am-10pm Mon-Fri.* **Map** *p156 O6* ⑥

Largely due to its location – down a barely marked alley between Hatton Garden's jewellers and Ely Place – this little traditional pub, the foundation of which dates to 1546, is a favourite of 'secret London' lists. There's always a good range of ales on offer at the tiny central bar, but people come for the atmosphere: lots of cosy dark wood and some overlooked curiosities, such as a cherry tree that Good Queen Bess is said to have danced around, but which now supports a corner of the bar.

♥ ZTH Cocktail Lounge

Zetter Townhouse Clerkenwell, 49-50 St John's Square, EC1V 4JJ (020 7324 4545, www.thezettertownhouse.com). Farringdon tube/rail. **Open** *7am-midnight Mon-Wed; 7am-1am Thur-Sat; 7am-10pm Sun.* **Map** *p156 P5* ⑦

The decor at Townhouse embodies a 'more is more' philosophy: every square inch of surface area is occupied by something lovely. The result: one of the most beautiful bars in London. The cocktail list is high quality; check out the Köln Martini. Service is friendly and helpful.

Entertainment

▶ *For details of the Barbican* ❶*, Europe's largest arts centre, see p155.*

♥ Fabric

77A Charterhouse Street, EC1M 6HJ (020 7336 8898, www.fabriclondon.com). Farringdon tube/rail. **Open** *11pm-6am Fri; 11pm-7am Sat; 11pm-4am Sun.* **Admission** *£10-£40.* **Map** *p156 P6* ❷ *Nightclub*

Fabric is the club that most party people come to see in London. Located in a former meatpacking warehouse, it has a well-deserved reputation as the capital's biggest and best club. Line-ups across the three rooms are legendary, with the world's most famous DJs bringing the finest low-frequencies and the deepest grooves, as the hip crowds that pack out the dancefloors testify.

LSO St Luke's

UBS & LSO Music Education Centre, 161 Old Street, EC1V 9NG (information 020 7490 3939, tickets 7638 8891, lso.co.uk/lso-st-lukes). Old Street tube/rail. **Box office** *(at the Barbican Centre) 10am-8pm Mon-Sat; noon-8pm Sun.* **Tickets** *free-£40.* **Map** *p156 Q5* ❸ *Concert hall*

Built by Nicholas Hawksmoor in the 18th century, this Grade I-listed church was beautifully converted into a performance and rehearsal space by the LSO several years ago. The orchestra occasionally welcomes the public for open rehearsals (book ahead); the more formal side of the programme takes in global sounds alongside classical music, including lunchtime concerts every Thursday that are broadcast on BBC Radio 3.

North London

A huge variety of people have been drawn to north London's mix of pretty, sleepy retreats and buzzing, creative party zones. First stop is normally **Camden Town**, with its markets, indie pubs and general alternative vibe, but there's further joy to be found in the regenerated area of **King's Cross**, a major rail hub and now a hip destination in its own right. Further to the north, the leafy squares of **Islington** make for pleasant exploration, while **Hampstead** and **Highgate** offer genteel village life and a glorious public space: **Hampstead Heath**.

Best for kids
ZSL London Zoo *p173*

Best for teens
Camden Market *p173*

Best for culture and calm
Kenwood House *p178*

Best cocktails
The Bar With No Name *p176*

Best night out
Almeida *p176*,
02 Forum *p174*,
Roundhouse *p175*,
Union Chapel *p177*

King's Cross

North-east of Bloomsbury, the once-insalubrious area of King's Cross has undergone massive redevelopment in the last decade. Behind George Gilbert Scott's grandiloquent red-brick frontage to **St Pancras International** station (much of which is now the St Pancras Renaissance hotel) is William Barlow's even more impressive Victorian glass-and-iron train shed. To the west is the **British Library** and, to the east, the much-improved entrance to King's Cross station (location of Harry Potter's Platform 9¾). It is the area to the north, however, that has been the most radically transformed, with the imaginative redevelopment of derelict land and buildings around the **Regent's Canal**. Hang out with art students among the choreographed fountains of **Granary Square**, shop and eat your way around **Coal Drops Yard**, or stroll along the tow path towards **Camden**.

Sights & museums

British Library

96 Euston Road, NW1 2DB (01937 546060, www.bl.uk). Euston or King's Cross St Pancras tube/rail. **Open** *9.30am-8pm Mon-Thur; 9.30am-6pm Fri; 9.30am-5pm Sat; 11am-5pm Sun.* **Admission** *free; donations appreciated.* **Map** *p169 M4.*

'One of the ugliest buildings in the world,' opined a parliamentary committee on the opening of the new British Library in 1997. But don't judge a book by its cover: the interior is a model of cool, spacious functionality and the collection is unmatched (150 million items and counting). The focal point of the building is the King's Library, a six-storey glass-walled tower housing George III's collection, but the library's main treasures are on permanent display in the John Ritblat Gallery: the Lindisfarne Gospels, a Diamond Sutra from AD 868, original Beatles lyrics. Upstairs are engaging blockbuster shows covering meaty themes such as sci-fi, Gothic literature and the English language itself.

House of Illustration

2 Granary Square, N1C 4BH (020 3696 2020, www. houseofillustration.org.uk). King's Cross St Pancras tube/rail. **Open** *10am-5.30pm Tue-Sat; 11am-5.30pm Sun.* **Admission** *£8.80; £4.40-£7.70 reductions; £19.80 family; free under-5s.* **Map** *p169 M3.*

The world's first gallery dedicated to the art of illustration has demonstrations, talks, debates and hands-on workshops covering all aspects of illustration, from children's books and scabrous cartoons to advertising and animation, as well as a regular programme of temporary

exhibitions, usually dedicated to a single illustrator: Quentin Blake, for instance, or EH Shepard, who drew the captivating pictures for *Winnie-the-Pooh*.

London Canal Museum

12-13 New Wharf Road, off Wharfdale Road, N1 9RT (020 7713 0836, www.canalmuseum. org.uk). King's Cross St Pancras tube/rail. **Open** *10am-4.30pm Tue-Sun (until 7.30pm 1st Thur of mth).* **Admission** *£5; £2.50-£4 reductions; family £12.50; free under-4s.* **Map** *p169 N3.*

Housed on two floors of a former 19th-century ice warehouse, the London Canal Museum has a barge cabin to sit in and models of boats, but the displays on the history of the ice trade (photos and videos about ice-importer Carlo Gatti) are perhaps the most interesting. The walk along the Regent's Canal (*see p172*; download a free MP3 audio tour from the museum website) to Camden Town is lovely, and in summer don't miss the tours – organised by the museum – that explore dank Islington Tunnel, an otherwise inaccessible Victorian canal feature.

Restaurants

There is a host of restaurants along King's Boulevard, around Granary Square and in Coal Drops Yard. Check out Bombay-style **Dishoom** (5 Stable Street, www.dishoom.com); tapas star **Barrafina** (Coal Drops Yard, www. barrafina.co.uk), and Mexico-via-Bermondsey darling **Casa Pastor** (Coal Drops Yard, www. tacoselpastor.co.uk). The station forecourt, Granary Square and the **Canopy Market** (canopymarket. co.uk) also host street food vendors for lunches on the go.

Caravan King's Cross ££

Granary Building, 1 Granary Square, N1C 4AA (020 7101 7661, www.caravankingscross.co.uk). King's Cross St Pancras tube/rail. **Open** *8am-10.30pm Mon-Fri; 9am-10.30pm Sat; 9am-4pm Sun.* **Map** *p169 M3* ❶ *Global*

This is an altogether bigger, more urbane operation than the original Caravan on Exmouth Market. The ethos is the same, however: welcoming staff and a menu of what they call 'well-travelled food'. Most are small plates – deep-fried

Coal Drops Yard

duck egg with baba ganoush, chorizo oil and crispy shallots, say, or grits, collard greens and brown shrimp butter – plus a few large plates and (at King's Cross only) a handful of first-class pizzas. The setting, overlooking the fountains of Granary Square, is another plus, and there's a good range of drinks, including cocktails.

German Gymnasium ££-£££

*1 King's Boulevard, N1C 4BU (020 7287 8000, www.german gymnasium.com). King's Cross St Pancras tube/rail. **Open** 8am-11pm Mon-Fri; 10am-11pm Sat; 10am-10pm Sun. **Map** p169 M3* ❷
European

England's first purpose-built gymnasium was constructed in 1865 for the German Gymnastics Society and hosted the indoor events at the Olympic Games in 1866. Today, the vast Victorian surroundings provide an inspired setting for three floors of stylish eating and drinking. There's an expansive Grand Café on the ground floor for poshed-up Germanic lunches; a sophisticated modern European restaurant on the first floor and glamorous cocktails in the Meister Bar. Going to the gym has never been more fun.

Pubs & bars

Booking Office

*St Pancras Renaissance Hotel, Euston Road, NW1 2AR (020 7841 3566, www.the-booking-office. com). King's Cross St Pancras tube /rail. **Open** 6.30am-midnight Mon-Wed; 6.30am-1am Thur, Fri; 7am-midnight Sat, Sun. **Map** p169 M4* ❶

Sit indoors at this smart cocktail bar and you'll gaze at Sir George Gilbert Scott's lofty interior; outside, under spacious canopies, you'll have a nearly ceiling-level

view of St Pancras International station. The cocktail list gives prominent place to traditional punches, served in mugs, but the list is a long one. Martinis are well made, and the Victorian Gimlet (vodka, lime juice and seasonal fresh fruit juice) is a wonderful and refreshing potion.

Spiritland

*9-10 Stable Street, N1C 4AB (020 3319 0050, spiritland.com). King's Cross St Pancras tube/rail. **Open** 8am-midnight Mon-Wed; 8am-1am Thur, Fri; 10am-1am Sat; 10am-10pm Sun. **Map** p169 M2* ❷

A true labour of love, Spiritland (named after a surprisingly funky Elkie Brooks song) puts its audiophile sound system, robust decks and rotary DJ mixer centre stage. At its core, it's a bar and eatery on Granary Square. But the quality of record selectors that pass through the space are on another level, and make it a truly rewarding destination for music lovers.

Shops & services

Coal Drops Yard (www. coaldropsyard.com) is the focus for retail therapy in this area, with posh shops like Cos, Rains, Aesop and sportswear specialist The Sports Edit all in residence. For something completely different, check out **Word on the Water**, a bookshop housed in a barge on the Regent's Canal.

Entertainment

Kings Place

*90 York Way, N1 9AG (020 7520 1490, www.kingsplace.co.uk). King's Cross St Pancras tube/King's Cross or St Pancras rail. **Box office** noon-8pm Mon, Wed-Sat; noon-5pm Tue; times vary Sun. **Tickets** free-£50. **Map** p169 M3* ❶ *Concert hall*

Beneath seven office floors and a ground-floor restaurant-bar (with prized seats on the canal basin outside), the 415-seat main hall is a beauty, dominated by wood carved from a single, 500-year-old oak tree and ringed by invisible rubber pads that kill unwanted noise that might interfere with the immaculate acoustics. There's also a versatile second hall and a number of smaller rooms for workshops and lectures. The programming is tremendous and includes curated weeks featuring composers as wide-ranging as atonalist Arnold Schoenberg and jazzer Kit Downes. Other strands include chamber music and experimental classical, and there are spoken-word events too.

Scala
275 Pentonville Road, N1 9NL (information 020 7833 2022, scala. co.uk). King's Cross St Pancras tube/rail. **Box office** *10am-6pm Mon-Fri.* **Tickets** *free-£25.* **Map** *p169 M3* ❷ *Live music*
Although the venue has vacillated between use as a picturehouse and concert hall, the Scala's one consistent trait has been its lack of respect for authority: its stint as a cinema was ended after Stanley Kubrick sued it into bankruptcy for showing *A Clockwork Orange*. Nowadays, it's one of the most rewarding venues in which to push your way to the front for those cusp-of-greatness shows by big names in waiting – names as varied as triple-threat Londoner MNEK and online sensation Poppy.

Camden & around

Tourists travel here in their thousands for the sprawling mayhem of **Camden Market**, while music-lovers come for rough-and-ready gigs in a host of legendary venues. West of Camden are **Primrose Hill**, with its expansive views and expensive properties, and the vast spread of **Regent's Park**.

Sights & museums

Regent's Canal
Stretching for 9 miles from the Grand Union Canal to the River Thames at Limehouse, Regent's Canal is a quiet and atmospheric waterway. It was built in 1820 to provide a link between east and west London for horse-drawn narrowboats loaded with coal. These days the towpath is popular with walkers and cyclists who appreciated this car-free route through the capital. From Camden Lock, you can catch a jolly tour boat run by the **London Waterbus Company** (020 7485 6210, www. walkersquay.com). These pass through London Zoo, Regent's Park and the short Maida Hill tunnel en route to Little Venice, home to a community of boat-dwelling Londoners.

Regent's Park
www.royalparks.org.uk. Regent's Park, Great Portland Street, Baker Street, St John's Wood or Camden Town tube.

Regent's Canal

Originally a hunting ground for Henry VIII, Regent's Park is one of London's most delightful spaces. Designed by John Nash in 1811, it remained a royals-only retreat until opening to the public in 1845. Attractions run from the animal and noises of **ZSL London Zoo** (*see below*) to the fragrant blooms of roses in **Queen Mary's Garden** and the enchanting open-air **theatre** (0333 400 3562, openairtheatre. com); rowing-boat hire, lovely waterfowl lakes, ice-cream stands and the **Espresso Bar** (020 7935 5729, 8am-4pm daily) complete the picture.

♥ ZSL London Zoo

Regent's Park, NW1 4RY (0344 225 1826, www.zsl.org/zsl-london-zoo). Baker Street or Camden Town tube then bus 274, C2. **Open** *daily, times vary; check website for details.* **Admission** *£31.50; £23.40-£29.25 reductions; free under-3s. Book online for 10% discount.* **Map** *p169 H2.*
London Zoo has been open in one form or another since 1826. Spread over 36 acres and containing more than 600 species, it cares for many endangered animals – part of the entry price goes towards the ZSL's projects around the world. Regular events include 'Animals in Action'

ZSL London Zoo

and keeper talks. In the fabulous 'In with the Lemurs' exhibit, you get to walk through jungle habitat with the long-tailed primates leaping over your head. Other major attractions are 'Tiger Territory', where Sumatran tigers can be watched through floor-to-ceiling windows, and 'Gorilla Kingdom'. Personal encounters of the avian kind can be had in the Victorian Blackburn Pavilion – as well as at Penguin Beach, where the black-and-white favourites are plainly visible as they swim underwater. Bring a picnic and you could easily spend the day here.

Shops & services

♥ Camden Market

020 3763 9900, www. camdenmarket.com. Camden Town or Chalk Farm tube. **Open** *10am-6pm daily.* **Map** *p169 J2.*
There are two main areas to Camden Market proper. **Camden Lock Market** (Camden Lock Place, off Chalk Farm Road, NW1 8AF, ❶) next to the Regent's Canal lock, is an arts and crafts haven packed with covered retail units and pop-ups specialising in scarves, shoes, hand-stitched leather goods, Fairtrade jewellery and loads more. It's also the place to go when you're hungry, thanks to the 30-plus global street-food stalls at West Yard (the cobbled bit next to the canal and behind Lock 17).

Further along Chalk Farm Road, the **Stables Market** (opposite Hartland Road, NW1 8AH, ❷) has undergone a multimillion-pound redevelopment. The grade II listed Horse Hospital (where horses injured from pulling barges along the canal were treated) and a warren of stables known as the Triangle are now home to an eclectic mix of cool urban clothing outlets, handmade crafts and one-off vintage items. North Yard has become a mecca for local epicureans. It's a relaxed

Camden High Street

space away from the main hustle, with restaurants, cafés and delis where you can watch artisans at work – from handmade fudge and chai workshops to butchery masterclasses and local brewery tastings.

To the south, on the corner of Buck Street and Camden High Street, the souvenir stands, T-shirt hawkers and throwback traders of **Buck Street Market** ❸ have long gone. In their place, 88 shipping containers have been re-purposed into a sustainable 'village' of eating, drinking and shopping units, with a rooftop garden and terrace; check @BuckStreetMkt for details.

Entertainment

Jazz Café
5 Parkway, NW1 7PG (020 7485 6834, thejazzcafelondon.com). Camden Town tube. **Live shows & restaurant** 7-10.30pm daily. **Club nights** 10.30pm-3am Fri, Sat. **Tickets** £5-£30. **Map** p169 J2 ❸
Jazz

In 2020, the Jazz Café will celebrate 30 years in business, having brought some of the most respected names in the jazz and soul world – D'Angelo, Roy Ayers, Bobby Womack – as well as Amy Winehouse and Adele to Camden Town. The programming focuses on funk, soul, R&B and electronic music, but there are also new and rising acts. With a capacity of 440, it's an intimate space, but the two-level layout offers you a choice: get sweaty in the downstairs standing area, or book an upstairs table for a bit of luxury and guaranteed good view.

Koko
1A Camden High Street, NW1 7JE (information 020 7388 3222, tickets 0844 477 1000, www.koko.uk.com). Mornington Crescent tube. **Box office** In person noon-5pm Mon-Fri (performance days only). By phone 24hrs daily. **Tickets** £10-£40. **Map** p169 K3 ❹ Rock & pop
Koko has had a hand in the gestation of numerous styles over the decades. As the Music Machine, it hosted a four-night residency with the Clash in 1978; the venue changed its name to Camden Palace in the '80s, whereupon it became home to the emergent New Romantic movement and saw Madonna's UK debut. Later, it was one of the first 'official' venues to host acid-house events and has hosted acts as diametrically opposed as Joss Stone and Queens of the Stone Age, not to mention one of Prince's electrifying 'secret' gigs. Nonetheless, the 1,500-capacity hall majors on weekend club nights – Guilty Pleasures and Buttoned Down Disco – and gigs by indie rockers, from the small and cultish to those on the up.

♥ O2 Forum Kentish Town
9-17 Highgate Road, NW5 1JY (information 020 3362 4110, tickets 0844 877 2000, www. academymusicgroup.com/ o2forumkentishtown). Kentish Town tube/rail. **Box office** In person 90mins before performance. By phone 24hrs daily. **Tickets** £10-£40. Rock & pop
Originally constructed as part of a chain of art deco cinemas with

a spurious Roman theme (hence the name, the incongruous bas relief battle scenes and imperial eagles flanking the stage), the 2,000-capacity Forum became a music venue back in the early 1980s. Since then, it's been vital to generations of gig-goers, whether they cut their teeth on Ian Dury & the Blockheads, the Pogues, Duran Duran, Killing Joke or the Wu-Tang Clan, all of whom have played memorable shows here.

♥ Roundhouse

Chalk Farm Road, NW1 8EH (tickets 0300 678 9222, www.roundhouse. org.uk). Chalk Farm tube. **Box office** *In person 9.30am-5pm Mon, Sat, Sun; 9.30am-9pm Tue-Fri. By phone performance days 9am-7.30pm Mon-Fri; 2-7.30pm Sat, Sun; non-performance days 9am-2.30pm Mon-Fri.* **Tickets** *£5-£25.* **Map** *p169 J2* ❺ *Music & performance*

The main auditorium's supporting pillars mean there are some poor sightlines at the Roundhouse, but this one-time railway turntable shed (hence the name), which was used for hippie happenings in the 1960s before becoming a famous rock (and punk) venue in the '70s, has been a fine addition to London's music venues since its reopening in 2006. Expect a mix of arty rock gigs (the briefly re-formed Led Zeppelin played here), dance performances, theatre and multimedia events.

Islington

There are no major sights here, but this area is worth a visit for its concentration of good restaurants and bars.

Restaurants

Ottolenghi ££-£££
287 Upper Street, N1 2TZ (020 7288 1454, ottolenghi.co.uk). Angel tube or Highbury & Islington
tube/Overground/rail.* **Open** *8am-10.30pm Mon-Sat; 9am-7pm Sun. Eastern Mediterranean*

Hit cookbooks have made this flagship branch of the burgeoning Ottolenghi empire a point of pilgrimage for foodies the world over. French toast made from brioche and served with crème fraîche and a thin berry and muscat compote makes a heady start to the day. Or there's a lively chorizo-spiked take on baked beans served with sourdough, fried egg and black pudding. In the evening (when bookings are taken), the cool white interior works a double shift as a smart and comparatively pricey restaurant serving elegant dishes for sharing.

Salut! ££
412 Essex Road, N1 3PJ (020 3441 8808, salut-london.co.uk). Essex Road rail. **Open** *6-11pm Tue-Thur; noon-3pm, 6-11pm Fri-Sun. Modern European*

Salut offers a relaxed take on modern European haute cuisine. The menu is understated but everything on it demonstrates exquisite attention to detail: king crab and watercress comes with unexpected crab roe foam and micro herb pesto; the 'selection of onions' with a juicy pork belly are in turn pickled, caramelised and charred to perfection; poached pear is perfectly complemented by fermented berries, rich fruit jelly, hazelnut crumble and white chocolate foam. These beautiful plates of food taste as good as they look – without breaking the bank.

Trullo ££
300-302 St Paul's Road, N1 2LH (020 7226 2733, www. trullorestaurant.com). Highbury & Islington tube/Overground/rail. **Open** *12.30-2.45pm, 6-10.15pm Mon-Sat; 12.30-2.45pm, 6-9.15pm Sun. Italian*

While evenings are still busy-to-frantic in this two-floored contemporary trattoria, lunchtime finds Trullo calm and the cooking relaxed and assured. Grills and roasts from the carte might include Black Hampshire pork chop and cod with cannellini beans and mussels, while pappardelle with beef shin ragù has been a staple since Trullo's early days and remains a silky, substantial delight.

Pubs & bars

🖤 The Bar With No Name

69 Colebrooke Row, N1 8AA (07540 528 593, www.69colebrookerow. com). Angel tube. **Open** *5pm-midnight Mon-Wed, Sun; 5pm-1am Thur; 5pm-2am Fri, Sat.*
It's not easy to get a seat here without booking. Punters come for the outstanding cocktails – some of which may push the boundaries of what can be put in a glass, but they always maintain the drinkability of the classics. Take the Terroir, for instance, which lists as its ingredients 'distilled clay, flint and lichen', and tastes wonderfully like a chilled, earthy, minerally vodka. It's made in the upstairs laboratory, which also produces bespoke cocktail ingredients such as Guinness reduction, paprika bitters, rhubarb cordial and pine-infused gin. There's a subtle jazz-age vibe in the small, low-lit room and – on certain nights – a pianist belts out swinging standards.

Earl of Essex

25 Danbury Street, N1 8LE (020 7424 5828, www.earlofessex.net). Angel tube. **Open** *noon-11.30pm Mon-Thur; noon-midnight Fri, Sat; noon-11pm Sun.*
The first thing you notice on entering this backstreet Georgian pub is the beautiful island back-bar with a 1960s 'Watney Red Barrel' sign; the second is the vast list of beers on offer. There are 13 on keg, three on cask, plus a couple of quality ciders. The range covers Britain (including a pouring from the on-site Earl's Brewery), Europe and the USA. Staff are happy to offer tastings and know their stuff. On the menu, dishes are all listed with beer recommendations. Whether you really need a suggested beer match for a fishfinger sandwich is a matter of opinion, but it's a nice touch.

Entertainment

🖤 Almeida

Almeida Street, N1 1TA (information 020 7288 4900, tickets 020 7359 4404, almeida. co.uk). Angel tube or Highbury & Islington tube/overground/rail. **Box office** *10am-7.30pm Mon-Sat.* **Tickets** *£10-£38. Theatre*
Since Rupert Goold took over as artistic director in 2013, the Almeida has been reinvented from something rather chintzy to London's hippest theatre, the leftfield programming doing nothing to staunch a seemingly endless stream of acclaimed shows that headed into the West End: *King Charles III*, *Oresteia*, *Hamlet*, *Mary Stuart* and *Summer and Smoke* are all recent transfer hits. The secrets of the Almeida's success are many: Goold's sheer audacity ranks up there, while associate director Robert Icke is probably the most exciting director of his generation.

Lexington

96-98 Pentonville Road, N1 9JB (020 7837 5371, thelexington.co.uk). Angel tube. **Open** *noon-2am Mon-Wed, Sun; noon-3am Thur; noon-4am Fri, Sat.* **Tickets** *free-£15. Rock & pop*
Effectively the common room for the music industry's perennial sixth form, this 200-capacity venue has a superb sound

Sadler's Wells Theatre

system in place for the leftfield indie bands that dominate the programme. It's where the hottest US exports often make their London debut: indie greats such as the Drums and Sleigh Bells have cut their teeth here in front of London's most receptive crowds. Downstairs, there's a lounge bar with a vast array of US beers and bourbons, above-par bar food and a pop quiz with guest host (every Monday).

Sadler's Wells Theatre
Rosebery Avenue, EC1R 4TN (020 7863 8000, www.sadlerswells.com). Angel tube. **Box office** *10am-8pm Mon-Sat.* **Tickets** *£12-£72. Dance* Built in 1998 on the site of a 17th-century theatre of the same name, this dazzling complex is home to impressive local and international performances of contemporary dance in all its guises. The Lilian Baylis Studio offers smaller-scale new works and works in progress; the Peacock Theatre (on Portugal Street in Holborn) operates as a satellite venue.

Screen on the Green
83 Upper Street, N1 0NP (0872 436 9060, www.everymancinema.com). Angel tube. **Tickets** *£16.20-£19; £11.20-£17 reductions. Screens 1. Cinema*
Do you like the smell of expensive leather? Everyman has half a dozen venues across London, each with plush seats, posh food and carpets you could lick without getting a stomach bug. It all started with the **Everyman Hampstead**, which has a glamorous bar and two-seaters in its 'screening lounges', complete with footstools and wine coolers. Everyman runs three former Screen cinemas, of which Screen on the Green retains its original name. It's another beauty, having lost seats to make space for the more comfortable kind, gained a bar and a stage for gigs, but kept its classic neon sign.

♥ Union Chapel
Compton Terrace, off Upper Street, N1 2UN (020 7226 1686, www. unionchapel.org.uk). Highbury & Islington tube/Overground/rail. **Open** *varies.* **Tickets** *free-£40. Rock & pop*
Readers of *Time Out* magazine have three times voted Union Chapel their top music venue – and it's easy to see why. The Grade I-listed Victorian Gothic

church, which still holds services and also runs a homeless centre, is a wonderfully atmospheric gig venue. It made its name hosting acoustic events and occasional jazz shows, becoming a magnet for thinking bands and their fans. These days, you'll also find classy intimate shows from bigger artists such as Paloma Faith. Watch out for the Daylight Music free afternoon concerts.

Hampstead & Highgate

Bordering **Hampstead Heath**, the hilltop villages of Hampstead and Highgate were absorbed into London during the city's great Victorian expansion. **Hampstead** was a favoured roost for literary and artistic types: Keats and Constable lived here in the 19th century, and sculptors Barbara Hepworth and Henry Moore took up residence in the 1930s. **Highgate** takes its name from the tollgate that once stood on the High Street, but it is best known for atmospheric **Highgate Cemetery**.

Sights & museums

Highgate Cemetery
Swain's Lane, N6 6PJ (020 8340 1834, highgatecemetery.org). Archway tube. **East Cemetery** *Mar-Oct 10am-5pm daily. Nov-Feb 10am-4pm daily. Tours 2pm Sat.* **West Cemetery** *by tour only (no under-8s), check website for times.* **Admission** *£4; free under-18s. East Cemetery tours £8, £4 reductions. West Cemetery tours £12; £6 reductions.*
The final resting place of some very famous Londoners, Highgate Cemetery is an enchanting overgrown maze of ivy-cloaked Victorian tombs and time-shattered urns. Visitors can wander at their own pace through the East Cemetery, with its memorials to Karl Marx, George Eliot and Douglas Adams, but the most atmospheric part of the cemetery is the foliage-shrouded West Cemetery, laid out in 1839. Only accessible on an organised tour (book ahead, dress respectfully and arrive 30 minutes early), the shady paths wind past gloomy catacombs, grand Victorian pharaonic tombs, and the graves of notables such as poet Christina Rossetti, scientist Michael Faraday and poisoned Russian dissident Alexander Litvinenko.

💜 Kenwood House/Iveagh Bequest
Hampstead Lane, NW3 7JR (020 8348 1286, www.english-heritage.org.uk). Hampstead tube, or Golders Green tube then bus 210. **Open** *10am-5pm daily.* **Admission** *free.*
Set in lovely grounds at the top of Hampstead Heath, Kenwood House is every inch the country manor house. Built in 1616, the mansion was remodelled in the 18th century for William Murray, who made the vital court ruling in 1772 that made it illegal to own slaves in England. The house was purchased by brewing magnate Edward Guinness, who was kind enough to donate his art collection to the nation in 1927. After extensive, splendid renovations, the interiors have been returned to a state that enhances such highlights of the collection as Vermeer's *The Guitar Player*, Gainsborough's *Countess Howe*, and one of Rembrandt's finest self-portraits (dating to c1663). There's a terrific kids' room with games and activities too.

Canary Wharf

East London

Despite, or perhaps because of, its long history of industrialisation, immigration and social deprivation, the East End now comprises much of what is most vibrant about the capital. On the doorstep of the City, **Spitalfields** and neighbouring **Brick Lane** mix upmarket shopping and dining with Bangladeshi cafés and boho boutiques. North of Spitalfields, **Shoreditch** and **Hoxton** retain some lively bars and clubs, although local hipsters have moved to **Dalston** for its innovative drinking, dining and dancing venues.

London's **Docklands**, once the busiest in the world, became the flagship of finance-led urban redevelopment in the 1990s. Now the Isle of Dogs is all shiny megabanks, with the landmark 'Canary Wharf Tower' almost lost between them. Follow the River Lea upstream to the north to reach the **Queen Elizabeth Olympic Park**, or cross the Thames south to **Greenwich** (*see p22*).

Best museum
Geffrye Museum *p180*

Best attraction
ArcelorMittal Orbit *p190*

Best market
Broadway *p185*,
Columbia Road *p185*

Best food & drink combos
Cub *p182*,
Happiness Forgets *p184*,
Sager+Wilde *p184*

Best nightlife
Dalston Superstore *p187*,
EartH *p187*,
Village Underground *p188*,
XOYO *p188*

East End & around

Sights & museums

Dennis Severs' House
*18 Folgate Street, E1 6BX (020 7247
4013, www.dennissevershouse.co.uk).
Liverpool Street tube/Overground/
rail or Shoreditch High Street
Overground.* **Open** *noon-2pm,
5-9pm Mon; 5-9pm Wed, Fri; noon-
4pm Sun.* **Admission** *Daytime
visits £10; £5 reductions. Evening
visits £15-£50.* **Map** *p181 S6.*

The ten rooms of this original
Huguenot house have been decked
out to recreate vivid snapshots of
daily life in Spitalfields between
1724 and 1914. A tour through the
compelling 'still-life drama', as
American creator Dennis Severs
dubbed it, takes you through
the cellar, kitchen, dining room,
smoking room and upstairs to the
bedrooms. With hearth and candles
burning, smells lingering and objects
scattered apparently haphazardly,
it feels as though the inhabitants
have deserted the building only
moments before you arrived.

❤ Geffrye Museum
*136 Kingsland Road, E2 8EA (020
7739 9893, www.geffrye-museum.
org.uk). Hoxton Overground.* **Open**
*From summer 2020; see the website
for details.* **Admission** *See the
website for details.* **Map** *p181 S4.*

Housed in a set of 18th-century
almshouses, the Geffrye Museum
has for more than a century offered
a vivid physical history of the
English interior. Displaying original
furniture, paintings, textiles and
decorative arts, the museum
recreates a sequence of typical
middle-class living rooms from
1600 to the present. It's an oddly
interesting way to take in domestic
history, with any number of
intriguing details to catch your eye
– from a bell jar of stuffed birds to
a particular decorative flourish on
a chair. There's an airy restaurant
overlooking the lovely gardens,
which include a walled plot for
herbs and a chronological series
in different historical styles, and a
new street-facing café with terrace.
The museum reopens in summer
2020 following major redevelopment
of the Grade 1-listed building as
well as new spaces for exhibitions,
events and collections.

V&A Museum of Childhood
*Cambridge Heath Road, E2
9PA (020 8983 5200, www.vam.
ac.uk/moc). Bethnal Green tube/
Overground or Cambridge Heath
Overground.* **Open** *10am-5.45pm
daily.* **Admission** *free; donations
appreciated.*

Home to one of the world's finest
collections of children's toys, dolls'
houses, games and costumes, the
Museum of Childhood is part of

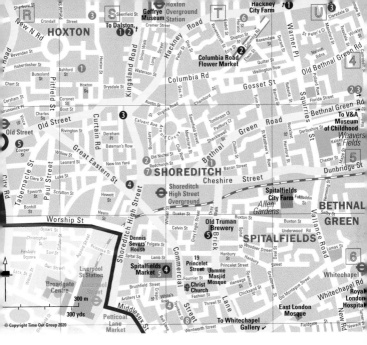

the Victoria & Albert Museum (*see p101*). It has been amassing childhood-related objects since 1872 and continues to do so, with *Incredibles* figures complementing bonkers 1970s puppets, Barbie dolls and Victorian praxinoscopes. The museum has lots of hands-on stuff for kids dotted about the many cases of historic artefacts, including dressing-up boxes and soft play areas, though the cases themselves may be of more interest to nostalgic adults than their spawn. Regular small exhibitions are held upstairs, while the café in the central space helps to revive flagging spirits.

Whitechapel Gallery
77-82 Whitechapel High Street, E1 7QX (020 7522 7888, www. whitechapelgallery.org). Aldgate East tube. **Open** *11am-6pm Tue,* *Wed, Fri-Sun; 11am-9pm Thur.* **Admission** *free. Temporary exhibitions vary.*

This East End stalwart, a perennial favourite of avant-garde aficionados and art students, continues to build on a stellar reputation as a contemporary art pioneer that began with exhibitions of Picasso – *Guernica* was shown here in 1939 – Jackson Pollock, Mark Rothko and Frida Kahlo. The Grade II-listed building underwent a 21st-century refurb that saw it expand into the similarly historic former library next door – rather brilliantly, the architects left the two buildings stylistically distinct rather than trying to smooth out their differences. As well as nearly tripling its exhibition space, the Whitechapel gave itself a research centre and archives, plus a café/ bar. With no permanent collection,

Geffrye Museum p180

there's a rolling programme of temporary shows, but an increasing number of artists have contributed permanently to the fabric of the building: a few years back, Rachel Whiteread added gold vine leaves to the gallery's frontage.

Restaurants

Hungry clubbers flock to the **Brick Lane Beigel Bake** (159 Brick Lane, E1 6SB, 020 7729 0616 ❶), which churns out freshly baked goodies 24hrs daily.

Brat £££

First floor, 4 Redchurch Street, E1 6JL (www.bratrestaurant. com). Shoreditch High Street Overground. **Open** noon-3pm, 6-11pm Mon-Sat; noon-3pm, 6.30-10pm Sun. **Map** p181 S5 ❷

A set of pokey steps go up to a room above a former pub, where you'll find glorious original features – wood panelling, arched windows, parquet floors – and chefs bustling around a large island kitchen. This is a handsome, buzzy chophouse serving a no-frills menu of meat and fish from a wood-fired oven, propped up by modern Brit small plates. Highlights include a subtle soused red mullet and an expertly cooked shorthorn beef chop.

❤ Cub ££

153 Hoxton Street, N1 6PJ (020 3946 7060, lyancub.com). Hoxton Overground. **Open** 6pm-late Wed-Sat. **Map** p181 S4 ❸ Plant-based

A collaboration between cocktail meister Mr Lyan and sustainable chef Doug McMaster, Cub serves a no-choice menu of inventive small plates teamed with equally creative cocktails, all made from sustainable ingredients. It's not technically a vegetarian restaurant, but the food is light and plant-dominated, with animal products only making fleeting guest appearances. There's a set menu featuring six food courses and six drinks for £67 per person. Super-friendly, savvy staff ensure the vibe is more like a house party than a restaurant.

Gunpowder ££

11 White's Row, E1 7NF (www. gunpowderlondon.com). Aldgate East tube or Liverpool Street tube/ Overground/rail. **Open** *noon-3pm, 5.30-10.30pm Mon-Sat.* **Map** *p181 T6* ❹ *Indian*

Despite its 'Curry Mile' reputation, it's surprisingly hard to find a good Indian restaurant in the Brick Lane area. This tiny family-run restaurant aims to bring quality small-plate eating to Indian food, ditching stomach-bursting breads and creamy sauces for delights such as *rasam ke bomb*, chilli cheese toast and Chettinad pulled duck served with homemade *oothappam*. The place oozes passion without a hint of pretension; at weekends it positively buzzes.

Kitchens £-££

Old Spitalfields Market, 16 Horner Square, E1 6EW (oldspitalfieldsmarket.com). Liverpool Street tube/Overground/ rail or Shoreditch High Street Overground. **Open** *11am-8pm Mon-Fri; 11am-6pm Sat; 11am-5pm Sun.* **Map** *p181 S6* ❺

As part of the Old Spitalfields Market refurbishment, ten kitchen units serve up first-rate nosh from some of London's highly rated eateries, all curated by superstar chef Nuno Mendes of Chiltern Firehouse. Look out for cult dumpings from the **Dumpling Shack**, nose-to-tail, open-fire cooking at **Flank** and possibly

the best sandwich in the city from **Monty's Deli**, also available at its permanent restaurant at 227 Hoxton Street, N1 5LG (020 7729 5737, www.montys-deli.com)

Marksman ££

254 Hackney Road, E2 7SJ (020 7739 7393, www. marksmanpublichouse.com). Hoxton Overground. **Open** *11am-midnight Mon-Thur; 11am-1am Fri, Sat; 10am-11pm Sun. Food served 6-10pm Mon-Thur; noon-3pm, 6-10pm Fri; noon-4pm, 6-10pm Sat; 10am-4pm, 6-9pm Sun.* **Map** *p181 T4* ❻ *Modern British*

Owned and run by head chefs Tom Harris and Jon Rotheram, the Marksman combines convivial pub surroundings with a first-rate modern British menu that strays far and wide from the standard gastropub script. Come for the unbeatable Sunday roast (£35 for three courses); at other times, try the signature beef and barley bun with horseradish cream or the curried duck with sourdough roti and tomato chutney. For dessert, the brown butter and honey tart is a masterpiece of culinary engineering.

Smoking Goat £

64 Shoreditch High Street, E1 6JJ (www.smokinggoatbar. com). Shoreditch High Street Overground. **Open** *noon-11pm Mon-Wed, Sun; noon-11.30pm Thur; noon-1am Fri, Sat.* **Map** *p181 S5* ❼ *Thai*

Got £5.50 in your pocket? Great. Because that's all you'll need for Smoking Goat's lardo-fried rice, aka the best fried rice in London: it's the colour of autumn, the taste of long-haul holidays and the ultimate hangover cure. The restaurant feels like the pub it once was, but with an open-counter kitchen in place of the bar and tightly packed tables that ensure a friendly, noisy buzz.

The food is in your face, featuring an abundance of volcanically hot chillies and heaps of fresh herbs. Try fragrant seafood *tom yum*; 'drunken noodles' – a twist on Cantonese beef *ho fun*; fish-sauce chicken wings, or, if you're reckless enough, the indecently fiery *laab*-style pork.

Som Saa £££

43A Commercial Street, E1 6BD (020 7324 7790, www.somsaa. com). Shoreditch High Street Overground. **Open** *5-10pm Mon; noon-2.30pm, 5-10.30pm Tue-Fri; noon-3pm, 5-10.30pm Sat.* **Map** *p181 T6* **8** *Thai*

Som Saa isn't somewhere you come for a cheeky green curry and a plate of pad thai – this is authentic, red-hot food from Thailand's north-eastern provinces. Take the deep-fried seabass with Isaan (north-eastern) herbs, for instance. The delicate flesh comes loose easily, leaving a cartoon fish skeleton and crunchy roasted-rice-battered skin, herbs (mint, coriander, Thai basil), mandoline-thin shallots and a puddle of sweet-sour-salt-fire sauce. The effect is thrilling: like setting off ooh-aahh fireworks of taste and texture.

Pubs & bars

♥ Happiness Forgets

8-9 Hoxton Square, N1 6NU (020 7613 0325, www.happinessforgets. com). Old Street tube/rail or Shoreditch High Street Overground. **Open** *5-11pm daily.* **Map** *p181 S4* **1**

From the moment you walk in, the staff will know how to make you happy. The short list of original cocktails is unfailingly good: lots of nice twists on classic ideas but never departing from the essential cocktail principles of balance, harmony and drinkability. Star

turns: Mr McRae, Perfect Storm and Tokyo Collins. But the classics are brilliantly handled too, the food is fabulous and so is the service. This is a very special place but not very large: booking is a good idea.

♥ Sager + Wilde Paradise Row

250 Paradise Row, E2 9LE (020 7729 6278, www.sagerandwilde. com). Bethnal Green tube/ Overground. **Open** *5-10pm Mon; noon-3pm, 5-10.30pm Tue-Fri; 11am-3pm, 5-11pm Sat; 11am-3pm, 5-10pm Sun.* **Map** *p181 U4* **2**

This bar-restaurant lies in a railway arch, low lit in the evenings, with a cathedral-like vaulted ceiling the colour of Carrara marble and a spacious courtyard that faces the traffic-free street. The wine list is intimidatingly vast, but staff are on hand to help you navigate it, plus there's a pleasing choice of cocktails. Abundant beverages aside, there's a simple but excellent menu of Italian dishes using the best of British produce.

Satan's Whiskers

343 Cambridge Heath Road, E2 9RA (020 7739 8362). Bethnal Green tube/Overground or Cambridge Heath Overground. **Open** *5pm-midnight daily.* **Map** *p181 U4* **3**

Satan's Whiskers might sound like a Captain Haddock curse, but it refers to a classic cocktail containing gin, orange and vermouth topped with Grand Marnier and orange bitters. It's a staple on the otherwise daily changing menu here, along with seductive alternatives – this tiny bar was set up by three bartenders, and they really know their stuff. Leather booths, an illuminated ice box and taxidermy for decor all add to the atmosphere.

Shops & services

Once a shabby Shoreditch cut-through, **Redchurch Street** has become a strong contender for London's best shopping street. Come here for civilised, independent-minded shopping – driven by art and fashion. Highlights include classic menswear at **Sunspel** (no.7) and **Hostem** (no.41), eminently wearable fashion at **Modern Society** (no.33), Aussie beauty products at **Aesop** (no.44), up-dos and manicures at the **Painted Lady** (no.65) and covetable home essentials at **Labour & Wait** (no.85).

❤ Broadway Market

Broadway Market, E8 4QL (broadwaymarket.co.uk). London Fields Overground or bus 236, 394. **Open** *9am-5pm Sat.* **Map** *p181 U4* ❶ *Market*
The coolest and most ridiculous of east London's young trendies can be found at this endearing market, where fruit-and-veg sellers trade alongside vintage clothes 'specialists'. It's as busy as a beehive, but the slew of cafés, pubs, restaurants and boutiques along the street – plus the market itself, plus the nearby Netil Market for further street food, plus Saturday's School Yard Market, plus the overspill of drunks and slumming may-do-wells on London Fields when there's even a whiff of sunshine – is a fine education in new London.

❤ Columbia Road Market

Columbia Road, E2 7RG (www.columbiaroad.info). Hoxton Overground or Bethnal Green tube/Overground. **Open** *8am-3.30pm Sun.* **Map** *p181 T4* ❷ *Market*
On Sunday mornings, this unassuming East End street is transformed into a delightful swathe of fabulous plant life and the air is fragrant with blooms and the shouts of old-school Cockney stallholders (most offering deals for 'a fiver'). It's worth shopping

Old Spitalfields Market p186

around; don't be afraid to barter, and prepare for it to get very busy. The market is popular with both locals and tourists; during the midday rush it is rammed with people elbowing their way to that perfect pot plant. If you can't bear crowds or just want to guarantee the pick of the crop, arrive when the market opens. Or wait till after 2pm to pick up bargains. When you've bought your blooms, head behind the stalls and down side streets to find cute cafés, independent restaurants, delis, shops, antique dealers, vintage stalls and small galleries, many of which follow the market's opening hours.

House of Hackney
131 Shoreditch High Street, E1 6JE (020 7739 3901, www. houseofhackney.com). Old Street tube/rail or Shoreditch High Street Overground. **Open** *10.30am-7pm Thur-Sat; 11am-5pm Sun.* **Map** *p181 S5* **3** *Homewares*
House of Hackney has the makings of a new Liberty (*see p123*): buy your future design classics now, we say. This is one of the most gorgeous retail establishments in London

– bedecked in the deliberately over-the-top juxtapositions of print-on-print-on-print that have made the brand's name, and with the entrance full of flowers. Upstairs, you'll find rolls of gorgeous paper, fabric, trays, mugs, fashion and collaborative designs with brands such as Puma; downstairs are generously proportioned sofas and plump armchairs in more-is-more combinations of print and texture.

Old Spitalfields Market
Brushfield Street, E1 6AA (oldspitalfieldsmarket.com). Liverpool Street tube/Overground/ rail or Shoreditch High Street Overground. **Open** *10am-8pm Mon-Fri; 10am-6pm Sat; 10am-5pm Sun. Shop opening hours vary.* **Map** *p181 S6* **4** *Market*
Old Spitalfields Market is one of east London's busiest shopping hubs. Built in the late 1800s, the market hall was restored and refurbished in the early 2000s and further revamped by Foster + Partners in 2017. Edging the giant covered space are numerous permanent boutiques from big brands such as Mac, Hackett, Dr

EartH

Martens and Chanel, but it's the heart of the market that's the most exciting. Here you'll find two concourses packed with traders selling arts, crafts, clothing and knick-knacks seven days a week. There's an antiques market every Thursday for vintage maps, books, furniture, fashion and collectibles, and a vinyl market twice a month. These days no London market is complete without a serious food offering: at Spitalfields it comes courtesy of The Kitchens (*see p183*).

Rough Trade East

Dray Walk, Old Truman Brewery, 91 Brick Lane, E1 6QL (020 7392 7788, www.roughtrade. com). Shoreditch High Street Overground. **Open** *9am-9pm Mon-Thur; 9am-8pm Fri; 10am-8pm Sat; 11am-7pm Sun.* **Map** *p181 T6* ❺ *Music*

The indie music label Rough Trade – perhaps most famous for signing the Smiths in the early 1980s – set up this 5,000sq ft (465sq m) record store, café and gig space in the noughties when the death of music shops in the face of internet price-cutting was widely accepted as

inevitable. Perversely, Rough Trade instead offered a physical space where music-lovers could browse a dizzying range of vinyl and CDs, spanning punk, indie, dub, soul, electronica and more, providing them with 16 listening posts and a stage for live sets. Now its triumph seems like it was always certain.

Entertainment

♥ Dalston Superstore

117 Kingsland High Street, E8 2PB (020 7254 2273, dalstonsuperstore. com). Dalston Kingsland Overground. **Open** *5pm-2am Mon; noon-2am Tue-Thur; noon-3am Fri, Sat; 10am-2am Sun.* **Admission** *varies.* **Map** *p181 S4* ❶ *Club*

This Kingsland High Street hangout is a bit of a face on the east London party scene. In true Dalston style it's home to all sorts: popular with a large and diverse LGBT crowd, but welcoming to everyone. A café during the day, at night you can expect queues for a hugely impressive roster of guest DJs spinning a typically east London mix of of pop and dance tunes to a floor that's pitch-black and intense. Regular dates, such as Saturday and Sunday's Disco Brunch (soul, disco and funk with all-day breakfast and cocktails), are well worth putting in the diary. Upstairs, alt-cabaret drag stars whip revellers into shape with sharp one-liners.

♥ EartH

11-17 Stoke Newington Road, N16 8BH (020 7422 7505, earthackney.co.uk). Dalston Kingsland Overground. **Open** *varies.* **Admission** *varies.* **Map** *p181 S4* ❷ *Music*

Launched in 2018, this self-styled 'multi-arts space for the 21st century' is an ambitious restoration of the formerly derelict Savoy Cinema. Its slightly ungainly name is short

for 'Evolutionary Arts Hackney', but so far the programming is trendy and accessible rather than too highfalutin. There are two atmospheric event spaces – the seated upstairs theatre and downstairs concert hall, which is standing only – and they're already proving a popular stop-off for discerning artists. Indie heroes Lambchop and soul siren Andreya Triana played EartH in 2019, while pop queens Little Mix launched their LM5 album here in late 2018.

Oval Space

29-32 The Oval, E2 9DT (020 7183 4422, www.ovalspace.co.uk). Bethnal Green tube/Overground or Cambridge Heath Overground. **Open** *varies.* **Admission** *varies.* **Map** *p181 U4* **3** *Club*

Located at the base of a disused gasworks off Hackney Road, this hangar-style space is one of the most impressive and exciting recent additions to London's nightlife scene. A mix of ace one-off parties and regular events mark Oval Space out: DJs regularly play spacey techno, twisted electronica, alt hip hop and glitchy house, while on-point events include Secretsundaze. Opposite is the more intimate gig and DJ venue, the **Pickle Factory** (www.thepicklefactory.co.uk).

♥ Village Underground

54 Holywell Lane, EC2A 3PQ (020 7422 7505, www.villageunderground.co.uk). Shoreditch High Street Overground. **Open** *varies.* **Admission** *varies.* **Map** *p181 S5* **4** *Club*

You can't miss Village Underground: four graffiti-covered tube carriages are perched on its roof. These and a series of shipping containers accommodate artists, writers, designers, film-makers and musicians, while a Victorian warehouse space hosts exhibitions, concerts, plays, live art and club nights.

♥ XOYO

32-37 Cowper Street, EC2A 4AP (020 7608 2878, xoyo.co.uk). Old Street tube/rail. **Open** *varies.* **Admission** *varies.* **Map** *p181 R5* **5** *Club*

There's live music during the week at this 800-capacity venue, but XOYO is first and foremost a club. The former printworks is a bare concrete shell, defiantly taking the 'chic' out of 'shabby chic', but the open space means the atmosphere is always buzzing, as the only place to escape immersion in the music is the small smoking courtyard outside. The Victorian loft-style space provides effortlessly cool programming and high-profile DJs, while the longer residencies – including drum-and-bass legend Andy C – is the best kind of old-school.

Docklands & beyond

Sights & museums

Museum of London Docklands

No.1 Warehouse, West India Quay, Hertsmere Road, E14 4AL (020 7001 9844, www.museumoflondon.org.uk/museum-london-docklands). Canary Wharf tube/DLR or West India Quay DLR. **Open** *10am-6pm daily.* **Admission** *free. Temporary exhibitions vary.*

Housed in a 19th-century warehouse (itself a Grade I-listed building), this museum explores the complex history of London's docklands and the river over two millennia. Displays spreading over three storeys take you from the arrival of the Romans all the way to the docks' 1980s closure and the area's subsequent redevelopment. The Docklands at War section is very moving, while the haunting

London, Sugar and Slavery exhibition explores the dark side of London's rise as a centre for finance and commerce. You can also walk through full-scale mock-ups of a quayside and a dingy riverfront alley. Temporary exhibitions are set up on the ground floor, where you'll also find a café and a docks-themed play area. Just like its elder sibling, the Museum of London (*see p159*), the MoLD has a great programme of special events.

Emirates Air Line

North terminal *27 Western Gateway, E16 4FA. Royal Victoria DLR.*
South terminal *Edmund Halley Way, SE10 0FR (tfl.gov.uk/modes/emirates-air-line). North Greenwich tube.*
Open *7am-9pm Mon-Thur; 7am-11pm Fri; 8am-11pm Sat; 9am-9pm Sun.* **Tickets** *£4.50 single; £2.30 reductions, free under-5s.*

Arguments for a cable car across the Thames as a solution to any of London's many transport problems are, at best, moot, but its value as a tourist thrill is huge. The comfy pods zoom 295ft (465sq m) up elegant stanchions at a gratifying pace. Suddenly there are brilliant views of the expanses of water that make up the Royal Docks, the ships on the Thames, Docklands and the Thames Barrier. Good fun and good value – but note that the cable car may not run in high winds.

♥ Queen Elizabeth Olympic Park

www.queenelizabetholympicpark.co.uk. Stratford tube/Overground/rail/DLR, Hackney Wick Overground

The site of London's 2012 Olympic Games, the park comprises immaculate landscaping to the north, laced by a network of paths and waterways. By the Timber Lodge café are the Tumbling Bay

Emirates Air Line

ArcelorMittal Orbit *p190*

Playground and the **Lee Valley VeloPark** (www.visitleevalley.org.uk) with a velodrome, BMX track and five miles of mountain bike trails. The 7,500-seat **Copper Box Arena** (copperboxarena.org.uk) is now a flexible indoor venue for sports and concerts. In the southern part of the park are the handsome Zaha Hadid-designed **Aquatics Centre** (www.londonaquaticscentre.org) and the landmark **ArcelorMittal Orbit** (0333 800 8099, arcelormittalorbit.com). The Orbit was designed by sculptor Anish Kapoor and engineer Cecil Balmond, with the addition of a spiral slide by Belgian artist Carsten Höller in 2016. At 274ft, this is the world's longest and tallest tunnel slide, taking a dozen turns around the Orbit in 40 seconds. The retooled Olympic Stadium, renamed **London Stadium**, is the home ground of West Ham Football Club, but it continues to host other major sporting events.

Restaurants

Giant Robot £-££

Crossrail Place, Canary Wharf, E14 5AR (020 7719 1325, ww.streetfeast.com). Canary Wharf tube/DLR. **Open** *11am-10pm Mon, Tue; 11am-11pm Wed; 11am-midnight Thur-Sat. Street food*

A big shiny box on a low-rise Canary Wharf rooftop, Giant Robot is from the Street Feast team, also responsible for hip outdoor food hangouts Dinerama and Model Market. It looks sort of like a boat. Or something with a massive quiff. Inside, it's like a cross between an airport departure lounge and a nightclub. Concrete floors, retro furnishings, groovy tunes. Plus four street food vendors, two bars and a coffee shack. Outside, there's access to the wharf's glorious 'rooftopia'. You've got it: a landscaped rainforest on a roof. It's all under a translucent, wood-framed dome, meaning shelter from the rain, but they've taken lots of panels out, so there's breeze and birds, too. This is the best eating option in Docklands by a mile.

Entertainment

O2 Arena & IndigO2

Peninsula Square, North Greenwich, SE10 0DX (information 020 8463 2000, tickets 020 3481 5503, www.theo2.co.uk). North Greenwich tube. **Box office** *In person noon-7pm daily. By phone 9am-7pm Mon-Fri; 10am-6pm Sat, Sun.* **Tickets** *£15-£70. Music & sport*

The national embarrassment that was the Millennium Dome has been transformed into the city's de facto home of the mega-gig. This 20,000-seater has outstanding sound, unobstructed sightlines and the potential for artists to perform 'in the round'. Shows from even the world's biggest acts (U2, Beyoncé, the reformed Led Zep, the mostly reformed Monty Python) don't feel too far away, and the venue seems to handle music, comedy and even sport (international tennis, boxing, basketball) with equal aplomb.

On the same site, IndigO2 is the Arena's little sister – but 'little' only by comparison. It has an impressive capacity of 2,350, arranged as part-standing room, part-amphitheatre seating and, sometimes, part-table seating. IndigO2's niche roster of MOR (middle-of-the-road) acts is dominated by soul, funk, pop-jazz and old pop acts, but it does also host after-show parties for headliners from the Arena.

London Essentials

British Museum *p147*

Accommodation

London continues to be a magnet for international hoteliers as well as their guests. Whether Brexit cools their ardour remains to be seen, but so far the pace of deluxe openings has hardly slowed, with a host of major new establishments opening their doors in Bloomsbury, the City and Bankside in 2019. The price of rooms in London is pretty shocking, but it's not all top-dollar activity. The pioneering **Hoxton** has an even better sister-hotel – the **Hoxton Holborn** – and the excellent Dutch **citizenM** chain is expanding its properties over here. **Qbic** and the **Z** hotels are other relative favourites for visitors on a budget.

Staying in London

Always research the location before you part with your money. Greater London is pretty huge and few people have a vision of their holiday that involves spending an hour on public transport to get to the heart of things. That said, there's no need to focus exclusively on the **West End**. Get somewhere to stay on the **South Bank** and you certainly won't regret it, and the **City** has plenty of business hotels offering great deals, particularly at weekends. **East London** retains some of its art-and-fashion coolness and is ideal if you're planning on some hard nights of clubbing. Or, if you can afford it, a stay in one of the grand old **Mayfair** hotels such as **Claridges** (www.claridges. co.uk) or the **Dorchester**

In the know
Price categories

Our price categories are based on hotels' standard prices (not including seasonal offers or discounts) for one night in a double room with en suite shower/bath.

Luxury	£350+
Expensive	£250-£350
Moderate	£130-£250
Budget	up to £130

(www.dorchestercollection.com) is a holiday without even having to step out of the door.

Money matters

As a rule, it's best to book as far ahead as possible, and always try the hotel's own website first: many offer special online deals; pretty much every business hotel will offer steep reductions for a Sunday night stay. Be aware that a few hotels – particularly at the top of the price range – don't include VAT (a 20 per cent sales tax) in the rates they quote. And watch out for added extras. Some hotels charge for Wi-Fi, some do not. Few central hotels offer parking and those that do charge steeply for it. It's also worth looking at hotel booking websites such as **uk.hotels.com**. And, if you are staying for longer than a weekend, or you fancy staying in one of the thriving neighbourhoods outside central London, then the myriad rental rooms and apartments offered by www.airbnb.co.uk and homeaway.co.uk are worth a look. For a more curated selection, check out www.plumguide.com, which cherry picks the top one per cent of holiday rental properties in the capital.

Luxury
The Beaumont
Brown Hart Gardens, Mayfair, W1K 6TF (020 7499 1001, www.thebeaumont.com). Bond Street tube. **Map** *p114 H7.*
Oddly, the Grade II-listed façade is the least impressive part of this hotel, set in the vast 1926 garage where Selfridges' shoppers used to get their jalopies tuned up. It is in the painstakingly rebuilt interiors that this art deco fantasia sings. There's smooth service and a lovely private bar/drawing room off the foyer. The staff gets the marriage of glamorous formality and approachability just right, and the owners' personal travel bugbears have created some really thoughtful touches, from the sliding screens that isolate beds from bathrooms to the free soft drinks, movies and shoeshines.

Towering over the handsome square in front of the Beaumont is the Antony Gormley-designed **ROOM**: on the outside it's a striking Cubist-influenced sculpture; on the inside it's a two-storey suite in immaculate art deco style, leading through to a low-lit, almost womb-like bedroom right inside the sculpture.

The Mandrake
20-21 Newman Street, Fitzrovia, W1T 1PG (020 3146 7770, www.themandrake.com). Tottenham Court Road tube. **Map** *p114 K6.*
Inspired by the plant it's named after and converted from a RIBA-winning building in Fitzrovia, this OTT hotel was an instant hit with the fashion crowd when it opened in 2017. And no

wonder: its dark, intimate and opulent styling is a feast for the senses: there are sumptuous and quirky elements, including a carefully curated private art collection throughout. The 30-plus bedrooms, set over four floors, are little works of art in their own right, featuring bespoke chandeliers, vintage furniture and contemporary trappings. They surround a beautiful hidden courtyard, dripping with jasmine and passion flower. Dining comes courtesy of Yopo, an Amazonian-inspired restaurant that offers modern European dishes with an exotic twist.

The Ned

27 Poultry, the City, EC2R 8AJ (020 3828 2000, www.thened.com). Bank tube. **Map** *p156 Q7.*

This five-star hotel and members' club is a collaboration between the Soho House Group and the Sydell Group (a US business behind the NoMad in New York). Together they have lovingly refurbished the Grade I-listed former Midland Bank building in the City to the tune of £200 million to create a seriously swanky spot that has moneyed hipsters swooning. The vast and opulent ground-floor banking hall hosts nine bars and restaurants. Above are 250 bedrooms and a members' area called Ned's Club that comprises a rooftop pool, gym, spa, hammam and late-night lounge bar. Phew! The accommodation ranges from fairly modest 'Cosy' rooms and 'Crash Pads' to more luxurious 'Heritage' rooms that feature French-polished walnut panelling, four-poster beds and other nods to 1920s opulence. It's worth noting that not all members' areas are open to guests in the cheaper rooms. And the name? The original building was designed by Sir Edwin Lutyens, known to his friends as 'Ned'.

Sea Containers London

20 Upper Ground, South Bank, SE1 9PD (020 3747 1000, www.seacontainerslondon.com). Blackfriars tube/rail. **Map** *p71 O8.*

Location's everything here: this hotel is right on the Thames, with the views on the bank side of the building among the best in London – low enough to feel part of the city, high enough to feel exclusive. The rooms are nicely furnished by Tom Dixon in a kind of postmodern deco style, minimalist without leaving you feeling the sharp edges. Public spaces are terrific and playfully ship-themed (not least the prow that encases the reception desks), and there are plenty of areas for meetings. The ground-floor cocktail bar, Lyaness (previously the world-famous Dandelyan), is still run by master mixologist Ryan Chetiyawardana, so expect the unexpected. There's a less accomplished restaurant on the ground floor, as well as a blingier bar in a glass cube on the roof (the 12th Knot, closed Mon, Sun), a basement spa and a cosy Curzon cinema.

Shangri-La at the Shard

31 St Thomas Street, Southwark, SE1 9QU (020 7234 8000, www.the-shard.com/shangri-la). London Bridge tube/rail. **Map** *p71 R9.*

The Shangri-La is unusual in many ways. The hotel proper starts on floor 35 with a spacious foyer and restaurant. The building's pyramid shape means every room is different, with most floor space and hence the poshest suites on 36 and 37, not at the top. And the rooms are priced by view: the most expensive look north, offering 180º Thames vistas. The views are amazing, as you'd expect: absorbing as dusk falls and the city lights come on, especially from the lobby and restaurant. The Skypool, fitness room and bar feel a bit remote, way up on floor 52. The decor is cosmopolitan Asian neutral, with some unimpressive bits of design offset by imaginative touches (binoculars for you to enjoy the view, torches to ease jetlagged room navigation in bedside drawers).

Expensive

Zetter Townhouse (49-50 St John's Square, EC1V 4JJ, 020 7324 4444, www.thezettertownhouse.com/clerkenwell) is a great option in Clerkenwell.

Boundary

2-4 Boundary Street, Shoreditch, E2 7DD (020 7729 1051, boundary.london). Liverpool Street tube/Overground/rail or Shoreditch High Street Overground. **Map** *p181 S5.*

Design mogul Sir Terence Conran's Boundary Project warehouse conversion was a labour of love. Its restaurants – which include ground-floor café Albion; Wilder, an elegant restaurant serving purely British ingredients; and a rooftop bar – are high-quality relaxed places, and all 17 bedrooms are beautifully designed. Each has a handmade bed, but all are otherwise individually furnished with classic pieces and original art. The five studios, lofts and suites range in style from the bright and sea-salt fresh Beach to modern Chinoiserie by Sir David Tang. The remaining bedrooms (the slightly larger corner bedrooms have windows along both external walls) are themed by design style: Mies van der Rohe, Eames, Shaker.

The Curtain

45 Curtain Road, Shoreditch, EC2A 3PT (020 3146 4545, thecurtain.com). Old Street tube/rail. Shoreditch High Street Overground. **Map** *p181 S5.*

Curtain's cool Manhattan-style surroundings are perfectly placed a stroll away from both Brick Lane and Hoxton Square. Red brick and glass predominate, creating a warehouse-meets-luxury feel. Overnighters won't want to miss the in-house Red Rooster restaurant (top-notch, Obama-approved, Southern-fried everything) before nipping down to the basement club (Skepta's been) or taking in the rooftop pool and terrace. Bedrooms have quality furnishings, gorgeous bathrooms (with rain showers) and fully stocked minibars.

Great Northern Hotel

King's Cross St Pancras Station, Pancras Road, King's Cross, N1C 4TB (020 3388 0800, gnhlondon.com). King's Cross St Pancras tube/rail.

Designed by Lewis Cubitt, the city's first railway hotel opened in 1854, part of the Victorian railway explosion. It has had plenty of rough times since then, not least the 12 years it was dark, but almost £40 million of renovation has recreated the place as a classic. The furniture is by artisans and, in many cases, bespoke: witness the Couchette rooms, each with a double bed snugly fitted into the window to playfully echo sleeper carriages; the neatly upholstered bedside cabinets; or the ceiling lights raised and lowered by fabulously steampunk pulleys. You're not expected to suffer the privations of a Victorian traveller, though: fast Wi-Fi, film and music libraries on the large TV, Egyptian cotton sheets and walk-in showers are all standard. There's no room service but each floor has a simply charming pantry, full of jars of vintage sweets, a stand of fresh cakes, tea and coffee, newspapers and books – even a USB printer. There's also Plum + Spilt Milk, a grand restaurant with Martini lounge on the first floor, while the busy ground-floor GNH Bar has direct access to King's Cross station.

London Edition

10 Berners Street, Fitzrovia, W1T 3NP (020 7781 0000, www.editionhotels. com/london). Oxford Circus or Tottenham Court Road tube. **Map** *p114 K6.*

The London Edition makes a big impact as you walk into its grand hall of a lobby, complete with double-height rococo ceilings, floor-to-ceiling windows and marble pillars. And there's more to the space: it's the setting for the lobby bar, with an eclectic mix of comfortable, snazzy seating – sofas with faux-fur throws and wing-backed chairs – plus a snooker table, a blackened steel bar, a real fire and a colossal silver egg-shaped object hanging where you might expect a chandelier. Off on one side is the equally opulent Berners Tavern, where Jason Atherton is executive chef. With banquette seating and many paintings, it has the vibe of a grand café and a brasserie-style menu to match. Hidden away at the back of the public area is the clubby, wood-panelled Punch Room bar, where the speciality is – you've guessed it – punch. Bedrooms are a contrast: akin to lodges or dachas, with matte oak floors, wood-panelled walls and more faux-fur throws tossed on luxurious beds. Larger rooms come with sofas, some have large furnished terraces, and all have rainforest showers, Le Labo toiletries (with the hotel's woody signature scent) and iPod docks.

Rookery

12 Peter's Lane, Cowcross Street, Clerkenwell, EC1M 6DS (020 7336 0931, www.rookeryhotel.com). Farringdon tube/rail. **Map** *p156 P6.*

The Rookery has long been something of a celebrity hideaway deep in the heart of Clerkenwell; its front door is satisfyingly hard to find. When Fabric (*see p166*) devotees are about the front rooms can be noisy, but the place is otherwise as creakily calm as a country manor. Once inside, guests enjoy an atmospheric warren of rooms, each individually decorated in the style of a Georgian townhouse: huge clawfoot baths, elegant four-posters, antique desks, old paintings and brass shower fittings. While the decor is dialled to 18th-century glamour, modernity is definitely not forgotten. There's an honesty bar in the bright and airy drawing room at the back, which opens on to a sweet little patio.

W London Leicester Square

10 Wardour Street, Leicester Square, W1D 6QF (020 7758 1000, www. marriott.co.uk/hotels/travel/lonhw-w-london-leicester-square). Leicester Square tube. **Map** *p114 L8.*

Where the old Swiss Centre used to be in the north-west corner of Leicester Square is the UK's first W Hotel, the entire building veiled in translucent glass that is lit in different colours through the day. The brand made its name with hip hotels around the world that offer glamorous bars, upmarket food and functional but spacious rooms. The London W is no exception: the

Perception Bar is a large nightclub/bar space with possibly the largest glitterball in town, offering classy cocktails, afternoon tea and a Sunday brunch party. There's also a branch of the deathlessly popular concept restaurant Burger & Lobster. The rooms – across ten storeys – are well equipped, with their own munchie boxes. FIT (the hotel's state-of-the-art fitness facility), placed next to the pale and serene Away Spa on the sixth floor, offers fine views over Soho. Oh, and there's a private 3D cinema.

Moderate

Hoxton Holborn

199-206 High Holborn, Holborn, WC1V 7BD (020 7661 3000, thehoxton.com). Holborn tube. **Map** *p145 M6.*

Shoebox, Snug, Cosy and Roomy. That's the choice you get when you stay at the Hoxton's trendy Holborn outpost, but who cares about room size when you're just about as close to the centre of London as it's possible to be. In truth, the rooms are so well designed you barely notice their size. Clever use of mirrors helps to enlarge the space, reflecting the rooms' dark walls, soft lighting and casually hip vibe. Add to that a snazzy TV and a lovely walk-in shower. The West End's bars and restaurants are right on your doorstep but the hotel bar, decked out in 1970s furniture, does a mean negroni to get you started.

Karma Sanctum Soho

20 Warwick Street, Soho, W1B 5NF (020 7292 6100, www.sanctumsoho.com). Oxford Circus or Piccadilly Circus tube. **Map** *p114 K8.*

In a former MI5 research building, Sanctum is Soho-club cool with its dark colours, bling room handles and deco lamps, sexed up with a handful of rotating beds and a no-questions-asked policy. The rooms follow one of four colour schemes, broadly deco or powder-puff boudoir in style, with plenty of mirrors and an unspeakable number of TV channels. The residents-only, 24hr-means-24hr bar is small but funky, opening on to a two-level terrace outside, which is topped off with a multi-person jacuzzi. The fun continues with a guitar-tuning service at reception, a smoothly run and darkly handsome bar-restaurant, louche art in each room and a screening room for hire downstairs.

The Pilgrm

25 London Street, Paddington, W2 1HH (thepilgrm.com). Paddington tube/rail.
Hate checking in? You'll love the Pilgrm. With this affordable (by London standards) 73-room hotel, Jason Catifeoglou – formerly of the Zetter group – has done away with reception, minibars and phones to create a hotel that has a personal feel and features super-fast Wi-Fi, Marshall speakers, 24-hour pantries and natural toiletries. (Plastics begone, we're using soap on a rope!) He has sensitively retained and restored original Victorian fixtures and fittings while adding interesting reclaimed ones to create a unique space that's a real winner. Head chef Sara Lewis (formerly of Grain Store) works wonders in the Lounge.

La Suite West

41-51 Inverness Terrace, Bayswater, W2 3JN (020 7313 8484, www.lasuitewest. com). Bayswater or Queensway tube.
A typical row of west London townhouses on the outside, La Suite has been transformed on the inside by designer Anouska Hempel, with sleek lines and a black and white palette. A discreet side entrance leads into a long, minimalist reception area with an open fire and a zen-like feel. An Asian influence persists in the rooms, with slatted sliding screens for windows, wardrobe and bathrooms helping to make good use of space (which is limited in the cheaper rooms). Thoughtfully designed white marble bathrooms, with rainforest shower and bath, give a feeling of luxury despite not being huge. The large terrace running along the front of the building, with trees planted for an arbour-like effect,

is a big summer asset for drinks, lunch or dinner, and the vegan Café Forty One is an unusual take on hotel dining. A great hotel for this price range. Highly recommended.

Shoreditch House

Ebor Street, Shoreditch, E1 6AW (020 7739 5040, www.shoreditchhouse.com). Shoreditch High Street Overground. Map p181 U5.
Shoreditch House perfectly catches the local atmosphere, with its unfussy slightly retro design. The rooms are a bit like urban beach huts, with pastel-coloured tongue-and-groove shutters and swing doors to the en suite showers. They feel fresh, bright and comfortable, even though they're furnished with little more than a bed, an old-fashioned phone and DAB radio, and a big, solid dresser (minibar, hairdryer and treats within, TV on top). There's the Cowshed Spa on the ground floor, plus guests get access to the fine eating, drinking and fitness facilities (including a gym and an excellent rooftop pool) in the members' club next door. Everything's put together with a light touch, from the 'Borrow Me' bookshelf by the lifts (umbrellas, boardgames) to the room grades: Tiny (from just £125), Small or Small+ (with little rooftop balconies from which to survey the horizon).

Zetter Hotel

St John's Square, 86-88 Clerkenwell Road, Clerkenwell, EC1M 5RJ (020 7324 4567, www.thezetter.com). Farringdon tube/rail. Map p156 P5.
Zetter is a fun, laid-back, modern hotel with some interesting design notes. There's a refreshing lack of attitude and a forward-looking approach, with friendly staff and firm eco-credentials (such as free Brompton bikes for guests' use). The rooms, stacked up on five galleried storeys around an impressive atrium, look into an intimate and recently refreshed bar area. They are smoothly functional, but cosied up with choice home comforts such as hot-water bottles and old Penguin paperbacks, as well as having walk-in showers with

REN smellies. The downstairs is home to Club Zetter, while the fabulous sister-hotel **Zetter Townhouse**, in a historic building just across the square, has a fantastic cocktail bar with a hip vintage feel (*see* p166).

Budget

citizenM London Bankside

20 Lavington Street, Southwark, SE1 0NZ (020 3519 1680, www.citizenm. com). Southwark tube. **Map** p71 P9.
This casually stylish new build is a superbly well-designed – and well-located – addition to London's affordably chic hotels. The ground floor is a slick yet cosy café-bar and reception area: self check-in, but with staff on hand to help and, where better rooms are available, offer upgrades. The rooms themselves are tiny but well thought through: there are blackout blinds, drench showers with removable sideheads, storage under the bed and free movies. The rooms are also fun: those blinds are automatic, controlled – as are the movies, air-con and funky coloured lighting – from a touch-sensitive tablet. **Other locations** 6 Holywell Lane, Shoreditch, EC2A 3ET; 40 Trinity Square, Tower Hill, EC3N 4DJ.

Dictionary Hostel

10-20 Kingsland Road, Shoreditch, E2 8DA (020 7613 2784, thedictionary hostel.com/en). Old Street tube/rail or Shoreditch High Street Overground. **Map** p181 S4.
Club kids, you've found your home: right at the axis of Kingsland Road and Old Street and so walking – or crawling – distance from Hoxton's best dance spots. There's a bar downstairs, Translate, and also a laundrette, a café, a cute, plant-covered interior courtyard and an intimate roof terrace. There are dorm beds and private rooms starting at £16 (with TVs, kettle and coffee). Jam-jar lighting, swings in the dorms and fairy-lit communal areas are quirky touches, which make for an enjoyable

stay. Breakfast is free and includes the highly prized bagels from nearby Brick Lane.

Qbic London City Hotel

42 Adler Street, Whitechapel, E1 1EE (020 3021 3300, qbichotels.com/london-city). Aldgate East or Whitechapel tube.
The Dutch invasion of stylish budget hotels continues with this Brick Lane offering, created by the incredibly rapid fit-out of a former office building using modular 'Cubi' bedrooms. Downstairs, Motley is a natty social space offering a low food miles, veggie-forward menu, with a selection of 'Waste not' dishes, craft beers and cocktails. The rooms are sold at four levels – starting at £69 a night for no view. Prices are pegged by keeping down the number of staff, which means self check-in and no cash accepted – even vending machines are card only. Still, the essentials are covered: TVs in each room, Wi-Fi throughout and free snack breakfast (or £15 for a continental). The location is gritty but great: minutes from Brick Lane.

Z Hotel Soho

17 Moor Street, Soho, W1D 5AP (3551 3701, www.thezhotels.com/soho). Leicester Square tube. **Map** p114 L7.
For the money, the Z is an absolute bargain. First, the location is superb: it really means Soho, not a short bus-ride away – the breakfast room/bar exits on to Old Compton Street. Then there's the hotel itself, which is surprisingly chic – especially the unexpected interior courtyard – and very cheerfully run, down to free wine and nibbles of an evening. The rooms are quite handsome, and have everything you need, from a little desk to free Wi-Fi, but not much more. Expect beds (perhaps a bit short for anyone over six-foot tall) to take up most of the room. A great little hotel – in both senses. **Other locations** throughout the city; see the website for details.

Getting Around

ARRIVING & LEAVING

By air

Gatwick Airport *0344 892 0322, www. gatwickairport.com. About 30 miles south of London, off the M23.*
The quickest link to central London is the **Gatwick Express train** (0345 850 1530, www.gatwickexpress.com) to Victoria; it takes 30mins and runs every 15mins 5am-11.30pm daily. Tickets cost £19.90 single or £37.80 for an open return.

Southern (0345 127 2920, www. southernrailway.com) also runs a rail service between Gatwick and Victoria, every 5-10mins (hourly 2-4am and every 15-30mins midnight-2am, 4-6am). It takes about 35mins, and costs from £16.70 for a single, £16.80 for a day return (after 9.30am) and £33.40 for an open return.

Thameslink Great Northern (www. thameslinkrailway.com), calling at London stations including St Pancras International and City Thameslink, costs from £16.70 single and from £33.40 for an open return.

For transfers by coach, **National Express** (0871 781 8171, www. nationalexpress.com) runs services every 30mins daily to Victoria from both terminals, from £6 single, £12 return, taking 95mins.

A **taxi** to the centre costs from £90 and takes a bit over an hour.

Heathrow Airport *0844 335 1801, www.heathrow.com. About 15 miles west of London, off the M4.*
The **Heathrow Express** train (0845 600 1515, www.heathrowexpress. co.uk) runs to Paddington every 15mins (5.12am-11.42pm daily) and takes 15-20mins. Tickets cost £22-£25 single and £37 return.

The journey by **tube** is longer but cheaper. The 50-60min Piccadilly line ride into central London costs £6 one way. Trains run every few minutes from 5.12am to 11.45pm Mon-Fri (3.17am-11.38pm Sat, Sun).

TfL Rail (0343 222 1234, tfl.gov.uk) trains also run to central London (same fares as the Tube). This service is due to become integrated with the new Elizabeth Line when it opens in late 2021 (*see p202* Crossrail).

National Express (0871 781 8171, www.nationalexpress.com) runs daily coach services to London Victoria (35-60mins, 4.20am-10.05pm daily), leaving Heathrow Central bus terminal every 20-30mins. It's £8 for a single or £16 for a return.

A **taxi** into town will cost £45-£70 and take 30-60mins.

London City Airport *020 7646 0088, www.londoncityairport.com. About 9 miles east of central London.*
The **Docklands Light Railway** (DLR) includes a stop for London City Airport and runs every 8-15mins. The journey to Bank station in the City takes around 20mins, and trains run 5.37am-12.17am Mon-Sat, 7.07am-11.17pm Sun. Tickets cost £4.90; £2.40 11-15s.

A **taxi** costs around £40 to central London.

Luton Airport *01582 405100, www. london-luton.co.uk. About 30 miles north of London, J10 off the M1.*
A 10min shuttle bus (£2.40/under 15s free) ride links the airport to Luton Airport Parkway station, from which **Thameslink Great Northern trains** depart for stations including St Pancras International and City Thameslink, 35-45mins. Trains leave every 15mins (hourly through the night) and cost £17.40 one-way, £19.50 return.

By coach, the Luton to Victoria journey takes 60-90mins. **Green Line** (0344 801 7261, www.greenline.co.uk)

runs a 24hr service. Tickets are £11.50 single, £17.50 return.

A **taxi** to London costs from £80.

Stansted Airport *0808 169 7031, www. stanstedairport.com. About 35 miles north-east of London, J8 off the M11.* The **Stansted Express** train, www. stanstedexpress.com) runs to and from Liverpool Street Station; taking 40-45mins and leaving every 15 mins. Tickets from £18.90 single, £29.90 return.

National Express (0871 781 8171, www.nationalexpress.com) is one of several coach services running to Victoria Coach Station; the journey takes 1hr 45mins and coaches roughly every 20mins (24hrs daily). A single is £10, an open return is £20.

A **taxi** into the centre of London costs from £60.

By coach

Coaches run by **National Express** (0871 781 8171, www.nationalexpress.com) and **Eurolines** (0871 781 8177, www. eurolines.co.uk) arrive at **Victoria Coach Station** (164 Buckingham Palace Road, SW1W 9TP, 0343 222 1234, tfl.gov. uk), a good 10min walk from Victoria tube station. This is also the destination for coaches to and from Europe.

By rail

Trains from mainland Europe run by **Eurostar** (0343 218 6186, www.eurostar. com) arrive at **St Pancras International** (Pancras Road, Euston Road, N1C 4QP, 020 7843 7688, www.stpancras.com).

PUBLIC TRANSPORT

Timetables and other travel information are provided by **Transport for London** (0343 222 1234, tfl.gov.uk).

Travel Information Centres
These offer help with the Tube, buses and DLR. Call 0343 222 1234 for more information.

Euston *opposite Platform 8.* **Open** *8am-8pm daily.*
Gatwick Airport *North Terminal arrivals hall.* **Open** *8am-4.30pm daily. South Terminal arrivals hall 8am-6pm daily.*
Heathrow Airport *Terminals 2 & 3 underground station concourse.* **Open** *8am-7.30pm daily.*
King's Cross *Western Ticket Hall, near St Pancras.* **Open** *8.30am-6pm Mon-Wed, Sun; 8.30am-6.30pm Thur-Sat.*
Liverpool Street **Open** *8.30am-5pm Mon-Wed, Sun; 8.30am-6.30pm Thur-Sat.*
Piccadilly Circus tube **Open** *9.30am-4pm daily.*
Victoria (main station) *opposite Platform 8.* **Open** *8.30am-6pm Mon-Wed, Sun; 8.30am-6.30pm Thur-Sat.*

Fares & tickets
London transport is becoming increasingly cash-free. Paper bus and tram passes, Travelcards and train tickets are still available from ticket machines but it's far easier (and cheaper) to use a pre-paid Oyster card or contactless debit/credit card (*see below*).

Tube and DLR fares are based on a system of six zones, which stretch 12 miles out from central London. The single adult fare is £4.90 for journeys within zones 1-3; £6 for zones 1-6; £7.40 for zones 1-7; £8.50 for zones 1-9. Using Oyster pay-as-you-go or a contactless card, journeys within zone 1 cost £2.40; zones 1-3 costs £2.80 (off peak)/£3.30 (peak); zones 1-6 costs £3.10

In the know
Routemaster buses

London's original hop-on/hop-off double-decker buses still run on Route 15 (between Trafalgar Square and Tower Hill; head to stop F on the Strand) on weekends March-September and bank holidays. You must have a ticket or valid card before boarding.

(off peak)/£5.10 (peak). Peak hours are 6.30-9.30am, 4-7pm Mon-Fri.

Oyster cards & contactless payments

You can buy and charge Oyster cards at Travel Information Centres (see above), tube stations, and some newsagents and rail stations. Cards are also available from tfl.gov.uk/oyster. A £5 refundable deposit is payable on new cards.

If you have a credit or debit card with the contactless symbol you can use it instead of getting an Oyster card – and you will pay the same fare.

Travelcards

If you're only using the Tube, DLR and buses, using Oyster to pay-as-you-go will always be cheaper than an equivalent Day Travelcard. However, if you're also using certain National Rail services, Oyster may not be accepted: opt, instead, for a Day Travelcard, a ticket that allows travel across all networks.

Anytime Day Travelcards can be used all day. They cost £13.10 for zones 1-4, £18.60 for zones 1-6. Tickets are valid for journeys begun by 4.30am the next day. The **Off-Peak Day Travelcard** allows travel after 9.30am Mon-Fri (all day at weekends and public holidays). It costs £13.90 for zones 1-9.

Travelling with children

The single tube fare for children aged 5-15 is 75p (off peak)/85p (peak) for any journey in zones 1-6. Under-5s travel free without the need to provide any proof of identity. Five-to 10-year-olds can also travel free, but need to obtain a 5-10 Zip Oyster photocard. An 11-15 Zip Oyster photocard is needed by 11- to 15-year-olds to pay as they go with reduced fares on the Tube/DLR and to buy 7-day, monthly or longer period Travelcards. Photocards can be obtained in advance from tfl.gov.uk/tickets.

London Underground

Trains are hot and crowded in rush hour (8-9.30am, 4.30-7pm Mon-Fri). Even so, the 12 colour-coded lines of the Underground ('the Tube') are the quickest way to get about. For fares, see p200.

Paper single or day tickets can be bought from self-service ticket machines in tube stations. To enter using a paper ticket, place it in the slot with the black magnetic strip facing down, then pull it out of the top to open the gates. Exit in the same way; tickets for single journeys will be retained by the gate on final exit.

To enter and exit the Tube using an Oyster or contactless card, touch it to the yellow reader, which opens the gate. You must also touch the card to the reader when you exit, or you'll be charged a higher fare when you next use your card. On certain lines, you'll see a pink reader (the 'validator') – touch it in addition to the yellow entry/exit readers and on some routes it will reduce your fare.

Timetables

Tube trains run daily from around 5.30am (except Sun, when they start an hour or so later, and Christmas Day, when there's no service). You shouldn't have to wait more than 10mins for a train; during peak times, services should run every 2-3mins. Times of last trains vary; they're usually around 12.30am (11.30pm on Sun). The Night Tube, offering a limited 24hr service, runs Fri and Sat nights on some lines (see below). Tubes also run all night on New Year's Eve. Otherwise, you're limited to night buses (see p202).

Night Tube

The all-night tube service started in 2016. Now almost all of the Central,

> **In the know**
> ### Travelling fines
>
> Anyone caught travelling without a ticket, Oyster or contactless card is subject to an £80 on the spot fine (reduced to £40 if you pay within three weeks).

Northern and Piccadilly lines, and the entire Jubilee and Victoria lines, have services through Fri/Sat and Sat/Sun. They are fast, frequent (roughly every 10mins) and you can continue to use your Day Travelcard (or capped pay-as-you-go card) until 4.30am in the morning after the day covered by that card.

Docklands Light Railway

DLR trains (0343 222 1234, tfl. gov.uk/modes/dlr) run from Bank station (where they connect with the Central, Northern and Waterloo & City lines) or Tower Gateway, close to Tower Hill tube (Circle and District lines). Stations are shown on the Underground map. Trains run 5.30am-12.40am daily, and there are lots of good views of Docklands to be enjoyed. Fares are the same as the Tube.

Overground

The **Overground** (0343 222 1234, tfl.gov.uk/modes/london-overground) is a patchwork of different rail services, some tracing a complex orbital route roughly following the boundary of zones 2 and 3 (the orange-and-white line on the tube map) and providing a useful service for areas with poor Underground coverage. The Night Tube now runs Overground services as well as Underground services, with a very useful link between New Cross Gate and Highbury & Islington, where it connects to the Victoria line.

National Rail services

Independently run commuter services co-ordinated by **National Rail** (03457 48 49 50, www.nationalrail.co.uk) leave from the city's main rail stations. Visitors heading to south London, or to more remote destinations such as Hampton Court Palace, use these services.

Fares

Travelcards are valid on these services within the right zones, but not all routes accept Oyster pay-as-you-go or contactless payments.

Crossrail

The dauntingly massive infrastructure project known as Crossrail (www.crossrail.co.uk) has been burrowing under central London since 2009 and is due finally to open to passengers in 2021. London's 12th tube line will be known as the Elizabeth Line and will whisk sleeper-town residents into central London from east and west at great speed. The underground section of the line has stops at Paddington, Bond Street, Tottenham Court Road, Farringdon, Liverpool Street, Whitechapel, Canary Wharf, Customs House and Woolwich.

Buses

Buses are now cash-free, so you must have a bus and tram pass, Travelcard or Oyster card/contactless card (for both, *see p201*). You can buy a Travelcard or pass from machines in tube and rail stations. All buses are now low-floor vehicles that are accessible to wheelchair-users and passengers with buggies. The only exception is Heritage route 15 (weekends and bank holidays Mar-Sept, heritageroutes.weebly.com), which is served by the historic and world-famous open-platform Routemaster buses.

Using an Oyster card costs £1.50 per trip; your total daily payment, regardless of how many journeys you take, will be capped at £4.50. Under-16s travel for free (using an Under-11 or 11-15 Oyster photocard, as appropriate; *see p201*). You can take a second bus journey for free if you board within an hour of touching in on your first bus.

Night buses

Many bus routes operate 24hrs a day, seven days a week. There are also night buses with an 'N' prefix, which run from about 11pm. Most night services run every 15-30mins, but busier routes run every 10mins or so. Fares are the same as for daytime buses; bus passes and

Travelcards can be used at no extra fare until 4.30am of the morning after they expire, with Oyster day-capping in effect until then too.

Water transport

Most river services operate every 20-60mins from 7am-9pm, more often and later in summer; see www.tfl.gov.uk. For commuters, **Thames Clippers** (www.thamesclippers.com) runs a service between Embankment Pier and Royal Arsenal Woolwich Pier boarded at Blackfriars, Bankside, London Bridge, Canary Wharf and Greenwich. A standard day roamer ticket (valid 9am-9pm) costs £19.80, £9.90 for a child (5-15s), while a single from Embankment to Greenwich is £8.70, £4.35 for 5-15s, or £5.80 for Oyster cardholders. Book online for reductions.

Thames River Services (020 7930 4097, www.thamesriverservices.co.uk) operates from Westminster pier, with trips to Greenwich and Tower Pier, and the Thames Barrier from May to Oct. A trip to Greenwich costs £13.25, £8.50 child. Travelcard holders get a third off. Book online for reductions.

TAXIS & MINICABS

If a **black cab**'s orange 'For Hire' sign is lit, it can be hailed. If it stops, the cabbie must take you to your destination if it's within seven miles. Fares rise after 8pm on weekdays and at weekends. You can book black cabs using the very handy free **mytaxi** app, or from **Radio Taxis** (020 7272 0272) and **Dial-a-Cab** (020 7253 5000; cards only).

Minicabs (saloon cars) are generally cheaper than black cabs, but can be less reliable. Only use licensed firms (look for a disc in the front and rear windows) and avoid drivers who illegally tout for business in the street: such drivers may be uninsured and dangerous. Check the price when booking, and with the driver before getting in. If you text HOME to 60835 ('60TFL'), Transport for London will reply with the numbers of the two nearest licensed minicab operators and

the number for **Radio Taxis**, which provides licensed black taxis in London (35p plus standard call rate). You can also use the **Uber** app to hail – and pay for – a minicab. After being banned from operating in London by TfL, Uber has been given a temporary reprieve until the end of 2019.

DRIVING

Congestion charge

Driving into central London 7am-6pm Mon-Fri costs £11.50. You'll know when you're about to drive into the charging zone from the red 'C' signs on the road. The restricted area is shown at tfl.gov.uk/modes/congestioncharging. You can pay at some newsagents, garages, NCP car parks or at tfl.gov.uk/modes/congestion charging, by phone on 0343 222 2222 or by SMS. You can pay any time during the day or, for £2.50 more, until midnight on the next day. Expect a fine of £160 for non-payment (reduced to £80 if you pay within 14 days).

Parking

Parking on a single or double yellow line, a red line or in residents' parking areas during the day is illegal, and you may be fined, clamped or towed. In the evening (from 6pm or 7pm in much of central London) and at various times at weekends, parking on single yellow lines is legal and free; look for a sign giving the local regulations. During the day meters cost upwards of £1 for 15mins, limited to two hours, but they are free at certain times during evenings and weekends. Parking on double yellows and red routes is always illegal. Use an app like **AppyParking** to help you find the nearest free car parking; otherwise, there are many **NCP** car parks (www.ncp.co.uk), open 24hrs a day.

Vehicle removal

If your car has disappeared, it's either been stolen or, if it was parked illegally, towed to a car pound by the local authorities. A release fee of £200 is levied for removal, plus upwards of £40 per day from the first midnight after removal. You'll also probably get a parking ticket, typically £130 (reduced by 50% if paid within 14 days). Contact **Trace Information Service** (0845 206 8602, freephone 0300 077 0100, trace. london). You can also text 'TRACE' followed by your car registration number to 66663 (you will be charged for this service).

CYCLING

London isn't the friendliest town for cyclists, but the **London Cycling Campaign** (020 7234 9310, www.lcc.org. uk) help to keep things improving.

Cycling tips are available at tfl.gov. uk/modes/cycling. TfL also runs the **Santander Cycles** scheme (0343 222 6666, tfl.gov.uk/modes/cycling/santander-cycles), nicknamed 'Boris Bikes' and recognisable by their red Santander sponsorship branding. These can be found at various 24hr docking stations. Touch the 'Hire a cycle' icon and insert a credit or debit card. The machine will print out a five-digit code, which you then tap into the docking point of a bike, releasing the cycle. A £2 fee buys 24hr access to the bikes; the first 30mins are free.

WALKING

The best way to see London is on foot, but the street layout is complicated. There's route advice at tfl.gov.uk/modes/walking/top-walking-routes (the map of walking times between stations, which can be downloaded from content. tfl.gov.uk/walking-tube-map.pdf, is particularly useful) or download the Go Jauntly walking app. Look out too for the yellowtopped 'Legible London' information posts (tfl.gov.uk/info-for/boroughs/maps-and-signs), which are oriented to the direction you're heading, rather than with north at the top.

Resources A-Z

ACCIDENT & EMERGENCY

In the event of a serious accident, fire or other incident, call **999** – free from any phone, including payphones – and ask for an ambulance, the fire service or police. If no one is in immediate danger, call **101**.

Emergency departments

If you need medical help or advice for conditions that are not life-threatening call 111. For life-threatening emergencies call 999. Listed below are most of the central London hospitals that have Accident & Emergency (A&E) departments that are open 24 hours daily.

Charing Cross Hospital *Fulham Palace Road, Hammersmith, W6 8RF (020 3311 1234, www.imperial.nhs.uk). Hammersmith tube.*

Chelsea & Westminster Hospital *369 Fulham Road, Chelsea, SW10 9NH (020 3315 8000, www.chelwest.nhs.uk). South Kensington tube.*

Royal Free Hospital *Pond Street, Hampstead, NW3 2QG (020 7794 0500, www.royalfree.nhs.uk). Belsize Park tube or Hampstead Heath Overground.*

Royal London Hospital *Whitechapel Road, Whitechapel, E1 1FR (020 7377 7000, www.bartshealth.nhs.uk). Whitechapel tube/Overground.*

St Mary's Hospital *Praed Street, Paddington, W2 1NY (020 3312 6666, www.imperial.nhs.uk). Paddington tube/rail.*

St Thomas' Hospital *Westminster Bridge Road, South Bank, SE1 7EH (020 7188 7188, www.guysandstthomas.nhs. uk). Westminster tube or Waterloo tube/ rail.* **Map** *p71 M10.*

University College Hospital *235 Euston Road, Fitzrovia, NW1 2BU (020 3456 7890, www.uclh.nhs.uk). Euston Square or Warren Street tube.* **Map** *p114 K5*

Dental emergencies

Guy's Hospital *23rd floor, Tower Wing, Great Maze Pond, SE1 9RT (020 7188 0124, www.guysandstthomas.nhs.uk/ our-services/dental). London Bridge tube/rail.* **Open** *8am-4pm Mon-Fri.* **Map** *p71 Q9.*

Queues start forming at 7.45am; arrive by 9am if you're to be seen at all.

Travel Advice

For up-to-date information on travel to a specific country – including the latest on safety and security, health issues, local laws and customs – contact your home country government's department of foreign affairs. Most have websites with useful advice for would-be travellers

Australia
www.smartraveller.gov.au

Canada
www.voyage.gc.ca

New Zealand
www.safetravel.govt.nz

Republic of Ireland
www.dfa.ie

UK
www.fco.gov.uk/travel

USA
www.state.gov/travel

Pharmacies

Also called 'chemists' in the UK.
Branches of **Boots** (www.boots.com)
and larger supermarkets will have
a pharmacy. Most keep shop hours
(9am-6pm Mon-Sat) but the Boots store
at 44-46 Regent Street, Mayfair, W1B
5RA (020 7734 6126) opens until 11pm
Mon-Thur, midnight Fri, Sat, 6pm Sun.

Useful websites

www.alcoholics-anonymous.org.uk
www.citizensadvice.org.uk
www.missingpeople.org.uk
www.111.nhs.uk
www.rapecrisis.org.uk
www.samaritans.org
www.victimsupport.org.uk

AGE RESTRICTIONS

Buying/drinking alcohol 18
Driving 17
Sex 16
Smoking 18

CUSTOMS

▶ *Post-Brexit customs arrangements
had not been finalised by the time this
guide went to press; for the most up-to-
date information, see www.gov.uk.*

Currently, citizens entering the UK from
outside the EU must adhere to duty-free
import limits:

• 200 cigarettes or 100 cigarillos or 50
cigars or 250g of tobacco
• 4 litres still table wine plus either 1 litre
spirits or strong liqueurs (above 22%
abv) or 2 litres fortified wine (under 22%
abv), sparkling wine or other liqueurs
• other goods to the value of no more
than £390

The import of meat, poultry, fruit,
plants, flowers and protected animals
is restricted or forbidden. There are
currently no restrictions on the import
or export of currency if travelling from
another EU country. If you are travelling

Climate

Average temperatures and monthly rainfall in London

	Temp High (°C/°F)	Temp Low (°C/°F)	Rainfall (mm/in)
January	6/43	2/36	54 /2.1
February	7/44	2/36	40 / 1.6
March	10/50	3/37	37 / 1.5
April	13/55	6/43	37 / 1.5
May	17/63	8/46	46 / 1.8
June	20/68	12/54	45 / 1.8
July	22/72	14/57	57 / 2.2
August	21/70	13/55	59 / 2.3
September	19/66	11/52	49 / 1.9
October	14/57	8/46	57 / 2.2
November	10/50	5/41	64 / 2.5
December	7/44	4/39	48 / 1.9

from outside the EU, amounts over €10,000 must be declared on arrival.

People over the age of 17 arriving from an EU country are able to import unlimited goods for their own personal use, if bought tax-paid (so not duty-free).

DISABLED

As a city that evolved long before the needs of disabled people were considered, London is difficult for wheelchair users, though facilities are slowly improving. The bus fleet is now low-floor for easier wheelchair access and all DLR stations have either lifts or ramp access. However, most tube stations still have escalator-only access; those with lifts are marked with a blue wheelchair symbol on tube maps. The Step-free Tube Guide map is free; call 0343 222 1234 or download it from tfl.gov.uk/accessguides.

Most major attractions and hotels have good accessibility, though provisions for the hearing- and sight-disabled are patchier. *Access in London* is an invaluable reference book for disabled travellers (£10 donation) from **Access Project** (39 Bradley Gardens, W13 8HE, www.accessinlondon.org).

Useful websites
www.canbedone.co.uk
www.disabilityrightsuk.org
www.tourismforall.org.uk
www.wheelchair-travel.co.uk

DRUGS

Illegal drug use remains higher in London than the UK as a whole, though it's becoming less visible on the streets and in clubs. Despite fierce debate, cannabis has been reclassified from Class C to Class B (where it rejoins amphetamines), but possession of a small amount might attract no more than a warning for a first offence. More serious Class B and A drugs (ecstasy, LSD, heroin, cocaine and the like) carry stiffer penalties, with a maximum of seven years in prison for possession plus a fine.

ELECTRICITY

The UK uses 220-240V, 50-cycle AC voltage and three-pin plugs.

EMBASSIES & CONSULATES

Australian High Commission *Australia House, the Strand, Holborn, WC2B 4LA (020 7379 4334, www. uk.embassy.gov.au). Holborn or Temple tube.* **Open** *9am-5pm Mon-Fri.* **Map** *p156 N7.*

Canadian High Commission *Canada House, Trafalgar Square, Westminster, SW1Y 5BJ (020 7004 6000, www. canadainternational.gc.ca/united_kingdom-royaume_uni). Charing Cross tube/rail.* **Open** *8am-4pm Mon-Fri.* **Map** *p85 L8.*

Embassy of Ireland *17 Grosvenor Place, Belgravia, SW1X 7HR (020 7235 2171, 020 7373 4339 passports & visas, www.dfa.ie/irish-embassy/great-britain). Hyde Park Corner tube.* **Open** *9.30am-12.30pm, 2.30-4.30pm Mon-Fri.* **Map** *p98 H10.*

New Zealand High Commission *New Zealand House, 80 Haymarket, St James's, SW1Y 4TQ (020 7930 8422, www.mfat.govt.nz/en/countries-and-regions/europe/united-kingdom/new-zealand-high-commission). Piccadilly Circus tube.* **Open** *9am-4pm Mon-Fri.* **Map** *p114 L8.*

US Embassy *33 Nine Elms Lane, Wandsworth, SW11 7US (020 7499 9000, uk.usembassy.gov). Vauxhall tube/rail.* **Open** *8am-5.30pm Mon-Fri.*

HEALTH

It's advisable that all travellers take out insurance before leaving home. Until the end of the Brexit transition period, EU citizens travelling in the UK can still use a European Health Insurance Card (EHIC), which entitles them to free or reduced cost medical care on the NHS. For further information, refer to www.gov.uk/guidance/healthcare-for-eu-and-efta-citizens-visiting-the-uk and p205, Accident & Emergency.

LEFT LUGGAGE

Airports
Gatwick Airport *01293 569 900.*
Heathrow Airport *020 8759 3344.*
London City Airport *020 7646 0088.*
Luton Airport *01582 808174.*
Stansted Airport *0330 223 0893.*

Rail & bus stations
London stations tend to have left-luggage desks rather than lockers. Call 0845 748 4950 for details or check www.networkrail.co.uk.

Charing Cross *020 7930 5444.* ***Open*** *7am-11pm daily.*
Euston *020 7387 1499.* ***Open*** *7am-11pm daily.*
King's Cross *020 7837 4334.* ***Open*** *7am-11pm daily.*
Paddington *020 7262 0344.* ***Open*** *7am-11pm daily.*
Victoria *020 7963 0957.* ***Open*** *7am-midnight daily.*

LGBT

London Friend *86 Caledonian Road, King's Cross, N1 9DN (020 7833 1674, londonfriend.org.uk).* ***Open*** *10am-6pm Mon-Fri.*
London Lesbian & Gay Switchboard *0300 330 0630, switchboard.lgbt.* ***Open*** *10am-11pm daily.*

LOST PROPERTY

Always inform the police if you lose anything, if only to validate insurance claims. Only dial 999 if violence has occurred; use 101 for non-emergencies. Report lost passports both to the police and to your embassy (see p207).

Airports
For items left on a plane, contact the relevant airline. Otherwise, phone:

Gatwick Airport *01293 223 457.*
Heathrow Airport *020 3761 1800.*

London City Airport *020 7646 0000.*
Luton Airport *01582 809174.*
Stansted Airport *0330 024 0099.*

Public transport
Transport for London *Lost Property Office, 200 Baker Street, Marylebone, NW1 5RZ (0343 222 1234, tfl.gov.uk/help-and-contact/lost-property). Baker Street tube.* ***Open*** *8.30am-4pm Mon-Fri.* ***Map*** *p114 H5.*
Allow two to ten working days from the time of loss. If you lose something on a bus, call 0343 222 1234 and ask for the numbers of the depots at either end of the route. For tube losses, pick up a lost-property form from any station. There is a fee to cover costs.

Taxis
The Transport for London office (see above) deals with property found in registered black cabs. Allow two to ten days from the time of loss. For items lost in a minicab or Über, contact the relevant company.

MONEY

Britain's currency is the pound sterling (£).

ATMs
Cash machines are found at banks, supermarkets and in larger stations. You should be able to withdraw cash from ATMs using any credit or debit card. Generally this is the cheapest form of currency exchange.

Credit cards
Credit cards, especially Visa, are accepted in most shops (except small corner shops) and restaurants. American Express and Diners Club tend to be accepted only at more expensive outlets. You will usually have to have a PIN number to make a purchase.

If you lose your card, call the relevant 24hr number:

American Express *0800 917 8047, www.americanexpress.com.*
Diners Club *0800 862 0935, www. dinersclub.co.uk.*
MasterCard *0800 964767, www. mastercard.com.*
Visa *0800 891725, www.visa.co.uk.*

Tax

Value Added Tax (VAT) of 20% is a sales tax added to most goods and services in the UK. This will be included in the prices quoted in shops, although it may not be included in hotel rates. Foreign visitors from outside the EU may be able to claim back VAT paid on goods via a scheme called 'Tax Free Shopping'. It was unclear at time of writing what arrangements will be in place for EU citizens after Brexit. Fill in a refund form at the time of purchase (till receipts are not sufficient) and get it verified by customs staff at the airport. You can then apply for your refund by posting the form back to the retailer or to a commercial refund company, or by taking your form to a refund booth to get immediate payment.

OPENING HOURS

Banks *9am-4.30pm (some close at 3.30pm, some 5.30pm) Mon-Fri; some also Sat mornings.*
Businesses *9am-5pm Mon-Fri.*
Post offices *9am-5.30pm Mon-Fri; 9am-noon Sat.*
Pubs & bars *11am-11pm Mon-Sat; noon-10.30pm Sun; many pubs and bars, particularly in central London, stay open later.*
Shops *10am-6pm Mon-Sat, some to 8pm. Many also open on Sun, usually 11am-5pm or noon-6pm.*

POLICE

For emergencies, call **999**. The non-emergency number is **101**.
London's police are used to helping visitors. If you've been robbed, assaulted or a victim of crime, go to your nearest police station.

Belgravia Police Station *202-206 Buckingham Palace Road, Pimlico, SW1W 9SX. Victoria tube/rail.*
Charing Cross Police Station *Agar Street, Covent Garden, WC2N 4JP. Charing Cross tube/rail.* **Map** *p114 M8.*
Holborn Police Station *10 Lambs Conduit Street, Bloomsbury, WC1N 3NR. Holborn tube.* **Map** *p145 N6.*
Islington Police Station *2 Tolpuddle Street, Islington, N1 0YY. Angel tube.*
Kensington Police Station *72 Earls Court Road, W8 6EQ. High Street Kensington tube.*
West End Central Police Station *27 Savile Row, Mayfair, W1S 2EX. Oxford Circus tube.* **Map** *p114 K8.*

POSTAL SERVICES

The UK has a reliable postal service. Some central post offices are listed below; for others, check the Royal Mail website www.royalmail.com.

Baker Street *no.111, Marylebone, W1U 6SG. Baker Street tube.* **Map** *p114 H6.*
Great Portland Street *nos.54-56, Fitzrovia, W1W 7NE. Oxford Circus tube.* **Map** *p114 K6.*
High Holborn *no.181, Holborn, WC1V 7RL. Holborn tube.* **Map** *p114 M7.*

PUBLIC HOLIDAYS

On public holidays (bank holidays), many shops remain open, but public-transport services generally run to a Sunday timetable. On Christmas Day, almost everything, including public transport, closes down. If Christmas Day, Boxing Day or New Year's Day fall on a weekend, a bank holiday is added to the calendar on the next working day.

Good Friday *Fri 10 Apr 2020, Fri 2 Apr 2021*
Easter Monday *Mon 13 Apr 2020, Mon 5 Apr 2021*
May Day Holiday *Fri 8 May 2020, Mon 3 May 2021*
Spring Bank Holiday *Mon 25 May 2020, Mon 31 May 2021*

Summer Bank Holiday *Mon 31 Aug 2020, Mon 30 Aug 2021*
Christmas Day *25 Dec*
Boxing Day *26 Dec*
New Year's Day *1 Jan*

SMOKING

Smoking is banned in enclosed public spaces, such as pubs, clubs, shops, restaurants and public transport.

TELEPHONES

London's **dialling code** is 020; standard landlines have eight digits after that. If you're calling from outside the UK, dial your international access code code (Australia 61, Canada 1, New Zealand 64, Republic of Ireland 353, South Africa 27, USA 1), then the UK code, 44, then the full London number, omitting the first 0.

Mobile phones in the UK operate on the 900 MHz and 1800 MHz GSM frequencies. US cellphone users need a tri- or quad-band handset.

Public payphones take coins and/or credit cards, but aren't widely distributed. International calling cards are widely available.

TIME

London operates on Greenwich Mean Time (GMT), five hours ahead of the US's Eastern Standard Time. In spring the UK puts its clocks forward by one hour to British Summer Time. In autumn, the clocks go back to GMT.

TIPPING

In Britain, it's accepted that you tip in taxis, minicabs, restaurants (some waiting staff rely heavily on tips), hotels, hairdressers and some bars (not pubs). Around 10% is normal, but some restaurants add as much as 15% if service has been included in the bill. Always check whether this is the case: some restaurants include an automatic service charge, but also give the opportunity for a gratuity when paying with a card.

TOURIST INFORMATION

See also Travel Information Centres, *p200*

City of London Information Centre *St Paul's Churchyard, City, EC4M 8BX (020 7332 3456, www.cityoflondon.gov.uk). Open 9.30am-5.30pm Mon-Sat; 10am-4pm Sun. Map p156 P7.*
Greenwich Tourist Information Centre *Visitor Centre, Old Royal Naval College, King William Walk, SE10 9NN (020 8305 5235, www.visitgreenwich.org.uk/tourist-information-centre). Cutty Sark DLR. Open 10am-5pm daily.*
Holborn Information Kiosk *89-94 Kingsway, outside Holborn tube, WC2B 6AA (no phone). Open 9am-6pm Mon-Fri. Map p145 M6.*
Twickenham Visitor Information Centre *Civic Centre, 44 York Street, Twickenham, Middx, TW1 3BZ (020 8891 1441, www.visitrichmond.co.uk). Twickenham rail. Open 9am-5.15pm Mon-Thur; 9am-5pm Fri.*

WEIGHTS & MEASURES

The UK is moving slowly and reluctantly towards full metrication. Distances are still measured in miles but all goods are officially sold in metric quantities. Nonetheless, imperial measurements are still more commonly used, so we use them in this guide.

Index

Picture credits

2 Engel Ching/Shutterstock.com, 3 (top) Dutourdumonde Photography/Shutterstock.com, 3 (middle) Gareth Gardner/Design Museum, 3 (bottom), 12 (top) Hutong, 6 Songquan Deng/Shutterstock.com, 11 (top) Club Mexicana, 11 (bottom), 89 Kiev.Victor/Shutterstock.com, 2 (bottom) GagliardiImages/Shutterstock.com, 12 (bottom) Mr Fogg's, 13 (top) Graham W Lacdao, 13 (bottom) Marc Brenner/National Theatre, 14 (top), 83, 95 cowardlion/Shutterstock.com, 14 (bottom) CLF Art Café, 15, 123 Liberty London, libertylondon.com, 17 Claudio Divizia/Shutterstock.com, 20 Britta Jaschinski/Time Out, 21, 119 Willy Barton/Shutterstock.com, 23 Mykolastock/Shutterstock.com, Sam Ashton/El Pastór, 28, 137 Andy Parsons/Time Out, 29 Ingus Kruklitis/Shutterstock.com, 31 KATE BEARD, 33, 140 The Shop at Bluebird, 34 Lewis Ronald/Selfridges & Co., 35, 79, 124 Alena Veasey/Shutterstock.com, 36 The World in HDRShutterstock.com, 39 © ROH/AKA, 41 Alastair Philip Wiper/Rio, 43 (bottom) Pedro Arnay, 44 Helen Murray/National Theatre, 46 © Photography by Jake Davis (fb.com/hungryvisuals) , 47 South London Soul train, 49 charliebard.com, 50 Michelle Grant/Corsica Studios, 51 Salvador Maniquiz/Shutterstock.com, 52 Andy119/Shutterstock.com, 53 Milind Arvind Ketkar/Shutterstock.com, 54 (top) Time Out, 54 (bottom) Bold Tendencies, 55 Georgethefourth/Shutterstock.com, 56 (left) © V&A. Alan Williams Photography, 56 (right) pcruciatti/Shutterstock.com, 57 (top) Fiona Hanson/Serpentine Gallery, 57 (bottom), 139 Christian Mueller/Shutterstock.com, 59 Historic Royal Palaces/Richard Lea-Hair, 61 Giles Smith, 63 Ms Jane Campbell/Shutterstock.com, 64 BBA Photography/Shutterstock.com, 67 khankanen/Shutterstock.com, 68 Melanie Major/Shutterstock.com, 72 FotoGraphic/Shutterstock.com, 73 Gimas/Shutterstock.com, 75, 162 Tony Baggett/Shutterstock.com, 76 Philip Bird LRPS CPAGB/Shutterstock.com, 78 Helen Cathcart/El Pastór, 35, 79, 124 Alena Veasey/Shutterstock.com, 81 National Theatre, 82 Morley von Sternberg, 87 Offcaania/Shutterstock.com, 90 Bikeworldtravel/Shutterstock.com, 93 schoukse/Shutterstock.com, 94 Anna Moskvina/Shutterstock.com, 97 elRoce/Shutterstock.com, 100 © Plastiques Photography, courtesy Science Museum Group, 101 Chrispictures/Shutterstock.com, 103 David Iliff, 104 Ioan Florin Cnejevici, 109 Farmacy, 111 Benjamin B/Shutterstock.com, 113 Anton_Ivanov/Shutterstock.com, 116 © The Wallace Collection, 121 Bubble_Tea Stock/Shutterstock.com, 128 ChameleonsEye/Shutterstock.com, 131 Kevin Lake/We Built This City, 132 Jonathan Perugia/Time Out, 135 John Gomez/Shutterstock.com, 136 Heike Bohnstengel/Time Out, 141 (top) © ROH/Johan Persson, 141 (middle) © ROH/Alice Pennefather, 142 a-image/Shutterstock.com, 143 Ben Gilbert/Wellcome Collection, 146 Miles Willis, 147 Patchamol Jensatienwong/Shutterstock.com, 149 Moro, 151 Cedric Weber/Shutterstock.com, 153 antb/Shutterstock.com, 161 ZGPhotography/Shutterstock.com, 164 Ming Tang-Evans/Time Out, 167 Eclecticism/Shutterstock.com, 170 Hufton + Crow/John Sturrock, 172, 174 I Wei Huang/Shutterstock.com, 173 marcela novotna/Shutterstock.com, 174 Philip Vile, 179 Richie Chan/Shutterstock.com, 182 chrisdorney/Shutterstock.com, 185 DrimaFilm/Shutterstock.com, 186 Luke Hayes, 187 Caro Gomes Pak, 189 (top) Sven Hansche/Shutterstock.com, 189 (bottom) Phillip Maguire/Shutterstock.com, 191 Luke David Williams/Shutterstock.com.

Credits

Crimson credits

Editor Nicola Gibbs
Contributors Sonya Barber, Megan Carnegie, Katie Dailey, Kitty Drake, Nicola Gibbs, Thomas Howells, Nick Levine, Andrzej Lukowski, James Manning, Ellie Walker-Arnott
Proofreader Ros Sales
Cartography Gail Armstrong

Series Editor Sophie Blacksell Jones
Production Manager Kate Michell
Production Designer Emilie Crabb
Print Manager Patrick Dawson
Design Mytton Williams

Chairman David Lester
Managing Director Andy Riddle

Advertising Media Sales House
Marketing Sophie Shepherd
Sales Lyndsey Mayhew

Acknowledgements

The editor would like to thank all contributors to previous editions of *Time Out London* whose work forms the basis of this guide.

Photography credits

Front cover Travel Pix Collection/AWL-images
Back cover Charles Bowman/Shutterstock.com
Interior photography credits, *see p215*.

Publishing information

Time Out London Shortlist 11th edition
© TIME OUT ENGLAND LIMITED 2020
March 2020

ISBN 978 1 780592 73 2
CIP DATA: A catalogue record for this book is available from the British Library

Published by Crimson Publishing
21d Charles Street, Bath, BA1 1HX (01225 584 950, www.crimsonpublishing.co.uk) on behalf of Time Out England.

Distributed by Grantham Book Services
Distributed in the US and Canada by Publishers Group West (1-510-809-3700)

Printed by Replika Press, India